SLEIGHT of HAND

Vicki Reed

LEXINGTON, KY

Text copyright © Vicki Reed 2025

This paperback edition:
ISBN: 978-0-9601243-4-3

ALL RIGHTS RESERVED

No part of this publication may be reproduced or transmitted in any form or by any means, electronic or mechanical, including photocopying and recording, or by any information storage or retrieval system, except as may be expressly permitted by the 1976 Copyright Act or in writing from the publisher. No part of this book may be used or reproduced in any manner for the purpose of training artificial intelligence technologies or systems. Requests for permission should be addressed in writing to:

Middleton Books, 832 Dana Drive, Coatesville, PA 19320

MIDDLETON BOOKS
www.middletonbooks.com

This book is a work of fiction. Names, characters, places, and incidents are either the product of the author's imagination or are used fictitiously, and any resemblance to actual persons, living or dead, business establishments, events or locales is entirely coincidental.

First edition 2024. Printed in the USA.

Cover and book design: Jonathan D. Scott

Cover artwork: Adobe Firefly

Library of Congress Control Number: 2025901842

For all the resilient kids who persevere and prosper because of—or in spite of—their involvement in the System. And for all the social workers, juvenile staff, lawyers, judges, advocates, and reformers who slug it out every day on behalf of these vulnerable youth.

Advance Praise for *Sleight of Hand*

"Written by someone whose life's work has been to improve a system that supports troubled youth, *Sleight of Hand* is one of the most engaging books I have had the opportunity to read. A fictional account that captures your heart and gives the reader insight into the life of a dual-system youth that is often fraught with chaos, pain and trauma. Reed brings to life lessons of complex cases and how trauma triggers behavior responses in situations that may seem benign on the surface. This book resonates with the importance of having one caring, committed adult in a foster child's life. Empathy, patience, and endurance – we all need more and this book shows why."

—**Michael A. Jones, Managing Director, National Partnership for Juvenile Services**

"Once I picked up *Sleight of Hand,* I couldn't put it down. I was too eager to see what happened next! Beyond the story, the book contains a lot of truth about the 'system' many children and youth find themselves in. As someone who works to improve that system, I was thrilled with how accurately and truthfully the book reads. Reed does a fantastic job bringing light to the incredible challenges before us. And she equips you with the opportunity to take action."

— **Melynda Milburn Jamison, Executive Director, CASA of Lexington**

"As someone familiar with the juvenile justice system, I am impressed by how well Vicki Reed has captured its struggles, losses, and victories involving youth. In *Sleight of Hand*, her follow-up to her two-time national award-winning debut novel, *The Car Thief*, Reed portrays the gradual transformation of Alex, a distraught teen with a dark past. Much like the metamorphosis of an ugly caterpillar into a beautiful butterfly, Alex slowly transforms with the help of his caseworker Sam and his foster father Matt, among others. The journey is not linear, often consisting of two steps forward and one step back, until Alex finally learns to think, hope, and care.

"The novel's title is particularly fitting, not only referring to Sam's card tricks to engage reluctant youth, but also because it serves as a metaphor for how many children in the system have been dealt a poor hand from birth. Readers will cheer for Alex as he defies the odds and learns how to stay in the game. Overall, this novel is compelling and will leave readers feeling they have been dealt a winning hand."

> — James B. Wells, retired Professor of Criminology and Criminal Justice, author of *Because: A CIA Coverup and a Son's Odyssey to Find the Father He Never Knew*

"With *Sleight of Hand*, Vicki Reed once again provides a 'can't put down' read that offers the reader first-person accounts of the foster care experience through the eyes of a foster youth, his foster parent, and his caseworker. The interweaving of their three unique viewpoints provides a rich and multidimensional look at a system that both serves troubled children and sometimes victimizes them. The book is both entertaining and informative. It will make you angry, and it will give you hope."

> —Pam Thomas, Senior Fellow, Kentucky Center for Economic Policy, former Juvenile Justice Specialist at the Kentucky Department of Juvenile Justice

"No one knows how to take a kid who has been dealt a bad hand in life and turn them around like Vicki Reed. I had the privilege of working alongside Vicki, advocating for therapeutic foster care, for many years. She knows how to take a broken system and a wounded child and breathe hope into both. In *Sleight of Hand*, she brings to life the raw, unfiltered reality of a fractured juvenile justice system and the young people caught in it. Through the eyes of a traumatized, vulnerable, and angry youth, readers experience the fear, self-doubt, and fleeting moments of joy that define the lives of so many at-risk kids. This story is a powerful reminder that it only takes one caring adult to change a child's trajectory forever. Vicky has spent her career being that person and creating positive systemic change in the nation's juvenile justice system. Through this book, she challenges all of us to do the same."

> —Beau Necco, Founder and CEO, NECCO

He drew a circle that shut me out—
　　Heretic, rebel, a thing to flout.
But Love and I had the wit to win:
　　We drew a circle that took him in!

　　　　—Edwin Markham

Chapter One

ALEX

A good day never begins with sitting in the back of a police car. Handcuffed. The sun barely up. You know it's only going to go downhill from here. As if picking up that thought, Meaty Jones, sitting next to me, says, "Well, Coffee Cup, we're in deep shit now."

My name is Alex Coffey, so Meaty thinks his nickname for me is cute or something. I just find it irritating. He's the only one who calls me that. A teacher at school overheard him once and told me I should tell him I don't like it. I'm sure Meaty, the same age as me at fifteen, would say, "Why, sorry Alex. I didn't realize you didn't appreciate it. Please accept my apologies, and I won't do it anymore." The more likely scenario would be he'd do it ten times more or think of something worse to call me.

Meaty's real name is Demetrie but no one calls him anything but Meaty. Not because he's chunky or anything like that; in fact, he's real skinny. He likes his nickname and has the tattoos to prove it. Him and me hang out together. I guess you could call us friends. He's useful to me because he is a reliable source for drugs and occasionally, when his father is passed out drop-dead-drunk, he lets me flop on his couch for the night. I'm useful to him because he thinks he can boss me around and get me to do whatever he wants. He's not wrong. I hate that about myself but there's lots of things I hate about me. That one ain't even near the top.

The day could be worse but the cops must be in a generous mood. They are charging us with misdemeanor drug charges and criminal trespassing, but not burglary, which is a felony. The house we spent the night partying in has been sitting empty for some time. It was easy to get inside through a broken window on the backside of the building. We aren't the first to help ourselves to the place, and I could hear the cops complaining about the absent landlord. Seems like they are madder at him than us.

A cop drives us up to the courthouse side entrance where we sit and wait. And wait. And wait. I'm not surprised at how long. I have a frequent flier pass. Can't say that about the cop. Marty Koontz is the name on his badge. He's drumming his fingers on the steering wheel. Keeps looking at his watch. He's practically screaming *get me out of here.*

He doesn't get any sympathy from the cops who have been at this longer. One older looking policeman walks past our car. Officer Marty hangs his head out the window and hollers, "Hey, I've been sitting here two hours!"

The older cop gives him a smirk. "Yeah, and you may be two more. That's what you get when you arrest kids. You'll learn to look the other way whenever you can."

Marty grumbles, "I don't see why I can't just drop them off at the station."

The older cop shifts his cup of coffee to his other hand so he can get a bite of his breakfast biscuit. It looks good to me. It's been some time since I've had anything to eat. He talks while he chews. "You had that in the big city where you first worked, but here in the sticks we don't have the space to separate juveniles from adults, so you get to babysit them in your car till the court folks do the processing."

As if on cue, the juvenile court worker strides out to the car with forms in his hands. Meaty catches a break. The call to his parents nets his mother, rather than his father, and she's going to come and pick him up. If his father had gotten the call, he'd have come too, but more than likely he'd beat the shit out of Meaty when he got him home. His mom will never be a mother of the year candidate herself, but the advantage for Meaty is he can easily get away from her as soon as they get home.

I don't remember my father at all. Mom had been an off and on guest of the county jail and women's state prison so she was no one to mess with. She was pregnant when she went to prison the second time and lucky me, I got to be born at the Cumberland Valley Women's State Prison. She got an early parole partly to come home and take care of me. It wasn't long after that my father ended up in prison. It was like they were playing tag team. A few years later he was released and rejoined our happy little family.

But it wasn't sunshine and rainbows. Good old Dad wasn't smart enough not to piss her off while she was higher than a kite with a gun in easy reach. The resulting manslaughter charge earned Mom a trip back to the joint. Her hepatitis, from all her drug using, got worse there and she died during the third year of her prison term. A great family legacy, huh?

This brings me back to the problem at hand and the never-ending question: Is it better to have lousy parents or none at all? In this particular situation, a shitty parent would be better than nothing. Because when the judge says *release to parents* that only works if you've got one.

What happens now?

I think I know.

After dealing with Meaty, Mr. Prescott, the juvenile court worker guy, looks at me and sighs. "Alex, we must quit meeting like this."

I smile. "Miss me?"

"Terribly. I called your social worker and she said the group home won't take you back since this is the third time you've run off from them. She doesn't have any foster home or other placement for you right now. So, you're going to have to go to juvenile detention until something else can be worked out. You understand?"

This is not happy news but completely expected. I know the drill.

"Yeah, I get it." I also get that Mr. Prescott is sugar coating it. *Something else can be worked out* isn't going to happen.

He knows it.

I know it.

After a few words with the fuming cop in the front seat, he goes back in the building. A short while later, when Meaty's mom arrives, he comes back out. At a gesture from Mr. Prescott, the cop gets out and opens the door on Meaty's side. Meaty's mom looks none too happy to see him. And she's even less happy as Mr. Prescott has her sign things and explains she needs to bring her son to court on Wednesday for an arraignment on the charges. She scribbles her name, then wads up the forms, and stuffs them in her large black bag. She turns and addresses Mr. Prescott and the cop at the same time.

"I hope you all are ready to come get my other kids when I lose my job and can't afford to feed them. I already had to leave early today and the boss ain't going to be happy when I have to ask for more time off."

"Yes, ma'am, I understand how troubling that can be." This isn't Mr. Prescott's first rodeo.

Stepping out of the police car, Meaty turns to me and says, "Later, Coffee Cup."

As Meaty gets in his mother's car, Mr. Prescott hands more papers to the cop, then we're merrily on our way. The car is warm and compared to other places I've been lately, fairly comfortable. I try and count my blessings. There's that matter of hunger. I'm starving, and where we're going I will get fed. It's been days since I've had a shower so that's definitely needed and I'll get that as well. I lean my head back and close my eyes. I'm not normally awake at this hour. Might as well get some sleep.

But it's a no-go. Seconds later I open my eyes and sit back up. I can't quiet my head enough to sleep. Thoughts keep popping up and I play whack-a-mole with them. As soon as I beat one down, another jumps up to take its place. Usually, all that matters to me is right here, right now. There's no sense thinking about the past and definitely, not thinking about tomorrow. But sometimes, I can't help myself.

Gazing out the window, I watch the scenery flash by. Soon I'll be seeing nothing but walls so I might as well take advantage of the views while I can. As we pass by fast food places, car lots, and the school I won't be attending tomorrow, a terrible emptiness wells up inside me and makes me feel sick. Like sick, sick. A jab of nausea hits me and my stomach rolls. I knock my head against the window glass to distract myself.

Don't think.
Don't hope.
Don't care.

I hit my head even harder.

"Hey, stop that!" The cop twists around to glare at me.

Instantly I feel better when I scream back at him, "I'll do whatever the fuck I want!"

He mutters something under his breath as he turns his attention back to his driving, but I ignore him. I'm back in control now. *Control.* That's all that matters.

As long as I have control, I can take anything. Haven't I been doing that all my life?

Chapter 2

SAM

If I had a lick of sense, I'd have said no. If I had an ounce of sense, I'd be on my way home to start my weekend instead of working late in the day on a Friday afternoon. If I had any sense at all, I wouldn't be staring across the table at this angry, insolent fifteen-year-old boy. But I promised the state child welfare agency I'd consider accepting him into our foster care program, so here I am at the local juvenile detention center when I should be home mowing grass.

I promised I'd come do this interview as a personal favor to Linda Snider, this boy's social worker, but I have no delusions I'll be calling her back to say, "*Why certainly, we'd love to admit him. When can I come pick him up?*" He'd be almost impossible to find a foster home willing to take him on. If I even get past that first step, this kid will probably either run off or get thrown out within days. Hell, within hours based on his past history. No, this will be a quick perfunctory visit and that will be that.

I look at the kid with the sneer on his face, slouched down into his plastic chair. He's tearing up the business card with my name on it and rolling the paper into little balls which he nonchalantly shoots at my chest with his finger and thumb. He's already torn through the Sam and is about halfway through the Murry. He is not showing any respect for the Field Director title under my name either. I suppose I could think less of him for it. But truth is, I admire the hell out of him.

I'd gotten to look at his file before I drove out to see him in person. It was thick with curled edges and miscellaneous scraps of Post-it notes about to fall out the side. His name on it, Alex Coffey, was speckled with what looked like tomato sauce. Like someone worked on it while they were eating lunch. After what I'd seen in that file, a lot of individuals who have gone through what he has would be flat out crazy, but no, he's not in the psych ward, just really pissed off. He has every right to be.

The agency dropped the ball on this kid years ago. What they've done to him is child abuse in itself and it's painfully obvious they've written him off as a lost cause. The case file was loaded with adjectives including *destructive, vindictive, uncooperative, hostile* ... and those were the better ones.

"Wow," I say. "Sixty-four previous foster care and residential care placements. That's a hell of a number. How did you manage it?"

He pauses long enough from launching his weaponry to curl his lip up. "*Nobody* tells me what to do."

I smile as all the automatic adult responses float through my head. *That's the kind of attitude that got you into a place like this ... Oh yeah? Well. I'm going to tell you what to do ... How are you ever going to get along in the world if you act like that?* But what I do is smile, slowly nod, and say, "Aaaah, an independent thinker. I get that. Good for you!"

He looks at me out of the corner of his left eye with what I think, and hope, is a flicker of interest. But then his eyes lower again. He hasn't looked me straight-on once. His head stays down a lot. He probably doesn't even realize how ingrained the behavior is. His right pupil is a floater and is usually resting at the corner of his eye by his nose. There's a name for the condition that most people know: a lazy eye. That nose, his chin, and pretty much the rest of his face is a study in bad acne. One of his front teeth is chipped in half. His brown hair is a short semi buzz, no doubt compliments of being in a correctional setting, which doesn't help his looks. He's not an attractive kid. Sad thing is, I can tell he knows it.

I motion to the book he has on the table next to him. Funny thing is my oldest son, who we adopted when he was sixteen, wrote it. "I've read that book. What do you think of it?"

The kid gives it a disinterested look and shrugs. "It kills the time."

High praise indeed. I'll have to pass that along to Kelly. So much for making chit-chat but I try again. Alex also has a lined composition book, the kind teachers often hand out for completing assignments.

I reach across the table and tap it. "Doing homework? Do you have a favorite subject?"

He puts his hand protectively over the booklet and slides it towards him. "Yeah, lunch."

Here's the thing. I can appreciate a smart-ass answer like this because you have to have a sense of humor and be reasonably intelligent enough to pull it off. I also get the larger picture: kids like this who know they are stuck in hell until they are at least eighteen and are happy to spread their misery to others. The juvenile correctional officer who has been sitting on the far side of the room, making sure Alex doesn't launch himself across the table to attack me, is not so understanding or appreciative. She shakes her head. "You might as well quit trying to get a civil word out of him. This is what we have to deal with."

Alex swivels in his seat to look at her and smirks. "Hey, I get released in three weeks. I'll be gone and you won't have to talk to me anymore."

She reaches down to adjust the volume on her radio which has begun to squawk letting everyone know Pod 3 is going to the gym, then glances back at Alex. "You won't be gone long. You'll be back. We'll leave the lights on for you."

I give her a look, but she's back to playing with the radio and doesn't see it. Inwardly, I wince. I hate it when people say things like that to a kid. But I'm not shocked. I've heard worse. Once it was a distraught thirteen-year-old girl threatening to kill herself. The officer responded with, "Oh, well. Do what you gotta do."

It's not that there aren't caring people in this line of work. I'd had a few words with his counselor, someone trying her best, who informed me that during his stay Alex hasn't made much treatment progress, despite individual and group counseling sessions. She said he has trust issues. *No shit Sherlock! Ya think?* Hell, I'd worry about him if he *didn't* have trust issues. How can you be trusting when you've been abused and tossed around like a ball all your life?

But I could tell she was giving it the old college try so kudos to her. Often staff do get jaded. Or they don't even realize the damage a few negative words can inflict. One of my best co-workers struggled during his adolescence. He told the story of having his dad come with him to meet with his teacher when he was having problems back in middle school. The teacher told his dad, *"I just don't think he's high school material."* Those casual words caused years of self-doubt, which he finally overcame. One of his proudest moments was strutting across the stage holding his diploma. But other kids take these words to heart and never recover.

As Alex turns back in his seat, his elbow hits his composition book, and it falls to the floor and lands by my feet. I pick it up and hand it to him before noticing a loose page has come out. As I pick it up, it's clear Alex has dropped his nonchalant persona. His whole body has gone rigid and his jaw is clenched.

Now I can't help but look at the page. From his reaction, I expect I'll see something he shouldn't be putting on paper, something that could get him in trouble if someone sees it. Doodling gang signs or drawing a picture of a gun. A list of people he hates or worse. But no, it *is* a list, but it's a teenage foster kid version of a bucket list. The top is *When I turn 18*. Listed in order are: Eat in a restaurant. Buy brand name sneakers. Get a dog from the humane society. See the ocean.

There's more but he's snatching it out of my hand. "That's mine!"

His face is flushed, and I know why. This is a kid who keeps his guard up and this is way more than he wants me to know about him.

Aw shit. It's more than I wanted to know, too. It speaks volumes. Because now I know while everyone else may have given up on this boy, he hasn't given up on himself. He has *plans*. The ability to look forward is often cited as the one difference between youth who may engage in a lifetime of violence and those that won't. There's one other factor that makes a difference in a life trajectory. Having one caring, committed adult in a child's life. Alex has no one.

But what if he did? Despite his voluminous file, just from these few minutes I've just spent with him, I can name things he has going for him. Take that novel he's got. I know he's changed schools countless times and despite that he reads at a high level. Wanting to rescue a dog shows he has compassion. He's endured all these placements and trauma but he's a survivor. He has *strengths*.

Feeling myself beginning to fall down the rabbit hole, I remind myself he entered the system when he was barely four years old. He was in five placements his first year, racked up another twenty by the time he was ten. He kept on accumulating them and this year alone he's managed to log in a whopping twenty-three before he got himself arrested on a drug charge. He's gone through eight social workers in addition to the sixty-four placements. I'd be a complete and utter fool to accept him into our program.

The only reason the child welfare folks contacted me is on the off chance they could pay my private agency enough to tempt us to take him. Three hundred twenty dollars a day. They're desperate. Juvenile justice has to release him in about three weeks because his time will be up and since he's a ward of the state he has to go to some placement, somewhere. If they can't find anything before Alex's discharge date, they'll end up sitting with him 24/7 in their office. They keep a cot for that purpose. I know of one office where the landlord won't let them house the kids at night, so as the sun goes down, the social workers load kids in a car and sit overnight in the parking lot of a nearby all night McDonald's. That's where they feed them and there is a bathroom.

Generally for these problematic teens, child welfare looks at some congregate care facility like a group home or residential center, usually operated by a religious organization, but Alex here has already trampled through every known church affiliation. Catholic Charities Youth Services. Baptist Home for Children. The Methodists and more. He is a non-discriminatory wrecking ball, tossed out of each and every one of them and they won't touch him now with a ten-foot pole. People who aren't in the biz are often surprised to find out it's foster care that is the last resort in these situations, because all it takes is getting one person or family to say yes, and presto, the kid has a roof over his head.

I can't keep my mind from thinking of possibilities. We do have a few homes that will take on some kids that no one else would even consider. Susan Jones, a single woman in her 70's, has stepped up for us several times before on tough cases. You might not think an older woman could manage tough teens but she has a way with them. She doesn't care about what's in their file. Said she'd use half of what was in there to line the bottom of a bird cage. She coined a phrase, *Paper Monsters*. Kids who on paper look terrible, but is that the real story?

I can tell by the way the light is coming through the one skylight in the ceiling that the sun is starting to go down. I really should wrap this up and get going but I find myself trying to make a connection with this kid with the chip—no, a boulder—on his shoulder.

Okay, time to up my game. My secret weapon. I reach into my pocket and pull out a deck of cards. "Want to see a magic trick?" I'm sure if I wait for an answer, he'll say no, so I just flip the cards with my thumb, showing him it's full of the usual hearts, diamonds, spades, and clubs and tell him, "Stick your finger in there wherever you want."

I don't make eye contact in an attempt to gain compliance. I don't have to. I've done this a couple hundred times and always get the same look from every kid. They don't want to cooperate but for some reason they just can't resist. True to form, the kid sticks his finger in the cards.

"Take the card your finger is on and look at it." I turn my head away. "Don't let me see it!"

The kid gives it a quick glance, still frowning at me. I hold up my hand with the cards. "Okay, put it back in the deck wherever you want."

Never taking his eyes off me, the boy puts it in about halfway to the bottom of the deck. I flip the cards a couple more times while looking at him studiously. "Are you thinking about your card? This is a mind-reading trick. I'm good at reading minds."

I read that his mind is most likely saying, *you're full of shit,* but I roll on.

"Hmm. Let me see. Yes, yes, I'm getting an image. It's becoming clear." I give it a dramatic pause. "Is it an ace of diamonds?"

He looks up in surprise, impressed despite himself. "How'd you do that?"

I shuffle the cards in front of him. "Want to try again?"

He pulls out the next card, looks at it, then his eyes narrow sharply at me. This never gets old. I put on an innocent look. "Is it an ace of diamonds?" As I say this, I flip the cards again and he watches all the jacks, two's, fives, and so on fly by. But then I put the deck on the table and give it a light tap. When I pick it up and flip it in front of him, this time all he sees are a whole deck of the ace of diamonds.

For just a few seconds he forgets himself. He forgets where he is. He forgets the image he has to put on to keep the world at bay. For a few heartbeats, he's just a kid. He sits up straighter. "Let me see that deck!"

I palm the cards and pull them in close to me. "Tell you what. I'll let you in on the secret eventually. I'll even teach you how to do it."

His guard comes back up. "How's that going to happen?"

Fools rush in. The deck I'm holding is a Svengali deck. Flip it one way and it looks like a normal deck. Flip it the other way and you see something entirely different. For a second, I get an image of each card as a time marker in this boy's future life. Flip it one way and it's another juvenile detention center, an adult jail, drug addiction, an adult prison. Flip it the other way and there are pictures of a high school graduation, his house, his wife, his kids.

My lawn is not getting mown today. And if I do the stupid thing I'm about to do, I'll be putting in a lot of extra hours over the next few weeks, if not months. Oh well, I didn't go into this line of work because it was easy.

I tuck the deck of cards back into their sleeve. Then I smile at Alex Coffey and slide over a promotional chocolate bar with *Phoenix Foster Care Agency: We Build Families* embossed in gold lettering on the front. "How about looking at us for placement number sixty-five?"

Chapter Three

ALEX

Geography. It's not the worst subject. It's sort of nice to know there's a bigger world out there beyond these walls, where I'm sealed off against the world, but since I've only left this state one time in my whole life, it's not like I've had much chance to put any of it to use. It wasn't like that one trip was any big deal—a trip to a zoo just across the river in a neighboring state. That was when I was in Placement Number 8. I acted badly. On the way home Mrs. Russell turned around in the front seat and yelled, "We are *never* taking you anywhere again!" That was a lie. Five days later they drove me to the child welfare office and dropped me off so I could head to Placement Number 9.

The teacher, Mr. Lang, is pointing to a spot that might be China, but my eyes drift past him to the calendar on the wall where I mentally put Xs through the days. It's been four days since the guy with the foster care agency came to talk to me. I remember his name was Sam Murry. An easy name. The last agency guy's name was Kirby Michalcyzk. Just on principle, I'm never going to trust a guy with that many consonants in his name. And forget spelling it.

In seventeen days, I will hit the magic four-month mark and because my committing offense was only a misdemeanor, by law, this joint will have to let me go. It doesn't matter that I haven't *cooperated with treatment goals and objectives*. It doesn't matter I'm still on Phase 2, just a step above Orientation Phase, and far removed from Phase 5 which is Graduation. Work my way through the phases to graduate early? What a joke. If I'd miraculously gotten to Phase 5 my second week here, I wouldn't have gotten out any sooner, so why bother? Children's Services would have told the juvenile staff *we're working on a placement,* and I'd have sat here for as long as they could legally keep me, regardless of how swell I acted.

I picture Ms. Snider, my child welfare worker, sitting at her desk. Maybe she's marking Xs on her calendar, too, thinking, *Damn, soon Alex Coffey is my responsibility again.* She might be the one who referred me to that Phoenix agency. No state foster homes will have me so they have to try and get one of the private agencies to take me.

Technically, the staff at this facility could petition the court to keep me here another four months for *lack of progress in treatment.* But I have no worries about that. Why? Because they don't like me. You might think that would make them want to make me suffer by extending my time. But no, then they'd be stuck with me and my mouth, so they'd rather roll the dice and hope the next kid that takes my spot is nicer.

I don't do *nice*. Oh, I used to. Thought if I did everything right, nothing bad would happen. If I was quiet, agreeable, likable, and made myself useful it was in my best interest. Eventually I figured out how stupid that was. Know what it's like to have no control over your life? Someone else decides everything for you regardless of how good or bad it is? I'd had enough of that. The only way to have control is to *not* do what they want you to do.

Take the group home I was just in. It had about a thousand stupid rules. If I'd followed them, been quiet and obedient, life would be miserable. Nope, nice gets you nowhere. The resident handbook says, "Don't open the refrigerator without permission." I learned if you bitched enough staff would often look the other way. They'd rather do that than have the hassle.

"Why can't I? All I want is a damn drink, what's wrong with that?!"

"The regulations say we get a snack every afternoon and I haven't had one. I want to file a grievance!"

"Mr. Hughes doesn't care if I get one. He let me do it last night. Why won't you?"

The big fear was I'd pitch such a fit they'd have to do a physical restraint on me and none of them wanted that.

My thoughts are interrupted when I hear a loud hacking cough. I make the mistake of glancing over at Darryl who's sitting on my right. A fellow *resident*. They call us that, I guess, because it sounds nicer than calling us *inmates,* but he's no friend. You don't have friends in here, just allies. Pretty much it's every man for himself.

"Who you looking at, One Eye?" he whispers.

Charming guy. I ignore him and look back at the calendar. If I'm lucky I might get placed a few days before the deadline, if there's a weekend involved. They usually don't make placements into foster homes on weekends if it's not an emergency.

I'm pretty much a walking encyclopedia on foster care regulations. Like anything in life, the way to get good at it is practice, practice, practice. In addition to all the placements I've had, I've gone through eight social workers. When I got committed to the Department of Juvenile Justice for the second time, I could almost hear my current worker, Ms. Snider, sigh in relief, knowing I'd be someone else's problem for a few months.

I'm actually surprised they are looking at another foster home for me. I figured it would be back to a private child care residential placement. Most of them are run by churches. Doesn't matter who runs them, I can find ways to get thrown out of them. Maybe there's a new one called *Church of What's Happening Now*. The cook here said that's where she wants to go to church. I like the cook. And the maintenance man. They're the only two staff here I ever really talk to. They're safe. They don't care about my treatment plan or whether I am *taking responsibility for my actions*. They fix food and repair the roof. Real things. Stuff that matters.

Mr. Murry called and talked to me on the phone a couple of days ago. He told me he's still looking for the right place, maybe a home with a single person with no kids. That's happened more as

I've gotten older, and it's harder for them to find homes that will take me. Placements Number 32, 38, 42, and 56 come to mind. There are advantages. I don't have to get into all the usual garbage of dealing with foster siblings or worse, the foster parent's own kids.

So, it's back into the foster home grind. Same old, same old. Fine, I'm ready to put on a good show. I'm all goody, goody now whenever I talk to Mr. Murry. *I'm ready for a fresh start. I promise not to run away. I've learned from my mistakes. Blah, blah, blah.* People usually eat that shit up, but I got a feeling Mr. Murry isn't exactly buying it. But it's still to my benefit to put on the act if I want out of here and not end up in another residential program. A foster home, even with the drawbacks, is at least like real life. Detention and other big group settings feel like you are not in the real world or completely out of it. Not fully alive, but maybe unfortunately, not dead either.

So yeah, I'm pleased to go to a foster home instead of some treatment facility. There are definite perks. Usually, the food is much better. Placement number 17 with the Sabbatinis had awesome Italian food: home-made pizza, lasagna, spaghetti. Mealtimes there were fun. Lots of joking around and laughter. I really liked it there and would have been happy to stay. But one of their other foster kids, who'd been there much longer, and I didn't get along and had some rip-roaring fights. Someone had to go. Guess who?

But the food's not always great. At Placement Number 21, I survived for many months on nothing but hot pockets and ramen noodles. I complained to my then social worker, Dave, but got no sympathy. He barely looked up from the papers he was studying and said, "They get paid to feed you; no one says you get to pick what it is. Lots of kids go hungry, you should be grateful you get a meal three times a day." The bastard probably went home and had a steak and fries.

The other perk of a foster home is getting to sleep in sometimes. Residential programs always get you up at the crack of dawn, or even before. Group homes may appear nice, and more home-like, but the rules at a lot of them aren't too much different than secure detention. If you're in a foster home, you can still do normal things like walk out into the backyard and sit in the sun, turn on the TV, get a snack when you want it. But in a lot of group homes you can't do any of that everyday stuff. Kids even have to ask permission to go to the bathroom. And you're supposed to live like that for *years*. It's no wonder so many of us run away.

I hear more coughing next to me and without thinking turn to look at Darryl. Darryl the Dick, Darryl the Prick, take your choice. He raises his middle finger under his desk and whispers, "Hey, zit face."

I look at the calendar. Seventeen days.

Chapter 4

SAM

It's Sunday evening, that time of night when my mind, unbidden, begins the transition from personal time to work thoughts. My wife is in the kitchen and my two girls are in bed. My son Kyle is still up, sprawled on the couch as only an adolescent boy can do. He has his eyes on his phone as he sits in front of the TV with a baseball game on.

From this spot at my desk, I glance up as the crowd roars. "Who's winning?"

Kyle doesn't seem to take his eyes off the phone but says, "Tied."

I look up at the clock on the wall. "Getting kind of late on a school night, isn't it?"

"Not my fault they went into extra innings."

Smartass. But I can't completely disagree with his logic. I walk over and scoot his feet aside to join him on the couch just in time to catch the home run that ends the game and clinches the win for the Braves. Kyle watches the ball sail over the fence then turns his attention back to his phone.

Knowing I'm treading into forbidden territory, I ask, "Who are you texting this late?"

"Nobody," he says as he hurriedly puts away the phone. "Guess I'll go to bed. Night, Dad."

"Night, kiddo." I smile to myself as he takes the stairs two at a time. Without a doubt, he's already got that phone out of his pocket to resume his texting with Tracy, his current crush. That's probably not the word kids use nowadays. How did I get so old? I knew it was happening when I no longer recognized any of the musical guests for Saturday Night Live. Worse, I couldn't make out a word they were singing.

I like Tracy. Much more so than the last girlfriend who was a little too … I don't know … *something*. She corresponded with a little rough patch we had with Kyle, so it's easy to blame it on her. Thankfully, the rough spot wasn't that bad. And as always, I'm thankful Kyle, who we adopted when he was thirteen, gets to be a typical teenager instead of the guy in charge, trying to take care of his two little sisters, who we also adopted.

That thought swivels my mind to Alex Coffey, the kid I saw on Friday. I pushed him out of my head all weekend, but now I'm going to have to try and make good on my promise to the child welfare folks that we'd take him. I should have never committed without a family firmly lined-up but I let my emotions get the better of me. He is a walking train wreck but I could also see he has potential. Neglected not just by his family, but by the state who was supposed to step in and take better care of him.

Sixty-four placements. Good Lord. I don't necessarily blame individual workers or their bosses, because they have to work within the budget parameters they are given by the legislature and the governor which is never close to what they need to really do the job. But someone needs to shake up the entire system. Stop accepting that shuffling kids between foster homes and facilities is "business as usual." Instead, there should be some alarm that goes off after say, two failed foster care placements, that prompts intense and vigorous efforts to find children stability. In most cases, that should always be a home, not a facility. Kids need stable, consistent loving adults, not a rotating cast of caregivers who come in for eight-hour shifts.

The question I really wanted to ask Alex Coffey is, why aren't you doing worse than you are?

Who the hell can I get to take him? The Robertsons are good but no, I just placed twelve-year-old Tim Montgomery with them. He has more mental health diagnoses than Santa has reindeer and they have their hands full.

There's always a balance to consider with your really good homes. You don't want to overload them with so many tough kids they burn out and step away. My sister is a fifth-grade teacher. She says about half her students are ADHD kids and if she gets one more she's going to scream. Every time she tells the special education director, *not another*, they tell her *oh, but you're so good with them*. The road to hell is paved with good intentions.

If only Susan Jones's mother hadn't fallen and broken her hip. Susan's had to take a foster care sabbatical while she cares for her ninety-four-year-old mom. Susan herself is no spring chicken, but at seventy-two she can still handle the toughest kids. Some people just have the magic touch and she's one of them.

With still no answer to my dilemma, I give up when my wife emerges from the kitchen and plops on the couch next to me. Bonnie Ziegler Murry. My kick-ass, take-no-prisoners lady, who plays tennis like it's a battle for world dominion then turns around an hour later and bakes the best brownies this side of the Mississippi.

She curls up next to me, tucking her feet under the throw pillows, and wraps her right arm around me before laying her head on my chest. "A penny for your thoughts. Unless they're about me, then they're worth a dollar."

I smile and pull her closer. "My thoughts aren't getting me anywhere. A problem with no easy solution. A kid with sixty-four prior placements. I need reminding not to take on challenges that rely on other people doing them."

She raises her head off my chest. "This getting carried away isn't involving me, is it? Or the girls or Kyle? Or even Kelly?" Her tone is teasing but I sense the warning underneath.

"Not to worry. I think four adopted kids is enough for us, even if just three of them are still under roof full-time, especially when we throw in all the other kids in the agency that are in some ways part ours too. But I'm sitting here running down the possible homes and nothing's clicking."

She pats my chest with her open hand. "Give it up for now. Sleep on it. You'll think better in the light of day."

"You're right. Obsessing on it isn't helping."

She gives me a smile and trails her finger down my arm. "Maybe what you need is ... hmmm ... a distraction."

I look in her eyes and smile the crooked smile I know she loves. "Yeah? That sounds good." Now I trail my finger down her neck. "Is there another ball game on?"

Her eyes narrow and she reaches over and grabs the TV remote from the arm of the couch, clicks the TV off, stands up, and sticks the remote in the back pocket of her jeans. "See if you can find the right channel."

Laughing, I fumble under the light shade to find the knob, and click off the lamp. "Now there's a challenge I'm willing to take on that doesn't rely on anyone else."

As I follow her up the stairs, I spot two large plastic containers on the dining room table.

"Good lord, how many brownies did you make?"

"With all the kids that will be there, probably not enough, but it's a potluck so between them and the gigantic birthday cake Carolyn ordered, no one should go hungry. Just don't blow the surprise. Make sure it's after six o-clock before you get Mike there. Park on Dupont Street but not too near the corner."

"I thought I'd park over on Hawthorne."

"Absolutely not, he might see the cars from there."

"Okay, okay. I'm not going to argue about it."

Continuing up the stairs, she says, "I'm not arguing. I'm explaining why I'm right and you're wrong."

I can't help but laugh. I give her a little poke in the back. "Do you ever get tired of being bossy?"

She turns to face me with her nose raised high. "I am *not* bossy. I just know what everyone should do and need to impart my knowledge."

I'm a man who understands what makes a successful marriage. Grinning, I give her a thumbs up. "I'm on it, Chief."

Mike King is my oldest friend and the pediatrician for all my kids. His wife decided at the last minute to throw him a surprise birthday party, a cook-out. I have been tapped to collect him after work tomorrow night and deliver him before the screaming masses, including his own two teenage boys, at Shillito Park's picnic pavilion on some ruse I haven't yet worked out. But I have a plan B, which I'm pretty sure will morph into Plan A. I'll tell him about the party then we'll arrive at the right time and hope his acting skills are up to looking astonished and surprised. I hate surprise parties. That, and restaurant staff singing at people on their birthdays. Bonnie and I have a pact that if either one of us does that to the other, it's grounds for divorce.

Reaching the bedroom, I see chocolate on the front of her Frank Little Memorial Tennis Tournament T-shirt. As she closes the door behind us, I nod at the direction of her chest. "You're wearing part of your potluck contribution."

She glances down and frowns. "Nice of you to point that out."

"That's me, a nice guy. And I'm going to be nice enough to help you take that T-shirt off."

"Well, aren't you considerate?"

I cradle her neck in my hand and pull her towards me. "I'll do anything to get that remote."

Chapter 5

SAM

It's Monday night. I'm no closer to finding a foster home for Alex Coffey, but I have fulfilled my duty to forcibly escort Mike King to his party at the picnic pavilion of Shillito Park. Out of a sense of obligation to his wife, I decided to try and come up with a lie to get him there, but it was so hard dragging Mike away from "one more minute" at his office, I gave it up and told him his ass and mine would be grass if we were late to his surprise party.

That did the trick. He hastened out of the office while thanking me for warning him. When we pulled up and the kids rushed out with their homemade happy birthday-banner, he did an admirable job of looking like he had *no idea* what was in the works. He did throw one little wink in my direction which had Bonnie squinting her eyes at me while I put on my best innocent look, knowing she wasn't the tiniest bit fooled.

After stuffing our faces, the adults are standing around the picnic tables with drinks in hand while the kids run around in the grass, armed with water blasters. I turn to the side and try to look busy when I see Mike's cousin Ray coming my way. He's one of those people you try to avoid because he greets you like he's your long-lost friend then proceeds to bore you to death. He sells real estate and is always pushing a sale, and when he isn't doing that he has several lines he uses over and over including *how about a frosty beverage*? But I can't escape him without looking rude, so I paste on a smile and face the inevitable.

"Sam, it's great to see you!"

"Hi Ray, how ya been?"

"Couldn't be better. You know, you should see this piece of property that just came on the market."

"Thanks, Ray. We're happy where we are." I must have told him this a hundred times in the past few years.

He reaches over to grab my elbow and vigorously shake my arm. "Never hurts to ask! Well, how about a frosty beverage?"

It's all I can do not to wince. I'm saved by Mike who drifts over to stand next to me and casually mentions that Mrs. Simmons, who is standing over by the last picnic table, just mentioned something about downsizing. Ray quickly leaves us looking for greener pastures.

Mike hands me one of the two soft drinks in his hand and produces the twitch that goes for a smothered smile. He glances at Ray's departing back. "He's annoying as hell, but he's one of their top salesmen, so I can't hold it too much against him."

He lifts his drink and takes a sip. "How's work going? I still can't believe you've gone from police work to adult corrections to running a foster care agency. What's next? Teaching kindergarten?"

I step aside in time to avoid a little girl about five dashing by me and laugh. "Now, *that* would be more dangerous than police work and adult corrections combined. Yeah, it's been a transition, but work's good. Other than always needing more foster homes. I'm constantly looking for candidates. You're great with kids but I'm waiting till your kids are out of the house and you aren't so busy with your practice before I hit you up."

Mike grimaces. "No thanks. When the kids are grown and I retire, I'm going to lay on the beach non-stop and do nothing. Except maybe some fishing."

We hear screams from the kids and from beneath the overhang of the picnic pavilion, we look down on a dozen or so kids waging war with their water blasters. The only adult with them is Mike's younger brother, Matt. First time I've seen him in a while.

Several years younger than Mike and me, as a little kid he was perpetually following us around. He gave that up long before Mike and I left for college. He had plenty of friends of his own by then, especially since he was the star of every sport he undertook. After conquering baseball and basketball, he concentrated on football and broke every record his high school had. An unfortunate incident ruined his prospective college football career, and what might eventually have been a pro career. Since high school he's had a series of different jobs, none lasting very long. I run into him now and again and we have a good laugh or two. I've always liked him.

I tip my drink towards the reverie on the lawn and say to Mike. "I haven't seen Matt in a while. What's he up to these days?"

Mike looks at his brother and gives a little sigh. "This and that. He gave up the construction job, and then his short run at selling used cars, before winding up at Carol Gray's landscape business. He lasted longer there. Carol retired and to all our surprise, Matt bought her out. It's left him strapped for cash. I offered to help him out but got shot down, which wasn't unexpected."

A kid aims his blaster at Matt who raises his arms above his head and prances to the kid like a monster. The kid shoots on the run, squealing in delight and mock terror.

"It's nice he's keeping the kids occupied."

Mike shakes his head and gives a rueful smile. "Yeah, he likes kids but I think he stays out there so he doesn't have to talk to Mom." Mike crushes the can in his hand and tosses it towards the recycle bin. It hits the edge and bounces out. "Damn. Losing my touch. I'm getting another drink, want one?"

"Nah, I'm good."

Mike goes to pick up his errant can while I go back to watching the kids. They are starting to get out of hand. Three of the bigger kids are zoning in on little Wesley Higgins for whom the phrase "non athletic" would be a charitable description. They've pinned him next to a shed and two other kids are on the way to join in the massacre. With a frown, I start to put my drink on the picnic table and head out there, but no need.

"Hey guys, you all couldn't hit the broad side of a barn," Matt yells as he diverts them away from Wesley. They are quick to grab the bait, firing jointly at Matt like something out of Ghostbusters, not caring if they cross the water streams.

Once they run out of ammo, he swoops in and tag-teams with Wesley. "Hey Wes, buddy, let's get 'em."

He managed to save Wesley without the older boys becoming more antagonistic and without making Wesley look like the victim. *Hmmm … interesting.* I keep watching as he guides the kids, stops other squabbles, and makes sure everyone gets to participate. More and more interesting.

Mike comes back with his drink and smiles at the gang and their battles. He raises his can and takes a quick drink. "Kids are having a ball. Maybe it's because Matt's never grown up himself, but he's always been good with them. He's great with mine. He hired them out for some work and managed to get them to toe the line, never easy with two teenage boys. They seem to know how far they can go with him, but no further. Too bad he's such rotten marriage material because he could actually be a good dad someday."

I keep my voice casual. "I saw a couple of garbage bags full of beer cans in the back of his truck. How much is he drinking?"

Mike sits down on a picnic bench. "Well, in spite of what happened, or maybe because of it, he's always very careful about that. I've never seen him drunk. Those cans are ones he picked up by the road near his place. Says he can't stand littering."

"He still out on Delaney Ferry Road? I haven't been to his place in a while. How many bedrooms does that cabin of his have?"

Mike has known me all my life so I don't get away with much. He turns and looks at me. "What's with your sudden interest in my not-so-little brother?"

I reach over and grab a handful of chips. Shoot Mike a cheesy grin. "Just thinking maybe he and I could help each other out."

Mike squints his eyes at me a few seconds and then shakes his head. "No! That is a bad idea."

"Why? You just said he's good with kids and would be a good dad."

"Yeah, like in the future … maybe twenty years. Right now, he's the same ornery cuss he's always been. He and Mom barely speak. I tried to talk some sense into him. Told him to go bury the hatchet but all he said to me was 'nobody tells me what to do.'"

I feel the corner of my mouth turn up but manage not to laugh outright. "Did he now?"

"Yeah. He's stubborn, selfish, immature. I'm telling you Sam, he might not do a kid any good at all."

I raise my eyebrows. "All that and more, huh? Well, maybe a kid might do some good for him." I think to myself that this is something I can personally speak to. It wasn't that long ago a kid did good things for me. I'd been stuck in a bad rut until the boy who we eventually adopted came into my life.

"You know you don't have to be perfect to be a foster parent. Everybody has their issues. Would he hurt a kid?"

"No! Never. But ..."

"Would he make sure he was fed? Clothed? Give him a kind word or two?"

"Of course, but ... still a bad idea."

Matt lets Wesley join in with the other kids to gang up on him. It's a universal truth that kids get great pleasure at beating an adult at anything. Matt takes their shots for a bit before dramatically falling down crying uncle. Then in one smooth move, he jumps up and indicates game's over. All the kids immediately drop their weapons and head up towards the pavilion to refuel on brownies and cake.

Mike scowls at me. "You aren't listening to me, are you? You're a stubborn bastard too. And crazy. I can't imagine my brother ever agreeing to such a thing but if he did, I pity the nice kid who might get stuck with Matt."

I crush my can, toss it towards the bin, hit dead center. "Oh, I'm not planning on a nice kid."

◆ ◆ ◆

Driving home with Bonnie, I'm preoccupied with my thoughts and realize I've committed the cardinal husband sin of not paying attention. Bonnie jabs my arm with her finger. "Have you heard a word I've said?"

"Sure." I make a stab at a high percentage answer. "Food was good."

"Nice try, champ. No, I said you spent lots of time with Mike. Any good gossip?"

"No, we spent most of the time talking about Matt."

Bonnie flicks the visor down to keep the sun out of her eyes and turns back to me. "Oh, now he should be good fodder for discussion. A bad boy from a good family. A hunk and not married. When he changed out of that wet shirt there wasn't a woman there who wasn't looking."

I turn my head and raise my eyebrows. She laughs. "Of course, I looked. I'm married, but I'm not dead. Black hair that's just a little too long and green eyes are a killer combination. But don't worry, I like my guys lean and lanky. Matt has the height but he looks more like the football player he once was."

"I was watching him with the kids. You know, I've known him all his life. He may not have gone the route of both his parents and Mike and become a doctor, but he's smart and despite his reputation, or whether he admits it or not, he's basically a good guy. He needs some money. It got me to thinking … maybe he and I could help each other out. Remember the kid I told you about, the one with all the placements?"

"Yes, and oh Sam, what are you thinking? That kid needs someone who's experienced."

Now as the sun strikes *me* full force in the face, I pull my visor down and reach for my sunglasses. "The boy's already had experienced. He's had inexperienced and everything in between. I think we need to shake things up and do something completely out of the norm. Throw him off guard. He already thinks all adults are good for nothing and only out for themselves. Whatever trick I can pull to keep him staying in one place for a while is a win. I'll try and line up other people to be on Team Alex. So what if nobody has tried a little sleight of hand before?"

Bonnie grins. "This sounds like the old adage, *the darn fool didn't know it couldn't be done, so he went and did it?*"

"Exactly."

"Yeah, what if the darn fool had tried swimming for the first time? The darn fool would have drowned. I hope you know what you're getting yourself into."

I reach over and grab her hand and lift it to my lips. "Well, the last time I played the darn fool, it worked out pretty well, don't you think? I ended up with you and a houseful of kids."

She laughs. "Right you are." She punches my arm. "Okay, go for it. What have you got to lose?"

"The usual. Nothing but my job and my sanity. So, no problemo."

As I drive, plans and strategies form in my head. I'm still a long way from landing Alex a spot, but I'm in a much better place than I was a few hours ago when I had zero prospects. I smile as one of my favorite Sherlock Holmes phrases pops into my head.

The game is afoot.

Chapter 6

MATT

When you want everyone to leave you the hell alone, you get a place in the country. Not just *in* the country, but *way* out in the country. I'd told my realtor one of my requirements was there couldn't be a single house in sight. When she brought me here after I'd turned down dozens of other places, she'd crossed her arms and said, "If this doesn't do it, I quit."

She didn't have to throw in the towel. I knew within three minutes this house and land was exactly what I'd been looking for. I put down a hunk of the money my father had left me on the down payment. Now this two-bedroom log cabin is all mine. The wood walls make it dark but the previous owner wisely put in enough skylights that the natural light brightens it up. It sits in a unique spot with the Elkhorn Creek about two hundred yards out my front door. I get to drive across my very own bridge to head to work every morning. Well, most days. The only problem with that creek is when the water is high, it overtakes the bridge. Then I'm either stuck here or have to anticipate it's coming and park my car about a quarter mile out the back and drive the long way around by Pisgah Pike to get to town. Most people wouldn't want to put up with that which meant the cabin came relatively cheap.

I took all the rest of my inheritance and put it into buying my own landscape business. I know everyone thinks this is some harebrained scheme. My resume doesn't exactly make me look like a stable, career-minded employee. My own mother thinks my executive skills are limited to slicing a pizza. But this time it's different. First, because it's mine. And second, because for the only time in my not-so-illustrious work life, something clicked.

First, I get to be outside all day. Okay, maybe not so great when it's freezing or rain is pouring down, but still preferable to sitting in some boring office all day. Likewise, I like the manual labor. Best of all, I like looking at something as it is, and imagining how much better it could be. Better for the eye, but also better for everything else-the air, the water, insects, birds, and animals. That's because Matt's Landscape Kingdom specializes in native plants and designs with a nod to restoring or improving the environment.

I laugh at myself. Who would believe Matt King would become an environmentalist? I think people would be less shocked if I told them I was secretly working for the CIA. The credit, or the blame, for my *aha* moment goes to Carol Gray. When I went to work for her, I didn't know a petunia from a rose. But I watched her work her magic and where once there had been a square plot of grass with no sign of life, I'd seen her transform it into a little piece of Eden, where butterflies fluttered, birds raised their babies, and in some cases even foxes took up residence. Carol, who despaired of finding someone to take over her business, initially hired me because she needed the muscle. The old adage *a strong back and a weak mind* was what she thought she was getting. Once she realized I was becoming genuinely interested, she'd thrown herself into developing her replacement.

Slowly but surely, I learned the names of the plants and which ones would be hosts for caterpillars that would in turn become moths and butterflies, which trees had berries that helped migrating birds increase their body fat for their long journeys. Doing this work, I feel … well … *purposeful*. Like I'm making a difference in the world.

Nationally, there's a growing number of homeowners who have seen the light and want a sustainable property. Folks who enjoy sitting on a patio in the morning with their cup of coffee watching fifteen kinds of birds come to their feeder. The other side of that coin is not everyone, or even the majority of folks in this neck of the woods, have made the conversion. Too many people think nature outside their house translates to a slab of lawn, a few foundation shrubs, and a Japanese Maple. Business isn't booming but I still think native plants are catching on. I believe the times will catch up to even this rural southern area. To help that along I'm doing as much educating as I can, like giving talks at the local library and to garden clubs where I pass out my business cards freely.

During my talks, I include a story that always makes an impact. Everyone loves chickadees and many people put out sunflower seeds in feeders for them. The truth is the babies can't eat seeds. They need insects to grow and survive. Insects are supplied by native plants. For instance, a native oak has hundreds of different caterpillars feeding on its leaves. Those Asian plants everyone is so fond of have almost none. A breeding pair of chickadees feeds 350-570 caterpillars a day to their young. Doing the higher math, it means it takes about 6,000-9,000 caterpillars to raise one clutch. The parents only fly so far and no further looking for food. Saddest thing I ever saw was a nest of dead chickadee babies covered in sunflower seeds. The desperate parents tried to feed them the only food they could find while the babies starved to death, no more able to eat the seeds than people can eat grass. This story hits folks in the heart.

I glance at my wrist. In just a bit, I'll be leaving to look at the Hanson's property to give them an estimate. They have thirty acres and loads of money. Landing this job could at least help me afford the new truck I desperately need. I start getting my things together and frown when a car pulls up in front of my house. Oh crap, now I remember, Sam Murry called and asked for a few minutes of my time. I forgot all about it. I glance at my watch again. I should still have ample time to make it to my appointment if I hustle him out pretty quick.

I close the door to the kitchen so Sam can't see the three days' worth of dishes stacked in the sink. Grabbing two of my jackets off the couch, I toss them in the bedroom and close the door just as I hear Sam's knock. The rat-tat-tat sets my black hound dog Sadie on a barking frenzy and she dashes to the door.

"Come on in, Sam," I holler from where I'm picking up my work boots to throw in my truck when I leave.

Sam walks in and bends over to rub the quivering dog's head. "Hi there, Sadie. You doing your watch dog thing?"

When I join them, Sadie sashays with her hind end twisting every which way over to me to receive her just due for her pathetic guard dog duties. "She won't bite you but if you break in during the night you might stumble over her while she's sleeping, so she *is* a burglar deterrent."

We make chit chat for a few minutes while I wait for him to get to whatever reason he has for coming and try not to look too impatient. I have to admit I'm curious. The thought crosses my mind he might hire me to do some work at his place since he's got some acreage. Deciding to take the direct approach, I ask, "You wanting to hire me out, Sam?"

Sam smiles, "In a manner of speaking. Not for landscape work, although if you call Bonnie, you might talk her into it. No, I've got something else in mind."

Intrigued, I tilt my head towards Murry. "I'm listening."

"Mike tells me you're a bit short on cash these days."

I squint my eyes at him. "Mike has a big mouth."

Sam grins. "Yeah, I know. You might be his brother but remember I've known him longer than you have. Okay, the money thing. Is it not true?"

I toss my boots by the door. "Yeah, it's true but I've got some irons in the fire. I'll be okay. What have you got in mind?"

"I've got something you could help me out with. See, there's this kid, a fifteen-year-old, who needs a roof over his head and someone to keep an eye on him. I don't have one of our usual homes for him right now. I'm a little desperate to find him a spot."

I know what Sam does for a living. It's not that I don't admire him for it but I think he's crazy. Now he wants me to sign on to Crazyville with him. "Wait. You're asking me to become a *foster* parent? You've got to be kidding. I'm not even married."

"Technically, yes. But I'm not asking you to become one like long-term for a bunch of kids. Just for this particular kid. For your information, plenty of foster parents are single. In this kid's case, think of it more as taking on a roommate. It's not as if he's some little tyke. You wouldn't have to potty train him or make sure he doesn't run out into the street. You just need to give him a room, feed and clothe him, provide some supervision. Look, I can make this financially worth your while."

"What bill of goods are you trying to sell me? I've read the paper and watched the evening news enough to know foster parents don't make diddly squat."

"Generally, that's true, but for special needs kids the state will pay a much higher rate."

Sam takes a piece of paper out of the folder in his hand and puts it on the table in front of me. "I could pay you this." I take a quick glance.

"Is that for a week or a month? Either way, I'm not tempted."

"It's for each day."

I look up at him with a snort. "You can't be serious. So, what kind of needs does this kid have that warrant this kind of pay out? Is he some sort of monster?"

"Not at all. With this boy, it's just a bunch of things lumped together. His age. Number of prior placements. A bit of some drug use that's gotten him in some trouble. He's sitting in a juvenile facility till I can find a place for him. And to be honest, he's snarky, stubborn, and obstinate. Sound like anyone you know?"

I give him a nasty look which he just ignores and talks on. "In fact, he reminds me of you so much I thought maybe he could actually be yours."

I scowl at Sam. "I'm thirty, I'd have to had him when I was fifteen."

Sam gives me a dry look. "If I recall, that's not out of the realm of possibility."

"Ha. Ha." I slide the paper back at him. "Still the answer is a firm and definite no. Besides I've got a major job coming up. Should help me pay the bills for some time." My patience has run out. "Look, I'm in a hurry here, so take your harebrained idea with you as you head out." I point my thumb over my shoulder as I turn my back on him and start picking up my stuff.

But he isn't making haste to leave. Just stands there shaking his head back and forth "Do you intentionally piss people off or is it a natural gift?"

Feeling a little contrite, I give him a grin. "Kinda comes natural, but I work at it too."

Sam pushes the paper back towards me. "You keep it. Mull it over a while." He takes a picture out of the folder and sets it on top of the piece of paper. "His name is Alex." With that he turns and takes a couple of steps to the door then stops as he puts his hand on the knob. "Matt, remember that time you said you owed me?"

Sam must be desperate to bring that back up. "It was years and years ago. I remember you said to forget it."

Sam pulls his car keys out of his pocket and shrugs. "Did I?"

Chapter 7

MATT

As soon as Sam's in his car, I'm grabbing my stuff and heading out to give an estimate on what would be my biggest job to date. I'm pissed at Sam for distracting me. Also, for dredging up unwanted memories of another kid who once sat in a cell waiting for someone to come rescue him. Murry is a manipulative son of a bitch. He knows just what buttons to push.

Sadie, sitting in the cab next to me, sees a couple of deer jump across the road and goes ballistic. As I shove her back to her side of the seat, I also shove thoughts of Sam and his troublesome kid out of my mind and concentrate on the job ahead. The prospective clients live on a private road and I turn at the green street sign that announces Rushing Wind Lane. Some guy probably named it that because it's at the top of a hill, making it breezy, but every time I drive by, I can't help but think of it as Fart Lane. Needless to say, I won't be sharing that little piece of information with the clients.

I pull up in front of the Hanson's big house at the top of a hill with the long winding drive. Find a shade tree to park under, roll down the windows, and tell Sadie to stay, before getting out. I feast my eyes on the view. It's a lovely piece of property. I can't help but think if I had gotten to play pro football and made a lot of dough, it might be me sitting up on that front porch. The house is framed on three sides by a wooded area, showing off its interesting angles and proportions. I can see all the possibilities. *I've got to get this job.*

The Hansons come out before I reach the door. They are both in their fifties. Nicely dressed like they took off from work. We say our hellos, shake hands, and they tell me to call them Jim and Lisa. We all turn at the same time to gaze at the rolling hills before us.

Unlike some jobs, I don't have to lie to be complimentary. "You've got a beautiful place here. I have some ideas but before I mention them, let me ask you. Have you given any thought to what you'd like to see done here?"

Lisa nods and her eyes light up. "Oh yes, definitely. We'd like to have a mix of shrubs and small trees lining the drive."

"Great idea. Ninebark would look great. There's a maroon leaf variety that stands out. Some serviceberry, dogwoods, and redbuds would all do well as understory trees with the shade you get from those big oaks, and they'd flourish once we chop out all that honeysuckle."

She waves her hand. "Oh, we want those big, old trees to come down. Don't want to bother with all the leaves. And we like the honeysuckle. It can stay. Smells so good, doesn't it? What we'd like to have in front of them is those bushes that get so lovely every fall. Oh, I know the name of them but it just left me. What are those, Jim?"

Her husband looks proud to have the answer. "Burning bushes."

Lisa laughs. "Of course, how could I forget? Those bright red leaves look like flames. And I'd like those nice pyramid shaped trees, the ones with the white blooms in the spring. The … uh … Callery Pears."

Jim gets his two cents in. "Yeah, and I want low maintenance under them. That shiny vine. You can mow right over it if you need too. Easy to grow. Well, dang, now the name of it isn't coming to me."

A feeling of complete dread comes over me. It's all I can do to say the word, "Wintercreeper?"

"Yeah, that's it! There you go. How does that sound to you?"

I want to say it's an apocalyptic vision that strikes at my very soul. It's like they've named the rogue gallery of invasive plants that are spreading across America with disastrous results. Worse, their property is sitting next to a woodland area where those plants would escape and take over and ruin a piece of Eden. I try to be diplomatic and use the technique Nancy taught me: Begin where the client is.

I nod and say, "I hear you. You want low maintenance and some color and maybe fragrance too. Great ideas." Then I try to move them away from the plants from hell.

Two hours later, after dropping off Sadie back at the house, I'm sitting at Dirty Ernie's bar nursing a beer and a headache. I used every trick in the book but couldn't get the Hanson's to budge. They wanted what they wanted and no amount of research or persuasion was going to sway them. Man, I needed that job, but I had to tell them to find someone else. I think if I'd tried to plant any of the plants they'd named, I'd have stuck the shovel right through my foot and chopped it clean off to end my pain. I just couldn't do it. Deciding I might as well have an early dinner, I order some potato skins. They are dry and overcooked but I eat them all without really tasting them. Or caring.

Afterwards, I get in the truck, turn the ignition, and hear a loud bang. The next time I turn the key, I get no sound at all. I lay my head on the steering wheel. *Shit!* Can this day get any worse? Turns out it can. After I get the truck towed to J & W Repair Shop, Wayne spends some time under the hood then stands up and wipes his hands on his oil-stained rag. He shakes his head. "I told you last time Matt, this old girl was on her last legs. You'd pay more for me to rebuild her than if you go buy a good used one."

The final straw on my terrible, horrible, no good, very bad day is I have to call my brother Mike and beg a ride home. He's sympathetic. I hate that. Worse, I hate knowing if this happened to him, thanks to his thriving medical practice, he could whip out his platinum card and drive a brand-new truck right off the lot.

Sadie greets me at the door. She never gives me bad advice, but she isn't the world's best listener. The worst thing about living alone is when you feel like shit, you have no one to complain to. I think of Mike on his way home to his wife and kids. All the noise and laughter in his house. This one seems awfully quiet tonight. Hell, maybe it wouldn't be so bad to have someone else around.

I walk over and pick up the picture of the boy Sam talked to me about this morning before the day went to hell. This picture had to be taken some time ago because he doesn't look fifteen, maybe twelve. The kid has his head down, like he didn't want his photo taken. Reminds me of the King family photo shoots my mother dragged us all to. *Matthew, quit sulking and look up and smile. The longer you don't cooperate the longer we'll be here.*

I feel a little stab of pity for this kid. Think about my family. They could be, and still can be, a pain in the ass but I have them. What would it be like to be so young and not have parents? Or siblings. I'm glad I don't have Sam's job where you witness so much sadness on a daily basis. More people *should* step up to help these kids out. Married, church-going, pillars of the community people. Not people like me.

With a flick of my hand, I toss the photo back on the table and go take a shower. Once I'm out, I grab my financial files and sit at the kitchen table. I've got to get a new truck but everywhere I look I can't find a corner I haven't already cut. There's no getting around it, I'm going to have to either take out a loan and try to make the payments, swallow my pride and ask Mike to loan me the money, or …

I meander back to the kid's picture and Sam's piece of paper with the daily per diem I'd get if I took in this boy. He isn't a great looking kid but he doesn't look like a monster either. Snarky, eh? A bit of trouble? That doesn't scare me off. It's having to be responsible for someone besides myself that scares the shit out of me. Surely, there's another way. Sadie is scratching at the door, so I let her out for her nightly constitutional, then lock up and decide to end this rotten day by going on to bed.

The sound of birds singing wakes me in the morning. Glad they're so damn cheery. I slept through the night but don't feel rested. I picture that kid starting his day in a juvenile facility where he wakes up to slamming doors rather than bird calls. I feel for him.

But right now, I need to worry about going to work. I'll have to take Mike up on his offer of the loan of his wife's car while she's out of town visiting her folks. Then what?

I stumble to the kitchen to get coffee started and listen to the satisfying gurgle of an impending caffeine hit. Throw on the clothes I wore yesterday and eat two-day old pizza. Wonder what the kid is having for breakfast? Maybe nothing as good as this.

An hour later, as the sun is burning off the morning dew and the bird chorus has only grown louder, I pick up the phone and call Sam Murry. Desperate times call for desperate measures.

Chapter 8

ALEX

I'm in the gym for our mandated one hour of exercise, when Ms. Hart, the treatment coordinator, comes to let me know Mr. Murry is here to see me. She's all smiles. She doesn't seem to hold any grudges against me, even though I've given her plenty of reason to, and to give her credit, she gave me her best shot. But I could see it in her eyes, she knew she was throwing a rubber ball against a wall. Nothing was sticking. What she was selling, I wasn't buying. *You need to think of your future. Let's talk about learning to trust people.* Like everyone else here, I know she'll be glad to see the door close behind me. Well, at least we have that in common.

Mr. Murry is sitting at one of the round plastic tables waiting for me. "Hi there, Alex." There's a 7-Up in front of him and after I sit down, I see there's a second one, which he plops on the table in front of me. "They let me get these from the vending machine. Hope it's a brand you like."

"Whatever," I tell him. What I don't say is I'm thrilled to have any soft drink. It's been a long time. Parents are allowed to buy one soft drink and one other vending item for their child when they visit. I get no visitors so I get no soft drinks. This does not seem at all fair. Maybe I should file a grievance about that. I try to file at least a couple every week just to piss off the staff. Having this soft drink and a visitor is the detention equivalent of going to

Disneyland. The sameness of our days is like the movie Groundhog Day. Anything to break up the boredom is welcome. In here there's nothing to look forward to unless you're the kind of person who gets excited about changing the sheets on Saturdays.

Murry looks back at the door like he's making sure no one can hear us. Uh oh, I'm going to get read the riot act. *You're going to get one chance and that's it. Don't think you're going to get away with this crap you've been pulling.* Well, let him start in on me. It's nothing I haven't heard before.

He leans in a little and says softly, "So, Alex, I'd like to propose a business deal."

I'm rarely surprised by any caseworkers, cops, or anyone else and have to admit he has me curious. I pause just a second before I ask, "What kind of deal?"

Murry puts his elbows on the table and leans further in. "Financial. The kind that involves money. How much would it cost me for you to stay in a foster home I'd put you in?"

What the hell? "Huh? What are you talking about?"

"It's simple. I'll make it worth your while if you stay. Not forever, but for a decent period of time, let's say … six months."

Here I thought this guy wasn't as nuts as some of the social workers I've had in the past. My bad. "You'd pay *me*. I don't believe that. Pay me what?"

"Money, moolah, greenback dollars. The real stuff. Believe it."

I shake my head. "You can't do that! Why would you do that?"

Now Murry leans back into the molded part of his plastic chair and spreads out his hands. "Like I said, it's a business deal. I head up a private foster care agency, you know about those?"

There's pretty much nothing I don't know about foster care. "Yeah, you get paid more money than the state pays their foster homes." It's time to get under this guy's skin. "You're kind of blood suckers, right?"

He smirks. "You got it. Here's the thing, the more success I have, the more referrals I get, the more money I make, right? With you, I see a real opportunity. No one at child welfare expects us to have any success with you. But if you stayed and were doing okay, can you see how they'd think, 'Wow, that Phoenix Agency is really good. Let's send a bunch more kids their way.' So even though I wouldn't make any money on you, in the long run it'd be more profitable. You'd kind of be like advertising. That's what's in it for me. What do you say?"

I'm still wrapping my head around this. It can't be on the up and up. "What if I say no?"

"Hey, in a business deal it only happens if both parties agree. You can choose to just come into care with us like usual; we'd give you the standard allowance we give all the kids." He steeples his fingers. "Or you can take a pass and turn us down completely. It's your choice."

Choice. What a strange concept. I take a slow drink of my 7-Up to buy time while I think. "So how much would I make?"

"You know about the level-system, right?"

"Yeah, I'm a level five, the highest." *Yay, me.*

"Yes, you are. Which means we make more money on kids like you than any others." He pulls a piece of paper out of his file and slides it in front of me. "Here are the current rates." He takes his pen and starts scribbling numbers. "I propose taking twenty percent off the top for my expenses then splitting the remaining money between you and the…" He holds his fingers up to do air quotes. "…foster father."

"It doesn't take a genius to know you're bummed out about foster care. Honestly, with all the placements you've had, I'd worry about you if you weren't. Here's my plan. We call this "foster care" to the child welfare folks but between us…" He looks back over his shoulder at the door again. "It's really more like finding you a roommate. Someone who can drive you to where you need to be, buy the groceries, and so on. You'd just be two guys who happen to live under the same roof. I've got somebody in mind. I'm making him the same deal, you know, doing it for the money. You can consider yourselves business partners. How's that sound?"

I look at the number before me. It's more money than I've ever seen in my life. More than I thought I'd ever have in my life. I could get Air Jordans, a phone, one of those cool jackets. Jesus, I could get a car after a bit. But cars are expensive. I look him in the eyes, something I hardly ever do to anyone. Well, not at least since my eye went wonky and I got tired of people looking at me funny.

Pushing the paper back in his direction, I say, "I want more. You get money when you aren't even there and whoever I get put with can sit around drinking beer on the dough. I have the hardest job."

He frowns and pulls out a little calculator. Starts punching on it then grunts and starts again. Looks at me and says, "I haven't used this in a while. Usually, I just use my phone. But of course, they wouldn't let me come in the building with it, so give me a second."

He works away at it some more. Frowns. "If I pay you more, I'll have to pay roommate guy more too, or he'll whine about it not being fair. I could take my cut from twenty percent to fifteen but that means I make almost nothing."

I lean back and cross my arms. "That's the deal."

Murry sighs and raises his eyes to the ceiling. "I don't know what classes you've been taking, but you ought to consider going into business. Alright, you drive a hard bargain, but I can manage that. Like I said, I won't be making any money anyway, I just don't want to lose too much in the bargain, even with the advertising perk. But that price includes everything, you understand? Clothing and food. Miscellaneous expenses you'll have to buy for yourself."

"When do I get paid? I want at least half up front."

"Hold on, I can't just hand you a wad of money."

"I knew it! You're just making this shit up! Trying to rip me off. I'll never see a dime."

"Yeah? And what's to keep you from ripping me off? If I pay you the money and you take off or get yourself thrown out in six weeks? I won't look good at all and I'll lose money in the bargain. I've thought about this and here's what we can do. Instead of assigning you to one of our usual caseworkers, I'll be your caseworker. I'll meet with you once a week since I'm required to do that anyway. We can go shopping for anything you want to buy based on how much you've earned up to then. I'll give you a bit of cash for anything you need to spend on for the upcoming week. The rest we'll deposit in a bank account. But remember, you have to stay in the placement for a minimum of six months to get the payout."

I look to the side at the concrete wall and shake my head. "A bank account in your name? I'm not that dumb."

Mr. Murry rolls his eyes. "Oh ye, of little faith. No. We'll open an account and put the money in your name and will require both our signatures to withdraw it. You can talk to the bank people yourself and they'll explain it."

This still sounds too good to be true. "So, what if I hate this guy you pick for me?"

Murry shrugs one shoulder. "Love him, hate him, the money's the same. But give me some credit here. I have to make sure no harm comes to my…" He points a finger at me. "…*investment*. I've got the perfect guy in mind."

At this he lowers his voice. "He's never been a foster parent and is not interested in being one. I recruited him just for you. He's someone I've known for years. A good guy who won't be hard to get along with if you treat him halfway decent. Remember, I know I have to keep you happy. 'Cause if you're happy with the arrangement you're more likely to put in the work to get along, am I right? You have to put some effort into being at least part-way agreeable. You'll be roommates so you'll need to pull your weight and do your share of the household stuff, keep track of your expenses, things like that. Think you can handle it? This is your decision, so you tell me whether this is something you want to do or not."

I keep running it all through my mind. Adults can't be trusted. I'm looking for loopholes. I can't see any but that doesn't mean they aren't there. But then again, what do I have to lose at this point? I also have to admit that being asked, not told, about a placement is having an effect on me. Only on rare occasions have I ever been asked my opinion on anything, and on those times, it was more like out of courtesy because then they go on and do whatever they want with me.

I make a decision. "Yeah, I guess. Just six months, right?"

"Yep." Mr. Murry stands up so I do too. He holds out his hand. "Deal?"

I look at it a few seconds. I don't usually touch people. Eventually, I reach out my hand.

"Deal."

Chapter 9

MATT

I'm doing this. I still can't believe I'm doing this. Sam put me on the foster parent fast track and has me jumping through one hoop after another. He sets me up with on-line foster parent training. New foster parents are mandated to have forty hours, and I spent part of every night working my way through the training components: attachment issues, adolescent brain development, the impact of trauma on behavior, a bunch of do's and don'ts. Most are easy. Don't withhold food as punishment. Do give him his own bed. Don't take away any of his personal property. Like I would do any of that anyway. I'd said that to Sam and he reached into his bottomless pit folder and pulled out a piece of paper.

"I once asked some kids to make a list of rules they'd want for wherever they lived, their own family or foster care."

When Sam hands me the list, I looked down the list and grimaced at what I saw. Number five and six really got to me.

Don't make me go to bed hungry.
Don't kill my pets.

I shook my head at Sam. "Jesus."

I'm just glad I got to complete the foster parent program alone on my computer, a by-product of the Covid pandemic, instead of sitting in one of those group circles with other prospective foster parents. I'm not a kumbaya kind of guy.

Once I completed the licensing application, gathered up financial papers, and listed personal references, I was fingerprinted and filled out the information for the records check. I raised my brows as I handed it over to Sam.

He gave me a little smile. "Not to worry. Juvenile records don't count."

Soon after, Sam sent someone from his office out to do my official home study. Sam had come out the day before with a cooler of beer and chips for a dry run. He'd made sure my gun was stored unloaded and locked up. Had me set aside an area for the kid to put his dirty clothes. Making himself completely at home in my house, he paws through my food pantry and refrigerator raising his eyebrows as he throws away some moldy bread.

In my defense, I say, "Hey, it's hard to use a whole loaf when it's just one person. They should make them smaller."

Sam grins. "Using up food is not going to be a problem for you for the foreseeable future, that I can promise you. Hey, remember the time you, Mike, and I ate every pizza in your Mom's freezer in one night?"

I laugh at the memory. "Yeah, she still talks about that."

Sam glances my way with a box of frozen waffles in his hand. "So, you two do talk?"

I frown at him, letting him know I'm not going to go down that path. "Now and then."

"How's she feel about this?"

I shrug. "Ah, you haven't told her." I take the box of waffles out of his hand and stuff them back in the freezer. "Someone else will tell her soon enough, I'm sure. Small town living. Everybody knows your business. It doesn't matter what she thinks anyway. She leads her life, I lead mine."

Sam is finally done with food patrol and says, "Okay, I think you're good, but one other thing. Lock up, or even better, take anything personal that's of value to you over to Mike's or your Mom's and store it there."

"Oh right, all my gold cuff links and Rolex watches."

He waves his hand in the general direction of all the rooms in my house. "I'm not talking about that kind of stuff. Personal things.

Things you couldn't replace. Pictures, diplomas, something your dad gave you. Sentimental items."

"I'll look around but I don't think I have much of anything like that."

"Think hard and look carefully. We had one kid who took his foster father's prize coin collection and used it in a vending machine to buy candy bars. Another kid found a baseball autographed by World Series players and used it in a pick-up game."

"Wow. Guess the poor kids didn't know what those things meant."

Sam pauses a beat and closes the last cabinet door before turning to look at me. "Believe me, they knew."

◆ ◆ ◆

Four days after my home study is completed, I get my official license. Sam and I talk about which day is best to bring Alex over. We decide a Friday afternoon will be good so I can have the weekend to get to know him. Sam assures me I can contact him anytime if I need assistance. I'm glad to hear it. The reality of this is hitting me and I feel ridiculously nervous. I'd made another grocery trip yesterday and loaded up on kid-friendly food. Feeling like someone pretending to be a parent, I even got some fruit and healthy stuff too.

By the time Friday afternoon rolls around, I'm even more antsy. It's past the time Sam said they'd probably be here. I've looked at my watch countless times and texted Sam three times with no reply. Forty-minutes later, I've decided the kid must have taken off before Sam ever got him in the car. Part of me feels relieved this isn't going to happen after all … and another part of me, for some strange reason, is vaguely disappointed. Maybe I'm worried about having to try and finance the truck after all. Yeah, that's probably it.

Just as I give up on them and go into the bathroom to take care of some business, Sadie erupts with barking. Isn't that always the way? I curse and pull up my pants while hurrying out to the living room. Sam's car stops out front and I scan it to see if it's just Sam or if there's a second occupant. There's two. Okay. Okay. I take a deep breath. Here we go.

I lock Sadie in my bedroom and walk back to the door to open it before Sam knocks. He's carrying a couple of duffel bags and a box and Alex has a bag too. Sam starts up the steps to the front porch and glances up at me with a smile, "Hey, Matt, sorry we're a bit late. I should have warned you institution time doesn't always coincide with real time. We had to wait quite a while to get processed out, didn't we, Alex?"

The boy doesn't respond to the question but Sam doesn't press it. "Alex, this is obviously Matthew King who prefers Matt. And Matt, this is Alexander Coffey, who prefers Alex."

I hold out my hand. "Hi Alex, good to meet you."

He manages to briefly grab my hand without making eye contact. "Hi."

"Can I help carry something?"

Sam shifts one of the bags in his arms. "I think we got it. Let's go put these things down somewhere then we can sit and talk a few minutes. Matt, how about on the way you give us the two-dollar tour?"

Glad to have something to do, I walk them through the place. Sam had prepared me for this. I show Alex his room and they dump all his stuff on the bed. I point out where he can put his dirty clothes, where the towels are in the bathroom. After a warning to Alex, and knowing Sam has prepped him I have a dog, I spring Sadie from captivity. She trots right up to Alex wagging her tail with enough speed to generate air flow. She needn't have bothered. He completely ignores her. That dashes my hopes she'd be an ice breaker for us.

I spend most of the tour in the kitchen. Open the cabinets and show the snack stash, figuring that will be of the most interest. "I made a stab at some chips and things. We can hit the grocery store in the next few days to get anything you'd like to have. Um … how about a soft drink? Sam, you too? Or something to eat?"

Sam is hoisting one of the chairs out from under the kitchen table. "We grabbed food through a drive-through because Alex got hung up waiting for a shift change while they processed his discharge, so missed out on lunch. But a drink would be good."

He turns his attention to the boy. "Alex, grab me one when you get yours, would you? Anything will do."

The kid hesitates just a second, throwing a glance my way, then opens the refrigerator and pulls out a couple of soft drink cans. For the first time beyond the initial "hi," he speaks to me. "Should I get you one?"

"Sure, I'll take a Coke." I take the one he offers to me, pleased to have made contact. Like a Star Trek landing party engaging with the planet's inhabitants for the first time.

We take our seats around the table and Sam leans over and distributes paper folders—a blue one for me and a red one for Alex. "Okay gentlemen, let's get started. I have a packet for each of you. First, the schedule for the next few weeks. Matt, you'll bring Alex to the Phoenix Office at 8:30 each morning for education services."

Alex is thumbing the side of his folder. "I don't see why I can't go to public school."

"We talked about this. There isn't a lot of time left in the school year so it would pretty much be a waste of your time. They are doing end of the year testing and it isn't a good time for new arrivals. Plus, you're pretty far behind your grade level which we need to do something about."

I see Alex's head go further down and I frown at Sam. That was kind of harsh.

If Sam notices my scowl, he doesn't show it. He keeps his attention on Alex. "Look, it's not your fault. Even Einstein couldn't switch schools as much as you have and not fall behind. But like Einstein, you're smart. With a little help and some effort on your part you can catch up. You'll like Ms. Miller. She'll tutor you and get you right up to speed. Here's the thing, you won't be doing school work all day every day. We'll get you involved in some activities you should like."

"Why can't I just go downtown and hang out till he…" He twitches his head my way like I'm an inanimate object. "…comes and gets me?"

"Yeah, that'd be easy, wouldn't it? But we can't have you running all over town unsupervised. Would look bad on the Phoenix Agency's image. Getting you involved in some great activities will look good, don't you think? Remember, we want to show how happy and successful you are with us. Get all those new referrals."

Alex appears somewhat mollified but also suspicious. "What things are you talking about?"

Sam pulls more paper from his folder. It seems endless and I'm not going to be surprised if there's a rabbit hidden down deep inside. "There's lots of possibilities. Here's a brochure from the Y and one from the city recreation department. Look over the classes and activities and decide what you'd like to do. Music lessons. Karate. Weight lifting. Underwater basket weaving." Sam glances again at the brochure and pushes his elbow on the table towards Alex, "Oops, sorry they don't have that one."

Funny guy. I want to join in and say something clever as well, but all I seem able to do is sit here like a gigantic blob. But I manage to roll my eyes at Sam's lame joke and catch Alex looking at me with maybe just the slightest lift of the right side of his mouth.

Sam returns to his spiel. "And Alex, since I'm assuming caseworker responsibilities with you, there will be a standing appointment with me on Thursdays at four o'clock."

Alex looks less than excited. "Every Thursday?"

"Hey, don't make that face. You'll be happy to see me. That's the day I'll be bringing you your weekly check. We'll go by the bank and deposit the bulk of it into your account and I'll give you your cash for the week. If there's something you want to go buy, I'll take you to get it. My wife and girls play tennis on Thursdays so we can grab an early dinner and that'll be one less meal you and Matt have to worry about."

I can see the talk about the money has brightened Alex up considerably, just like it would for any kid. And I'm thinking, hey he *is* just a kid. All Sam's talk about precautions and special needs seem over inflated. I don't know what I was expecting, for the boy to have horns coming out of his head? I almost feel guilty. This could be the easiest money I've ever made in my life. It could even be fun. Maybe the kid and I could hit the nearby lake and rent a boat one weekend. Bet he'd have a big time. We could fish, swim, and maybe even do a little skiing. I'm ready to finish up this meeting and get

Sam on his way but no, he's still going on and on. I never knew he could be so chatty.

"Okay, let's get to the medical part. You had a physical while you were in the facility so we can skip that for now, but we need to set up an appointment with a dentist to fix your broken tooth."

"My social worker said all I get from a dentist is two cleanings a year unless I get a cavity."

"Well, good thing you came to Phoenix, huh? We will take care of it."

Sam leans in towards the boy. "Alex, your medical needs have been neglected. In addition to the dentist, we'll take you to a dermatologist, a skin doctor, to get you some acne medicine. Dr. Fuller has worked wonders with some of our other teens. And the biggest thing? I have an appointment scheduled for you with an ophthalmologist to get your eye repaired."

For the first time the kid begins to look mutinous. "Forget it. I've had the eye patch and the stupid glasses and did all those dumb eye exercises. I'm not doing any of that shit again."

Sam sighs. "How many times do I have to say it? How you look reflects on Phoenix so we have to get you looking your best. I'm not talking about a half-ass fix. We're going for quick and permanent. I already checked it out. One little surgery and you'll be good as new. You don't even have to go into the hospital; it's done as an outpatient. Takes just about an hour, not that you'll care; you'll be asleep during the whole thing. Easy-peasy."

There's an expression on the boy's face I can't quite describe. Disbelief? Wary? Hopeful? Sam had talked to me about the eye, and he was angry about it. *Why would they let that boy suffer with this for so long when it could be fixed so easily? Can you imagine the teasing and bullying he's had to endure?* Remembering middle and high school, I cringe. Partly because I can imagine the remarks made to this poor kid. More so, because I was the type of kid that would have been saying them. I'm not proud of it.

Sam makes a final dip into his folder then closes it up and pushes it to the side. He holds up a piece of plastic. "And as a down payment on our financial arrangement, here's a prepaid visa card for you to go shopping. New clothes, new shoes, the works." He holds it out to Alex who takes it from his hand and clutches it in his own. I don't look at Sam for fear I'll give away a confidence he shared. That all foster kids get an initial clothing allowance, so this isn't really any special perk Alex is getting, but let him think it is. The card is usually given to the foster parent, not the kid.

Fifteen minutes later we've had question and answer period, talked about how the Braves' baseball season is going, and Alex has even answered some of my questions about what he likes to eat. As Sam starts to pack up to go, Alex turns to me and asks if he can use the restroom.

"Sure," I hurry to tell him. "Make yourself at home. I mean this is your home now."

He gives me a toothy grin and in a very cheery voice says. "I really appreciate that. And of course, you taking me in out of the goodness of your heart." I'm not sure what to make of this, but behind the boy, Sam's eyes roll to the ceiling. I decide to take the wisest course, and say nothing back.

I follow Sam out to his car. He opens the door and glances back at the house. "Drop me a text tonight and let me know how it's going."

It's going to be a nice evening and looks to be a beautiful weekend. I'm feeling better about everything. Now that this initial awkwardness is over, I think I'll do just fine with this boy. Hell, I've done things worse than him. It's sad really, how people have made this kid out to be such a bad egg.

I give Sam a thumbs up. "Sure. We'll be fine. He seems like a pretty nice kid. This isn't going to be so difficult."

Sam steps into his car and rests his elbow on the open window. He turns the ignition then mutters something as he puts it in gear. As he drives away, I'm pretty sure what I heard was, "Keep that thought."

Four hours later, I text Sam.

He went into his room right after you left and has only come out once which was to go to the bathroom. I asked if he'd like to go for a walk He said no. Later I

asked if he'd like a snack. He just yells through the door I'm good. It's almost bedtime.

I watch the little dots swirl, indicating Sam is reading my message. In a few seconds his answer pops up.

Congrats. You've already had him longer than at least 8 other placements.

Dammit Sam. Quit joking around. Tell me something constructive. My fingers start tapping.

That's all you've got to say. What should I do?

More swirling.

Go to bed.

Chapter 10

ALEX

Blissful aloneness. It's the first time in months I'm totally by myself for longer than it takes to take a poop or get a shower. I walk around the room and look out the window. Nothing in sight but trees and stuff. I wonder if Murry picked this guy because he knew any city kid, kids like me, would think twice before trying to hoof it out of here into the great nothingness. There could be bears out there for all I know. No, I'm not planning on leaving tonight. Or for that matter anytime soon. Yeah, I want that money. I want all the things it can get me.

But there's another reason I'm staying put. After being locked up for several months, I feel off my game. For now, I've lost the momentum to just keep blitzing through one placement after another. I need some time to map things out.

My sixteenth birthday is pretty close. The next year I'll be seventeen. The birthday after that, my eighteenth, is when I officially become an adult. I try not to think about it. The future is a big black void. My child welfare caseworker will probably be more than happy to drop me at an adult homeless center and speed away as fast as she can. As much as I hate foster care, the thought is terrifying. I've seen and read about what happens to other kids. The options aren't pretty: shelters, the street, jail, prison … or dead. I feel the time ticking away. I need a plan, but for now I'll hang tight. See how long this place can last before I get the boot. That leaves it up to Mr. King to decide when he's had enough of me. That means giving up control. I hate that.

I'm not going to suck up, but I'm going to try and not be awful. If I can help it. Can I help it? Am I really always in control of the things I do? Can I fake it till I make it? Earn some money. Get a car. If I have a car, I can live out of it when I turn eighteen.

Then there's the matter of the bed. I try to remember the last time I didn't sleep in a bunk bed, other than when I was in detention. I sit on the bed and bounce a little. Not only is it not a bunk bed, it's a double bed. I've never slept in a bed this big. The pillow looks new. In all these years in the state's care I don't think I've ever had a new pillow. The room is good too. A log cabin home is interesting. I've gotten tossed out of at least five homes for punching a hole in the wall. Won't be trying that here unless I want to break my hand.

Footsteps sound in the hall. I tense up, waiting for the door to open. But there's just a light knock. "Alex, you need anything? A snack or something?"

I relax my muscles. I'd had a flashback to Placement Number 28 when the foster father used to burst through my door without knocking, like each time he was going to catch me doing something I shouldn't be doing. I direct my voice to the door. "I'm good."

"Okay, I'm going on to bed. See you in the morning."

After a second the footsteps go away and so does the click click of the dog's nails on the wood floor. When I'm eighteen, once I get a car and maybe a job somewhere, I'm going to get my own dog. I like dogs a lot but I don't want anything to do with this one. My motto is no attachments and that includes the dog.

I should put my stuff away. I'll do it tomorrow. Or the next day. Make sure I'm still here then so I'm not doing it for nothing. I *could* see what's in the mysterious box Mr. Murry gave me. There's an envelope on top but not sealed. I flip it open and pull out the card.

Dear Alex,

Welcome to Phoenix. We're glad to have you with us. Here are some things that we hope will help you settle in. Remember if you need to speak to your caseworker, you can do that any time, day or night, at the number listed below. I look forward to meeting you at the Phoenix summer picnic next month.
Best Wishes,
Margo Richards, Chief Executive Officer

A handwritten note. Another first. I fold it up and put it with my personal things to keep because it's sort of like getting a letter. Never gotten one in my life. I can see now why the other kids in detention who had parents or guardians write to them, got excited when the mail came.

I look behind me at the door before I open the box. I don't know why. It's mine. Maybe it's because if I'd opened this at the detention center, I'd have to fight for any scrap that would be left once the vultures descended. Not of course, that the people who run the place would *let* you have a box in the first place. I shake my head at my foolishness and flip it open. The first thing I see is a red and black checked fleece blanket. It's brand new with the tag still on it. I rub it against my cheek. *So soft.*

I set it on the bed next to me and dive back in, reaching in and bringing out the contents one by one. A journal. A drawing pad and set of markers and colored pencils. A Rubik's cube and deck of cards. Bottle of water and gummy fruit snacks. Peppermint sticks. Twizzlers. A word-find puzzle book. And at the very bottom, a pair of pajamas.

For a few minutes, I fight the urge but give up and put them on. They aren't in keeping with my image but Jesus, they feel incredibly comfortable. I tear the tag off the blanket and wrap it around me like all this softness can wipe out the past months of nothing but metal and stone.

The last time I had real pajamas, I was what, maybe seven? I vaguely remember being that little kid years ago. Mostly, I don't think about him anymore, but sometimes I get a glimmer. One thing I remember is how when you're little everything seems amazing. But what once seemed amazing becomes ordinary. What once seemed awful becomes ordinary too. That's a good thing. It's how I survive.

I'm too excited about being out of detention to want to sleep but I finally get into bed and turn off the light, welcoming the darkness. At the detention center, the lights are barely dimmed at night. Staff said they have to be able to look in the window and see us when they do the fifteen minute required checks. Said it keeps us safe. Maybe, but it also makes it very hard to sleep. And when I don't sleep, I get cranky. Honestly, I kind of just always stay cranky, because nobody likes a cranky person, and I don't want to be liked.

I stare up at the ceiling and wait for sleep to come. I strain my ears listening for sounds. It's good not to hear slamming doors and other kids screaming, but it's weird being in a place so deadly quiet. The good thing is, I should hear any footsteps or my door opening. I noticed earlier it squeaks a little. I've never had a foster parent try anything, but in Placements number 24 and 32, another foster kid tried to sneak into my room with bad intentions. Each time, I'd read the signals and was ready for them. I busted the nose of the older teen in number 32. I got thrown out of that home for assaulting him. He didn't say why he was in my room and I didn't say either. What was the point? I just packed the next morning and moved on.

I didn't get any bad vibes from Matt King but I'll keep my guard up just in case. Constant vigilance is the name of the game. Lying in the darkness, I can feel my earlier exhilaration fading into depression. The bed is great, sure, but it's just another bed. Another house. Another stop on the way to nowhere, with no end in sight.

Chapter 11

MATT

Two weeks have gone by since Alex graced my front door. He spent the rest of that first weekend almost entirely in his room. He'd come out to grab any food I fixed and carry it back to his lair, firmly shutting the door. If he had his own bathroom, I wouldn't know if he was alive or dead between meals. So much for bonding.

I feel more like a glorified chauffeur than I do a foster parent or even a roommate. I ferry him to the Phoenix office Monday through Friday mornings and pick him up later. We make brilliant conversation:

Me: *How'd it go today?*
Him: *Shrug.*
Me: *What'd you do for fun this afternoon?*
Him: *Stuff.*

That's on a good day. He won't talk about himself so I end up telling him things about me. About my parents and my brother Mike being doctors. About different jobs I've had. About my hopes for my business. He looks about as interested as someone watching sand in an hourglass but I keep hoping to eventually have a real conversation. Most of the time during our drives he wears earbuds and ignores me. As soon as we get home, he goes straight to his room and shuts the door. I'm getting paid a hunk of money for this, so why should I care, but it's driving me insane for some reason.

Today's drive is much more important than usual. I'm taking him to the outpatient clinic for his eye surgery. I glance over at him a couple of times. For once he doesn't have in the earbuds and he's absorbed in looking out the window. He's wearing his perpetual tough guy look but I watch him play with his fingers, pop a few knuckles, take a few deep breaths. He's nervous.

"I'm sure it'll all go fine," I say, "but it's normal to be a little apprehensive."

"What do you know about it? Guess you weren't smart enough to go to medical school like everyone else in your family, huh?"

Youch. So much for trying to be nice. I manage to keep my poker face on. That was a nasty little shot. I flash to one of the sessions I had with Sam while he prepared me for this. *I'm going to warn you that whatever is your Achilles Heel, he'll find it. Just prepare yourself for it. I had one woman who was very fit, rail thin for twenty years, but had been a chubby teenager and was very sensitive about it. The girl placed with her started calling her Porky and she about lost it. How the kids figure these things out I'll never know, but they do.*

And damn, if he didn't. I've been hearing this all my life. *His parents are doctors you know. His brother too. But Matt didn't really even graduate high school.* But I did graduate. Officially. It's just my diploma doesn't read Western Hills High School. It reads Passage Academy. Over eleven years of regular public school but I'd been tagged for the rest of my life with the diploma from the alternative school where I'd spent my final days of high school. So yeah, the zinger he sent hits the mark but I refuse to give him any satisfaction from it.

To deflect, I give him a big grin. "Probably not. But I've got a pocket knife. I'd be happy to have a go at the surgery if you'd like. I promise I'm cheaper. And quicker."

That earns me the tiniest of smiles. A major score.

Matt 1. Brat 0.

Sam meets us at the clinic to sign some papers but as soon as Alex is prepped for surgery, he leaves and I'm left in the waiting room reading today's newspaper and old issues of magazines. The kid's words and being in this medical setting gets me thinking about my parents. Dad was a cardiologist up until his death and my mother still has her own general practice. I guess medicine is what got them together in the first place.

During the summer between my junior and senior year, with Mike in college, we moved to a new house, one with a bedroom in the basement that had a separate outside entrance so coming and going endured less parental monitoring. There was also a rec room and my own bathroom. During the day, when Dad and Mom were both at work, I'd entertained frequently. Several cheerleaders, at least ten percent of the dance team, and one long-legged blonde tennis player who, for a while, I was sure I was in love with.

One afternoon the toilet in my bathroom quit working. Fixing household items was a competitive sport in our house. Mom viewed it like a human disease to be solved and Dad wanted to put on his man-of-the-house act. He got a plumbing snake and with me watching and mom giving instructions over his shoulder, he threaded it into the bowl until he hit a clog.

"I've got it snagged," he proclaimed, pleased with himself. As he pulled the clog to the surface it looked like a bunch of translucent worms. Those worms started separating until they floated to the top and filled the whole toilet bowl. Gradually they started looking less like worms and more like what they were: condoms. There was a stunned moment of silence while the three of us stared. I tried to think of something to say but there were no words that seemed adequate. My mother could only come up with six.

"Oh, Matt!" she wailed. "What were you thinking?"

Honestly, I didn't think she'd like to know what I'd been thinking. Mom turned to Dad and said, "*You* handle this," and fled the room. Dad grinned, winked, and punched me on the shoulder before saying in his firmest voice, raised to be sure Mom could hear, "Young man, you and I are going to have a serious talk about this later." He looked down in the bowl before half whispering, "Meanwhile, you can clean this up."

He grinned again and left me standing there trying to decide the best way to get rid of the evidence of my transgressions. I grabbed the little blue bathroom garbage can and seeing nothing else for it, dipped my hand in the bowl and pulled them out by the fistfuls, plopping them in. I waited till the cover of darkness before emptying them into a bag and putting them in the outside garbage.

If my folks had a fight about this when they were alone, I never knew. They fought half the time anyway as standard household procedure. They divorced shortly after the start of my senior year of high school. I did wonder why my mother instigated the change to a new house shortly before they split up. The answer came later when I found out she'd been seeing someone else. I guess it made sense to down-size before making her move and filing for divorce. Scott, her dipwad boyfriend, moved in for a while until they too split up. Dad rented a house near the hospital and I moved in with him until he died of a heart attack—ironic considering his job—a year later.

My thoughts are interrupted when a nurse pushes open the door to the waiting room, and beckons me down the hall to Recovery where Alex lies awake in his hospital bed. The nurse flutters around the room adjusting this and that. She turns to Alex to say, "Look, here's your Dad now." She glances at me from the sides of her eyes while scribbling on a clipboard. "Everything went fine and the doctor will be in to talk to you both in a minute." With a click of her pen, she marches out of the room.

I take the chair next to the bed. "Hey, Champ, how are you feeling?"

"Can we leave now?"

"Hopefully so. We'll see what the doctor has to say. He might let you go or want to observe you for a while longer. I'm sure he'll discharge you by sometime this afternoon at the latest."

The boy is sliding his hand across the top of the sheet. "Sadie won't like being home alone all this time."

This catches me by surprise. He's hardly ever given any indication he knows she's alive, much less cares.

"She's fine. If you don't get discharged till later, I can always call my neighbor, Mr. Parkins, to go let her out."

There's a little tap tap on the door and the doctor, dressed in his blue scrubs, walks in. He's followed with the nurse who was here earlier. I'd met the doc in the pre-op office visit a couple of weeks ago where he'd taught me a lot about Alex's condition. The term is a tongue twister: strabismus. It's been called lazy eye, but he informed me that's not an accurate term. It's more that the muscles of the eyes aren't working together. As a result of not being held in place properly, the eye heads off on its own and the brain stops doing the right communication with the misaligned eye. Some kids have it develop while they are a baby, but in Alex's case it was caused by a head injury when he was ten years old. Apparently, another foster kid accidentally whammed him in the head with a baseball bat. Sam said there are occasional notations in Alex's file about referrals to doctors. They tried some eye exercises and prescription glasses but when those didn't work, they left it at that.

The doc gives a rundown of the surgery, discussing details I'd rather not hear concerning the adjustment of the muscle around the eye. My own eye starts to throb just thinking about it.

"Alrighty then, we're going to let you get dressed in a few minutes and get on out of here. Mr. King, Nurse Hamilton here is going to give you a prescription for some antibacterial and steroid eye drops that'll help reduce the swelling. We've already dosed him good today so wait until tomorrow. Leave the eye patch on till then too. Alex, your vision will probably be blurry for a week or maybe two. Your brain has to catch up with the changes to your eye but once it does everything should right itself. You might get a headache now and then, just take some Tylenol as needed. We'll also set you up with a follow-up appointment with us. Any problems in the meantime just give us a call. Any questions?"

I look at Alex who says nothing so I speak for both of us. "I think we're good. Thanks for your help."

The doc smiles at us as he slides out of the room. "Glad to do it. Alex, you're going to look good, buddy, but maybe stay away from a mirror until the redness goes away."

By bedtime, I've spent more time with Alex in this one day then I have in just about his entire time here. The sun is shining brightly into his room because I've never bothered with curtains on any window in the house. His eyes are sensitive so I set him up on the couch in the darker living room. I bring him lunch and later fix us dinner and eat across from him, using the coffee table as a dining table. It's the first two meals we've had together. He sits up to eat but lies back down when he's finished, looking totally worn out. I know from my own prior experiences that anesthesia can wipe you out for an extended time. As I reach over to take his plate away, he speaks and it's so soft I have to lean over to hear.

"Thanks, Matt."

It's the first time he's called me by my first name. Damn, if it isn't a thrill.

The couch is dog-height friendly. Sadie walks over and lays her muzzle on the couch cushion right in front of Alex's face. I make a movement to shoo her away, but before I can, Alex raises a hand to her head and gently strokes it. The old girl quivers and never takes her eyes from his face. It's like she knows this is a momentous change in their relationship. I know how she feels. Once again, Sam's words of wisdom seem to be on target. He'd told me when kids are sick or otherwise vulnerable, it's when they'll often let down their guard, and it's an opportunity for us adults to step up to the plate and prove ourselves worthy.

I view Alex from a spot in the room where he can't see me. His hair has grown out a bit. His broken tooth was fixed within his first week with me, which made a huge change in his appearance. The acne medicine kicked in right away and his face is much improved. With the eye repaired, he's going to look like a totally different kid.

For the first time in a long time, I think about my mother and the nights she sat up with me after my various sports surgeries.

For the first time, if for no other reason than I drove him to all those medical appointments, I feel like a parent.

For the first time, I get an inkling why some people might just be crazy enough to voluntarily sign up for this.

Chapter 12

MATT

Alex has come out of his room. I want him to go back. Like now. Like permanently. His mouth curls downward as I set some toast on the table for breakfast. "Toast again? And you burned it up. Again."

"It's not burnt. It's ... well done."

"Since when is black not burnt?"

I make a concerted effort to not raise my voice. "If you don't like it, there's the toaster; you're welcome to cook your own."

His frown gets even deeper. Doesn't seem possible but then he's made an art out of it. "The deal is I do the dishes and you do the cooking."

"So, I cooked. And by the way, half of last night's dishes are still in the sink."

"They're soaking."

I start to say something back but he starts buttering his toast and shuts up so I consider I'm in the scoring column. What's sad is I've begun keeping score. I strongly suspect I'm losing. He has made irritating me a full-time job. The kid starts up at breakfast and never gives it up till one of us goes to bed. I find myself turning in earlier just not to have to listen to his mouth.

"This place is boring. Why do you want to live out here in the sticks?"

"I wanted pop tarts. Why didn't you buy them?"

"Why can't you get HBO?"

"Why have you never been married? Why don't you have a girlfriend?"

And the worst thing? He's started calling me Doc. "Hey Doc, Sadie wants out." "Hey Doc, when will dinner be done?"

I recall his first days here when he said almost nothing. Rather than just keeping my big mouth shut, I filled up the space with mindless chatter. He may not have been talking, or even looking interested, but he listened. And damn, if he didn't hone in on it. Just like Sam warned me, he found the one thing that would really bug me. The fact that everyone else in my immediate family is a doctor but I never even went to college. That I'm considered the failure of the family.

To add insult to injury, Alex, as instructed by Sam, did pick out a recreational activity to sign up for. He waited to make sure I was there when he informed Sam.

He held up a brochure. "Okay, I picked. This is it."

Sam took it from his hand. Glanced at Alex then at me. His mouth twitched up. "Okay, are you sure this is what you want? It looks rather demanding."

"Yep."

"Okay. I'll take care of it."

Alex's eyes are practically dancing out of his head. I'm glad to see something has made him so excited, since low-key, aka slumping, is his usual default mode. Then I do a double-take. He's asking to be a junior volunteer EMT. It means he'll be closer to being a doctor than I ever will.

Sam and he are both gauging my reaction. I refuse to give either of them the satisfaction of knowing Alex hit the mark he was aiming for. I make a point of reading the details on the brochure. "Yeah, this looks interesting."

Okay, my response was lame, I admit it, but best I could do on the spur of the moment.

I can tell him why I don't have a current girlfriend but he might not like the answer. What woman would want to be here and listen to him mouth off twenty-four seven. Not to mention, he is such a complete pig. Sadie loves him because he leaves crumbs wherever he goes while she follows behind with her nose to the floor like his own personal Roomba machine.

Apparently, he has no idea what a garbage can is for. An empty chip bag gets put on the counter when the can is less than a foot away. His room is a disaster area. There are more clothes on the floor than in his closet. One time when he was gone I braved going in there and saw a trail of ants marching under his bed. I peeked under and discovered half of a peanut butter sandwich which the bugs were having a jolly old time enjoying.

Compared to him, I'm Mister Clean-and-Neat. I find the messier he is, the neater I'm becoming. This is concerning. I hear my mother in my head when I say things like, "Is it that hard to hold your hand under a cookie when you're eating it?"

We had an argument about some silly thing and he hollers, "You're ruining my life!"

Forgetting all the advice Sam gave me about getting calmer and quieter when the kid gets louder, I holler back, "I haven't known you long enough to ruin your life. Give me time!"

Maybe Sam's advice comes with a grain of salt. I'd done the wrong thing, but it worked. A side of Alex's mouth actually turned up and he piped down.

Most times I can't shut him up, but other times, I can't get him to answer a simple question. The last time it happened I thought I'd go for humor again saying, "You don't want to talk, that's fine. Show me one finger for yes, and two for no."

Without lifting his eyes from the video game he was playing, he held up his middle finger. Well, stupid me, I guess I asked for that one.

I can't complain to most people because it would dispel the myth I'm this great guy who has taken on an older foster child out of the goodness of my heart. Telling them that I'd like nothing better than to drop the little shit back off at the Phoenix office would be, well, disillusioning to say the least. Therefore, Sam gets the burden of my complaints. Two days ago, I had him alone for a few minutes while waiting for Alex to get done with tutoring and got the chance to unload.

Sam pastes on his patient face while I go into my rant. "He's manipulative, egotistical, self-centered, stubborn …"

While I search for more adjectives, Sam interrupts, "Of course he is. He's had to be to survive. I know that doesn't make it any easier for you, but at least you can understand where it comes from. It's not personal."

I grumble, "It sure feels personal. He doesn't do anything he's supposed to do. Like he's expected to wash his own clothes but he keeps putting them in the dryer with a fabric sheet rather than running the washer. He wads up his towel after a shower and stuffs it back in the closet sopping wet!"

Sam asks, "Did you set down the household expectations like we discussed?" While I searched for a non-incriminating reply, he made the correct assumption. "Ahh, you didn't. He's going to walk all over you if you don't set down some ground rules. Even your standard issue teenager is going to test limits. Alex is going to test them even more. He's fifteen. For at least two-thirds of his life he's had an abnormal existence at foster homes, group homes, residential treatment, psychiatric facilities, and juvenile detention facilities, not to mention just living on the street. Always remember that, but don't allow his background to hold you back from doing what all parents need to do. Things like establishing expectations and setting boundaries."

I took Sam's little lecture to heart. Today, driving him to drop off at Phoenix, I man up and lay it on the line. As I hear myself talk about consideration, about responsibility, I can almost swear I hear my mother laughing. But it seems to work. After dinner, Alex heads straight to the sink and starts doing the dishes. He was surprisingly quick and is soon strolling towards his room.

I look up from the game I have on TV. "That was fast."

"I cleaned as good as you cooked." Before he closes his door, I catch his smirk. I know that look. As a kid, I owned that look. Steeling myself for what I'm likely to see, I enter the kitchen. *Well, what do you know?* I'm going to have to mentally apologize to the kid. Everything is as it should be. No dirty dishes in sight and the counter wiped down. Even the sink is washed out. I pat myself on the back. I've got the kid coming along, no doubt about it. I should have had that little talk about responsibility sooner.

I decide to reward myself with one more bite of the cake I bought from the band bake sale in the lobby of the grocery store yesterday. Opening the cabinet to the left of the kitchen window, I reach for one of the little plates, but as I'm pulling it out, it almost slides right out of my hand. It's slick with some oily substance. I glance and there's glued on crumbs over the entire front. *What the hell?* I pull out one of the larger dinner dishes and it's worse. So is the next one, and the next. I tug open the drawer where the silverware is stored and there's meat still sitting between the tines of the fork on top.

That little shit! "Alex! Get in here."

Well, *of course* he doesn't come. Fuming, I stomp down the hall to his room. I'm reaching to yank it open, possibly off the hinges, when out of nowhere the invisible hand of reason holds me back. Instead, I take a deep breath and give two sharp raps before turning the knob.

"Alex, you need to redo the dishes."

"I already did them."

"You didn't do them right."

"The deal is I do them, nobody said they had to be perfect."

The hand of reason has lifted from my back and his first cousin, the hand of I-don't-give-a damn has taken its place. "You know they aren't anywhere near perfect. You get in there and do them right if you want to have any more meals eaten on them."

Alex lazily turns the pages of his book and doesn't even bother to look up as he nonchalantly says, "You can't deprive a foster child of food. It's in the regulations."

Screw the regulations stops just before coming out of my mouth. I repeat my earlier try. "The deal is I cook, you clean."

He repeats a version of his earlier response. "Well, your

cooking isn't all that great so if my cleaning isn't great, it equals out."

I attempt to up my game. "You can use that argument if you ever choose not to eat what's put in front of you, which so far, you've never done. Now go do those dishes the right way."

His mouth tightens and he looks straight at me. "No."

I stand there staring, my face I know is turning red. With my size there's grown men who would be intimidated, but it doesn't scare him. He looks ... *satisfied?* My blood is boiling but what can I do? I can't hit him. I can't drag him there by his ears, as appealing as that vision is. I can't ground him because he doesn't get to go anywhere on his own anyway. Saying go to your room would obviously be silly since he's already there. All that's left is a total wuss out.

"I'm going to call Mr. Murry."

His eyes get wide. His mouth makes a little circle. "Oooh, I'm trembling."

I show him my back, shutting the door behind me. Proud of myself for not slamming it because, well, I'm supposed to be the adult. I stomp back to the living room before my baser instincts take over. Decide against going back in the kitchen because I am *not* going to go do those dishes. I know if I do, he'll have me in his back pocket forever, so I go make good on my not-so-scary-threat, if for no other reason than to vent.

I step outside and punch in Sam's number. He answers on the fifth ring right when I'm about ready to give it up. Maybe he was away from the phone or more likely he saw my name on the screen, rolled his eyes, groaned, and debated whether he could get away with ignoring it.

But he answers with his always cheery voice, and that is irritating in and of itself, "Hey Matt, what's up?"

I need a target for my anger and Sam more than fits the bill. He's the one who talked me into this insane scheme. "I'll tell you what's up. You aren't paying me enough!"

"Uh oh, what's he done?"

I fill Sam in, repeating Alex's and mine's interaction word for word.

After I'm done, there's a pause before he says, "I'm sure that was upsetting."

My mouth goes to full snarl. "Don't be pulling that condescending psychological crap on me, Murry."

"Sorry, sorry. Force of habit. But I am glad you called me instead of doing something you'd regret. How about I come out in the morning? Can you keep the peace till then?"

"If he stays in his room all night, probably."

"Okay, I've got to run by the office first, but I'll be out around ten o'clock."

I take a few more steps away from the house. "What are you going to do?"

Why I'm asking I don't know. What do I care what he does? I hope he helps Alex pack his bags and hauls his rotten little ass out of my sight forever. Money isn't worth this amount of grief. I've had it. I don't care what happens to the brat. He deserves whatever he gets. No wonder he's had sixty-four previous placements. The number sticks in my head.

Sixty-four, how awful!

No, don't let him off the hook just because life's been a bit tough.

A bit?

I shake my head to get the warring voices to shut up.

Sam replies. "Ehh, play it by ear. Don't enter the battle anymore tonight. Now that you've backed off, he might go wash them tonight or in the morning. Either way, I'll come out."

Fat chance that's going to happen. As expected, Alex shows no intention of completing the chore. In the morning, he takes a dirty bowl out of the cabinet and fixes some cereal in it. Fine. Hope he gets food poisoning. We don't speak to each other.

At ten sharp, Sam arrives, looking disgustingly unconcerned. I'm torn between wanting Sam to solve this dilemma and wanting to see him fall flat on his face, just like me. Alex is wearing his favorite sweatshirt with, despite the warmth of the day, the hood pulled up over his head. Most of his face is hidden, but the part that isn't looks sulky and defiant. I think my face might look the same.

But Sam's all relaxed and smiles. "Hey guys. How's it going?"

I stare at Sam and Alex just turns his head away. Neither of us answers him.

"That good, huh? Let's head into the kitchen, shall we?"

Once there, Sam opens the upper cabinet door and takes down some of the dirty plates. He leans against the counter and shakes his head with a sad look on his face. "Alex, Matt and I owe you a big apology."

Alex looks suspicious and I squint my eyes at Sam. I'm *not* apologizing. What game is he playing?

"You know I said as roommates it was important to share the chores, but it sure wasn't fair of us to ask you to do something you didn't know how to do. And of course, it's important you learn how to do some things to prepare you for independent living. Man, the Phoenix agency would look bad if we didn't. Can't have that now, can we? But don't you worry, I know just how to fix this. We'll just break it down into steps. It looks like you didn't understand the scraping the food off part of the process so I'll demonstrate that."

Sam goes into a full out explanation like somehow this is quantum physics, which bores me to death if it doesn't do it to Alex. But I do learn something.

Sam pulls a plastic hotel key card out of his back pocket. "Here's your secret weapon. This works better than anything. I brought you one. We just rinse it off afterwards and leave it by our sink at my house. The problem we have today is that by now the food is glued on from sitting so long, so we'll have to do more of step two which involves hot water and soap."

Sam is plugging the sink and turning the spigot. "Alex, step on over here. We'll let you do this part today." Sam hands him a dishcloth and moves aside.

I practically hold my breath.

I watch the boy weigh his options. There's a dangerous two-count. Then he moves, like a sloth, but he eventually arrives at the sink. Sam starts pulling dishes out of the cabinet and stacking them to the left of the sink. He scrapes the first one then slides it into the soapy sink.

"Matt, you don't mind drying just this one time, do you?" After today, I think Alex will have the hang of it."

Alex doesn't look like he wants to get the hang of anything. He gives the plate two half-ass swipes then hands it to me. Sam looks over and taps the upper right side. "Whoops, missed that spot at two o-clock, bud."

The plate goes back into the water and the next time he hands it to me, it's good enough for government work.

Sam is like an annoying pit bull. "There ya go. Now you're talking."

Eventually, we get all the previously dirty dishes taken care of but Sam continues to reach in various cabinets and drawers pulling out dishes that haven't been used since I moved in.

Alex knows it. "Hey, we didn't eat off those."

"Oh, I know, but they've been in there overnight with those dirty ones and might have gotten contaminated. We at the Phoenix agency don't want you to get sick, not with all we've invested in you. I believe social services regulation number 601 on household hygiene requirements comes into play. Besides, practice makes perfect. By the time you do these, I think you'll be totally proficient. The better you get at this, the faster you'll go, and then you and I can head to Phoenix for school. But hey, if you need to go slow to get it right, I've got plenty of time."

Sam turns his back on Alex and says to me, "Did you catch the game last night? I can't believe Quinn tried to get that extra base."

Sam and I talk baseball until Alex finishes up. Alex leaves to get his books out of his room and walks a lot faster than he usually does outside to Sam's car. I linger with Sam by the front door. Nod my head and say, "Okay, you're clever. I'll give you that. But what would you have done if he still said no?"

Sam grins, "Oh, I have other tricks up my sleeve. This one technically has a name. It's called overcorrection. Don't you remember Mrs. Finney back in seventh grade? If you threw a piece of paper on the floor, she made you pick it up and anything else on the floor to boot. She just didn't have a fancy name for the technique."

"Well, obviously I don't have any tricks. I just got mad."

"That's a natural reaction. Give yourself some credit. You stayed calm and didn't let him get the better of you. You did the right thing by calling me. A lot of times with these kids they need someone or something to make the interaction less personal. I have one foster parent of a problematic six-year-old. Whenever she gets at loggerheads with the kid, she just pulls out a stuffed Elmo doll, goes into a high-pitched voice, and lets Elmo serve as the intermediary. It works every time."

He pulls his keys out of his pocket. "When you pick up Alex this afternoon, don't bring this back up unless he does."

"Okay, but he did completely defy me. You got the dishes done but didn't deal with that."

Sam smiles as he opens the door. "Small steps. Kids often need a bite of the apple at the beginning to see that success brings further success. If they've never experienced it, they don't know what they're missing. Let's take our victories where we can."

Sam's grin gets bigger. "You don't want him to pee on the dishes out of spite, do you?" With that parting comment, Sam jogs down the steps and joins Alex at the car. Maybe I should invest in a dishwasher. One with a very large sanitizing button.

Chapter 13

MATT

After that incident, Alex and I settle into a frosty truce, with me trying to be the one to take the high road. For instance, at one of my client's restaurants where I landscaped the patio area, I bought Alex a T-shirt I thought he might like.

Tossing it at him, while keeping my voice casual, I tell him, "Picked this up yesterday for you. I think it'll fit you but let me know if it doesn't and I'll exchange it."

He doesn't say thanks but actually smiles as he holds it up to take a look. That made me feel good for less than twenty-four hours. The next day, I'm taking out the garbage. When I dump the kitchen can into the outside receptacle, I see the T-shirt. He'd sliced it into about twelve pieces. I think that disturbed me more than anything else he's done so far. I much prefer the in-your-face defiance to doing something that seems so deliberately vicious.

I stood there with a couple of the pieces of fabric of the shirt in my hand. Thought about walking in and confronting him, but don't know what I'd gain. I could give him a withering look but he eats those for breakfast. After staring at the massacred shirt a few more seconds, I just tossed it in and closed the lid. Never said a word to him.

I ought to just shut up, take the money, and be satisfied, but I seem to be a glutton for punishment. Why do I feel compelled to keep reaching out to this kid who has made it plain he wants nothing to do with me? Maybe I can't resist the challenge. The times I do make some headway with him can be satisfying. Like someone putting coins in a slot machine, I keep at it for the payoff that occurs just enough times to keep me plugging away.

On Thursday after Sam brought him home, I asked how his day had been.

He threw his backpack onto the couch. "Shitty. Like always. What the fuck do you think? Any other goddamn, stupid questions?"

Sam raises an eyebrow at me, so I feel compelled to say something constructive, but I know *"I'm sorry to hear that"* or *"please find a more respectful way to tell me how you feel"* aren't going to work.

I look at Sam. "It's so cute when he uses his little potty mouth. Makes me just want to hug him." I open my arms and walk toward Alex who backs away in horror.

"Get the fuck away from me!"

I put an *ahhh* expression on my face. "Oh, there he goes again. *Sooo* adorable. C'mere you!" I open my arms even wider and take another step.

Alex darts behind the couch so I go to one end, which predictably has him sliding to the other end. I pivot, and he pivots. Sadie has gotten excited about the game and is jumping around barking. Sam is laughing his head off and to my complete delight, Alex starts too.

"Stop it," he says, between his laughter. "I mean it."

I make a dejected face and lower my arms. "Shoot, he's not cussing now. There goes the hug."

Proud of myself, I shoot Sam a little smug look. Yeah, I used some reverse psychology.

It's late spring and past time to start indulging in one of my favorite activities, biking. With some coaxing and bribing, I talk Alex into joining me. He slows me down and I can't go as far, but in addition to trying to do some relationship building, I don't want to leave him in the house alone. God knows what damage he could do. I also have the thought it could be good for him. When I told Sam, he agreed.

"Matt, that's a great idea. I went to a workshop on trauma not long ago and the instructor even talked about that. Yoga has proven beneficial to help kids regulate their emotions, and cycling has been shown to bring relief from negative thoughts and help them develop better impulses. Kids see and hear things they didn't notice before. The speed and movement can help remind them how good it can feel to be alive. Do you need Phoenix to buy him a bike?"

"Nah, I've got a few and no sense investing in a new one when he might just give it up."

During our first expedition, Alex made it into a competition. Didn't want to admit when he was worn out so I said, "I've had enough," just to keep him from killing himself. I didn't inform him I'd gone half the speed I normally would. By golly, if the rest of the day he wasn't actually rather pleasant company. Plus, it wore him out and he went to bed early. Now we're biking whenever there's some spare hours and the weather is good.

I soon decide this biking stuff is the best decision I've made since the kid graced my doorway. I try to remember it wasn't that long ago, but it already feels like he's been here forever. There are times when I really look forward to when he's gone, but there are times when that makes me feel … I don't know … a sense of loss?

His endurance has picked up, so we've gone from riding one after the other to mainly side by side, at least when traffic allows or we're on a designated bike trail. We're having *conversations.* Like real ones, talking about all sorts of things. Ever so often his guard slips and he shows a glimmer of something of his former life. I always keep my eyes straight ahead. Looking at him would end the talk immediately. I feel compelled to tell him something of mine too, although there's the concern he's filing it away under *things to use against Matt* for a later time.

It's a beautiful Sunday morning, perfect for a bike ride. Riding along a country back road, the green grass smell is in the air. It's a special sweetness like nothing else in the world. In the suburbs it's the smell of fresh-cut lawns, but in the rural valleys it's the age-old perfume of new hay curling in the sun.

I'd packed some drinks and snacks and we stop under a shade tree for a little break. The drinks are in my bike bag and I hand him one. The granola bars are in his bike bag and he tosses one at me. I catch it and tease him. "Oh sure, throw food at me. Fine, out here, as long as you know better than to do it in a restaurant."

He takes a swig of his drink and shrugs his shoulders. "I wouldn't know. I've never eaten in one."

He looks down and starts unwrapping his granola bar, and I'm glad he doesn't see my face. *He's fifteen and has never eaten in a restaurant? What else has he never done that I just assume all kids his age have done?* I vow to take him as soon as possible and two days later we eat at an Applebee's. We do the whole shebang. Appetizers, an entrée, then dessert where I introduce him to the triple chocolate meltdown.

I enjoy the outing.

I enjoy watching him wolf it down.

I enjoy watching him enjoy himself.

We've had one of those spells when summer makes an early debut, hitting into the eighties. Wednesday, after picking up Alex from Phoenix, I decide to capitalize on his recent good mood by feeding him his favorite take-out fast food, chicken nuggets and fries.

Saturday, Alex helps me finish up a big job and we still have the time and energy for a bike ride before dinner and then watching a ball game. I bring out drinks and chips and Alex falls asleep during the sixth inning, with Sadie laying on top of his legs on the couch. She's polished off the crumbs. Really, what does someone do without a dog to do important tasks like that?

Today is Sunday and I have to run over and pick up some trees for a job that starts Monday. I won't be gone but a couple of hours. Alex is sleeping in and I know getting him up will be a long process filled with everything from mumbles of *few more minutes*, to *go away*, to the ever popular *fuck off*. I decide I'll leave him home alone and hope the place is still standing when I return. I try to take Sadie with me, but she's sprawled across the bottom of

Alex's bed with all four feet in the air and isn't inclined to get up. She doesn't respond when I say her name. Like Alex, her hearing becomes selective when it suits her.

I call one last time then give it up. *Okay, you're on your own. Take your chances.*

The job takes longer than I thought, and I get increasingly anxious as time ticks by and it gets closer to the lunch hour. I called and Alex didn't answer his phone. That could mean he's burned down the house, he's still sound asleep, or just as likely, that he's fucking with me, one of his favorite activities. It's like his little waiting game where he's always late, knowing it drives me crazy. I should have just made him go with me.

I pull in the drive, throw the truck into park, and quick time it to the door. All is quiet.

"Alex?"

I look in the living room. No sign of him. Or in the kitchen. Go to his bedroom door and let out a breath I didn't know I was holding. He's still in bed. And so is Sadie. Lazy bums both of them, but I'm relieved all is well. Sadie jumps down, wagging her tail, making for the door. I imagine the outdoors is calling.

"Hey Alex, I'm home. I'm going to let Sadie out. Time to get up."

By the time Sadie has taken care of her business, Alex is up, yawning, but up and dressed.

"Did you eat any breakfast?"

"Wasn't hungry."

"Okay, well let me run out to the shed and put up some of these things, then I'll fix us something."

"Don't bother. I'll fix something for myself."

"Great." Fine with me.

When I get back to the house, I hit the bathroom, then head towards the kitchen. I stop and sniff the air. There's a bad smell. A really awful stench that soon has me covering my nose. The closer I get to the kitchen, the stronger and more terrible the smell is.

Alex is sitting at the table eating. I look around trying to determine where the hideous odor is coming from. Finally, I focus on what's in front of him, the cardboard tray with chicken nuggets.

I point at them and ask. "Where did you get those?"

He barely looks up from his chewing. "I saved them from the other day."

"Where?! I didn't see them in the fridge."

He shakes his head. "They were still in your truck."

I look at him with disbelief. *Oh my God. The truck? It's been hotter than hell out and you could fry an egg on the dashboard. They've been there for days!*

I walk over and grab the cardboard tray. Pull the half-eaten one out of his hand. "Hey," he protests.

Jesus Christ, they're green! They stink so bad I don't dream of putting them in the kitchen garbage. Instead, I run them outside to the large can on the side of the house, stuffing them down deep and securely closing the lid.

Alex is still sitting at the table when I walk back in, taking a big drink of his Coke. My eyes still don't believe what they've witnessed. "Why would you eat those the way they looked and smelled?"

His lips turn down. "I love chicken nuggets. They weren't so bad."

To think he complains about my toast. "Do you feel okay? You don't feel sick or anything?"

"I feel fine. But I'm still hungry," he complains.

"There's ham in the fridge and there's peanut butter. Fix a sandwich."

We take a bike ride and he seems fine. Guess he's got a cast iron stomach. Or, maybe he didn't eat enough to do any damage. But at dinner time he says he's not hungry. Shortly after, he goes and lies down on the couch. "I don't feel so good."

Uh oh, I was afraid of this. "Do you feel like you need to throw up?"

His hand goes to his mouth. "Shut up!"

"It's probably best you do."

He gives me one of his scathing looks, but two seconds later bolts up and makes a dash for the bathroom, barely making it to the toilet. I grimace as he hugs the bowl and wretches over and over. When he finishes, I bring him some water to rinse his mouth out. "Feel any better?"

He leans back against the wall. "Yeah, I'm okay now."

But he's not. He made it back to the couch but ten minutes later bolts again. This time he closes the door. After a couple more times of running to either throw up or sit on the can, he just stays in the bathroom slumped on the floor by the toilet bowl, cradling his head in his arms. I hand him a towel. "I'm going to call Mike."

He doesn't protest. His expression says *kill me now*. This is his own damn fault, but I can't help but feel sorry for him. Pitiful is not his usual look. He looks like what he is, a sick kid.

I call Mike. Don't get him. *Of course.* But I leave a message and in a couple of minutes, he calls me back.

"Mike, can you come over. Alex is really sick at his stomach. Food poisoning. "

"Sorry, I'm at a wedding. Out of town. But you know who you can call."

"Shit."

"Suck it up." The phone clicks off.

I disconnect and stare at the phone. A moan from the bathroom has me taking a deep breath and dialing a familiar number.

It rings three times. "Matt?"

"Hi, Mom."

Chapter 14

MATT

Through most of my childhood the battle lines were drawn. Mom and Mike on one side. Dad and me on the other. After the divorce, Mike stayed with Mom and I went with Dad. I didn't stay with him long because a short time later he had a heart attack, right there in the middle of the operating room. In the middle of an operation. Surrounded by doctors and nurses, he was dead on arrival. In my teenage mind, I blamed Mom … because I had to blame someone to make sense of it. I'm old enough now to realize how illogical my thinking was.

Forced to move back into Mom's house, I made it my mission to make life miserable for Mom's boyfriend, Scott. Whether it was me, her, or whatever, he exited our domestic scene pretty quickly. I was glad to see him go but even after he departed, I always felt like the third wheel, especially as Mike, following the family tradition, entered medical school. I finished high school at the alternative school and moved out as soon as I turned eighteen, staying with some friends in a ratty rented house. I knew it embarrassed my mother where I was living. That was fine with me.

I avoided her more and more. The funny thing is, Mom and I never had some big knock down and drag out fight. I just felt a dripping disapproval. Of everything. How I lived. How I made money, or often in my case, didn't. As the years went by, I went home less and less ... called less and less. Until it got to be a two-hour visit at Christmas, an hour on Mother's Day, and an hour on her birthday. The last one I barely made. It was like *sorry I'm late, I didn't want to come.* I had the good sense not to say it out loud, but that's what I was thinking.

This is the first time she's seen this place. She pulls into the drive in her snazzy little BMW. Even though it's a Sunday afternoon and I know she was home when I called, she looks like she's going to the country club. Well, maybe she was, how do I know? Not a hair out of place. Gold bracelets and necklaces. She always dresses in three colors. It's her trademark look. I glance down at my sweatshirt with at least three holes in it. I brush at the dirt on my jeans with the palm of my hand.

I open the door before she can knock or open it herself. "Thanks for coming."

"I came as soon as I could. Matt, what were you thinking, feeding him moldy chicken!"

Geeze Mom, I'm not an idiot! I want to slap my forehead but refrain and just say, "I didn't *feed* them to him. He *ate* them!"

Her expression says she's not buying it, and even I admit my words sound lame. She cuts to the chase. "Where is my patient ... my grandson?"

I haven't talked to her about Alex, but I know Mike has kept her informed. When I asked what she'd said when he told her, he seemed to enjoy telling me, going into a high mocking female voice, "*What is Sam Murry thinking giving him a CHILD?!*" Her confidence in me has always been overwhelming.

When I take her to Alex, he doesn't blink when I introduce them. I imagine he feels so bad he wouldn't care if I said Santa Claus was here to see him.

She pins me with a look. "Can we take him off the bathroom floor?"

I go over to help Alex to his bed but say defensively, "Well, it's where he's spending most of his time."

"Get him a pan. And bring some ice chips."

I do as I'm told, she is my mother after all, so that's more or less ingrained. The pan is easy. Ice chips? I have ice cubes. I grab a hammer from the drawer next to the stove, wrap an ice cube in a dish cloth, and give it a couple of good whacks then dump them in a coffee cup. I hear her talking to Alex. "You poor baby. Let's get you feeling better."

She won't be calling him baby when he cusses her out. But when I get back with the pan, he's lapping up the attention and being sweet as pie. She, in turn, is playing the cross between loving grandmother and Doctor Great-Bedside-Manner. Putting a cool washcloth on his head. Tucking the sheet up around him. If I didn't know better, I'd think I'm feeling a twinge of jealousy.

She waves one of her bracelet-covered hands, directing me to place the pan at the top of the bed, then she takes the ice chips and pivots back to Alex. "Here sweetie, have some of these. Take it slow."

I lean against the door jamb, but only for a second because I'm again tapped as errand boy. "Matt, I've got some bottles of Gatorade in my car. Go bring them in."

Like a well-trained lapdog, off I trot. Maybe the emergency room wouldn't have been so bad after all. By the time I get back, Alex has apparently polished off the ice chips and has that drowsy look indicating sleep is near.

Before I can warn her she might lose that hand, Mom leans over to push Alex's hair off his forehead. "You get some rest, darlin'. You'll feel better in the morning."

Alex doesn't protest the touch. Maybe he was already asleep. Mom and I head to the kitchen with Sadie trotting beside us, excited about unexpected company. She snaps her doctor bag shut, finds the one empty spot on the table where there's room to set it down, then looks up at me.

"I gave him some Imodium for the diarrhea. I think he's already purged most everything out of his system but if he gets worse, let me know. We might need to administer IV fluids. If he wakes later and is thirsty, he can have small amounts of the Gatorade. Start him on some saltine crackers in the morning and be very careful what he eats until his stomach gets truly settled."

"Thanks Mom, I appreciate you coming on such short notice."

"I'm happy to help out." A pause. "At least I get to see where you're living."

Here we go. I'm suddenly aware of every dirty spot on the counter. At least, thanks to Sadie, there are no crumbs on the floor, just black dog hairs. Okay, I did sweep the floor yesterday but the dog is a full-time shedder. It's her best trick.

Making herself at home, Mom opens the refrigerator door. "Do you not have any food? Why did he think he had to eat old chicken nuggets?"

The fridge is not lacking for food, but it could use some cleaning. I push the door shut. "Mom, there's plenty to eat. I'm sorry, I didn't think he needed to be told he shouldn't eat old, green chicken nuggets."

My sarcasm is lost on her. "Well, I worry about the two of you, way out here, with no one else around to help you."

"This isn't outer Alaska, Mom. We do fine."

Her tone softens. "Well, he seems very sweet."

Sweet is not a word I would generally use when describing the Holy Terror, but I don't try to give her the low down on all the things Alex does, and has done, to make him worth Sam paying me an arm and a leg to keep him. All I say is, "He's coming along." Maybe I even believe it a little.

"Well, you should bring him over for dinner one night."

A smart guy might lie and a dumb one might tell the truth. *Not happening.* Me, I hedge. "Yeah, maybe we could sometime. It's my busiest season with work so I put in hours into the evenings lots of days."

An awkward silence follows. Should I offer her something to drink? A Coke? But she'd probably want a glass and I don't know if there's one clean enough for her standards.

Mom picks up her bag. "I guess I should get going so you can get some rest too."

I walk her out to her car. It's dark and she's not familiar with the place. Plus, she's older. That suddenly hits me. She still looks trim and fit, but there are wrinkles I hadn't noticed before and some gray in her hair, which I'm sure she'll pay premium dollars at the hair salon to get fixed on her next visit.

She opens the car door but stands there, lit by the interior light. "Matt, you were always great with kids, but it certainly surprised me when Mike told me you'd become a foster parent." She reaches over and pats the hand I have resting on top of her car door. "You're doing a good thing."

I squirm a little inside thinking about the money and my not so high-and-mighty motives for taking in Alex. It's becoming more and more like some dark secret.

With that parting remark, she steps into the car. I release my hold on the door and softly close it as she gets seated behind the wheel. She gives me a smile and a little wave as she starts to back the car around. I raise my hand to wave back. Watch her tail lights fade into the blackness of the night.

I stand a moment with the stars twinkling overhead. There is twinkling closer to the ground too. During the day there are small, drab beetles that do no harm and are seldom noticed. When darkness comes on warm early summer nights, they take to the air over suburban lawns and rural meadows, and the darkness comes alive. Firefly nights. Or lightning bugs, as we like to call them around here. Sadly, their numbers are diminishing, a victim of too much mowing and way too much pesticide sprayed on the ground by lawn care companies

As a kid I'd capture them and put them in a jar, but Mom always made me release them within a short period of time so they wouldn't die. "Matt," she'd say, "some things are meant to be free." I'd screw open the lid while she stood next to me and together we'd watch them fly up into the sky. I'd like to stay out here and enjoy the night and the memories, but I turn to go back to the house.

Alex might need me.

Chapter 15

ALEX

At first, I thought this is one of those times where I may have outsmarted myself. I picked the Junior EMT program just to jab at Matt. Turns out I should have studied that brochure a lot harder. Mr. Murry was right. It *is* challenging. I thought I'd just get to ride in a fire truck and they might let me turn on the siren. Turns out I had to fill out a bunch of forms, pass a physical test, and yeah, pass a drug test. I couldn't help but smile about that, knowing it's probably the first time in a long time I could do it.

Then it turns out there are classes, homework … shit, it's like being in school. After the first session, I was ready to quit. Only reasons I didn't were pride and worrying Matt would get some satisfaction from it if I did. So, I gritted my teeth and kept going. Consoled myself with the thought at least it gets me out of the house.

But here's the thing. Now I like it. I really like it. During the third session something just clicked. The instructors treat us like adults. You listen to what they tell you, then you have to show you can do it or you don't move on. They don't make you feel bad if you can't perform adequately, but there's also no over the top praise if you do. You get your turn to show you can do CPR. If you can't do it right, then it's "Study up and try again next time," and if you do it correctly, it's watching them check the mark on the form while they say, "Good job. Next!"

Once we have mastered some of the basics we even go out on real calls. There was a big fire at a recycling center. The conditions were tough with the heat and all the equipment fire fighters have to wear. Us Junior EMTs manned the backup station providing food and drinks, cleaning tools, and refilling air packs. The feeling of doing something important is something I've never experienced before. The best part of all? As we were packing up to go, citizens (that's what we call them in the biz) came up and thanked us just like they did the firemen and real EMTs. One guy kept pumping my arm so hard when he shook my hand, I thought he'd yank it off, but I guess he was just so grateful the fire didn't spread to his nearby house.

We even get to wear uniforms. It was kind of pricey and no way was I going to pay for it, but when I handed the order form to Mr. Murry, he said, "I'll take care of it."

A few weeks ago, Mr. Murry and I went shopping and I used some of my newly earned money to buy the sneakers I've always wanted. It's the first time in my life they weren't bought at some discount place. The first time I've had ones I'm proud of. Ones that don't scream, *"He's poor!"* Adults don't get it. Nothing screams who has money and who doesn't at school like what shoes you have on your feet.

I bought a nice jacket too and best of all, thanks to Matt, I got a phone. When he handed it to me, I guess I didn't hide how surprised I was. I waited for him to say something like, *"You should be grateful because I didn't have to do this"* or *"You don't really deserve this but here it is."* But all he said was, "You can buy your own case for it, presuming you know what you'd like to have."

This makes me nervous. I've learned to deal with the usual shit of cruelty and meanness. Kindness is trickier. It creeps up around you and can stab you in the back when you're least expecting it. Friendly eyes. Smiling faces. Be careful. Keep your guard up. Defenses against kindness are much tougher.

I get the most antsy at night. It's when bad memories lie waiting to haunt me. Tonight is one of those nights. Where I'd like to try and outrun the memories. Like I've done at other foster homes, where I just pack up and take off. I could do it. I could take the stuff I've gotten so far and cut my losses on the rest. I went to my room early tonight, giving the excuse I was tired, but I just wanted to be by myself. I play a game or two on my phone, then toss it on the bed, too restless to concentrate.

I hear Matt let Sadie out one last time then go to his room. I stretch out on my bed with my hands behind my head and hope to get sleepy. After a while I give it up and pick up a book to read but I can't get interested. If I had some drugs to get high, that would help me knock myself out. A couple of beers might do it just as well. Too bad Matt doesn't keep any in the house.

Moving over to the bureau, I stare at myself in the mirror above it, still amazed to see both eyes staring straight back at me. I lift my lips into a smile that has all its teeth. My face no longer is covered in ugly zits. If for this and nothing else, it's been worth being here. I feel slightly less like damaged property, at least on the outside.

Sometimes I think if Matt lived downtown instead of out here in the wilderness, I couldn't help myself from walking out the door into the darkness when the itch to run comes over me. A thought pops into my head. Okay, there's a middle ground here. I don't have to run but I don't have to stay within these four walls either. Tonight, they are closing in on me, reminding me too much of being locked up. I could just go to the kitchen or the TV room, but I need to *move*.

Going to the window, I pull it all the way up. The screen pops out easily and I take care to quietly set it on the floor next to the wall, then step out into the night. I close the window behind me almost all the way, allowing enough room to get my hand under to pull it back up when I return. Excited to be out, I look around to see which way I should go. I thought I might be afraid but I've been here long enough to know monsters aren't lurking about … it's just darkness. Probably far less to be afraid of out here than in town. What was it Matt told me? Oh yeah. *City folks are afraid of things on four legs; country folks are afraid of things on two legs.* I get that. No drug dealers or would-be muggers hanging out here in the trees.

It's actually kinda nice out here. It's very still and the sky is lit up with lightning bugs. The moon is so bright, I can easily see my way around. I decide to walk to the creek and take the little path that winds around Matt's property line. I feel adventuresome, like a pioneer or explorer.

I come to the creek and cross the bridge then turn right. In a bit, I come to a place where there are two paths mowed through tall grass. Oh right, now I remember I should turn left here. I think that's right. The grass is brittle. Matt says we really need some rain. I recall there's another spot where I should be turning right. Seems like I should have hit it by now, but surely, I didn't miss it. I keep going. Abruptly, the path ends. *Shit*! I somehow missed a turn.

Okay, no big deal, I'll just turn around and find it on the way back. A breeze has picked up and out of nowhere a bank of clouds covers the moon. It's now much harder to see. I feel a little panicky but tell myself to get over it. I'm not lost, not really, not like *they found his body days later*.

The house is on the other side of that tree line, but there's an unmown stretch of about twenty-five yards that's taller than I am and full of brambles and tall weeds. There's no way I'm getting through there. I'm just not sure how to return to the house without taking another wrong turn and being out here all night long circling around like an idiot.

The sky suddenly lights up and there is a low rumbling thunder. The breeze is stronger now too. Just my luck. It hasn't rained in forever, but now it's going to storm. I pick up the pace, my heart starting to thump in my chest, and my breathing more labored. Another streak of lightning, this one closer, followed by a loud crack, and I jump out of my skin. I start going faster even though I don't know where I'm going.

As I near a grove of trees, I hear a rustle in the leaves and stop in my tracks. Probably a deer, I tell myself. *Please be a deer.* Suddenly, a black blob pops out from the trees and barrels towards me. Terrified, I freeze. The black blob jumps up on me. The black blob starts licking my face.

"Sadie!" I hug her tight, my knees weak with relief. She's excited to see me too and gets the zoomies, streaking all around me in as big a circle as the mown path allows. Now nothing seems scary. I laugh at her and call her back to me, sitting down and rubbing her ears.

"Hey, Sadie, let's go home, okay? Home, Sadie, home." She takes a few steps then stops and looks back at me.

"Chewy, Sadie. Let's get a chewy."

That does it. She's on full scale run. I worry for a second she'll leave me in her dust. But no, she never gets too far ahead of me, running back to make sure I'm still in the game. It's obvious she completely knows the way. I decide I'll buy her a whole box of chewies myself when I get the chance. When I see the creek, I know we're almost there. The bridge is in sight and silhouetted against the sky … Matt.

Uh oh. I stop just before the bridge while Sadie runs to him, excited to have all her people out in the night and having a good time. I wait to get reamed out, but all Matt says is, "Sadie heard you go out, and she couldn't stand missing an outing, so I gave up telling her to go back to sleep and opened the door. Speaking of doors, next time, you can use one instead of a window. I sometimes like a night time walk myself when I have trouble sleeping."

Taken by surprise by his nonchalant attitude, I don't say anything. Matt looks up at the sky then back at me. "Ready to go in? Unfortunately, I think most of the storm is going to miss us, but we might get a little rain out of it."

I set foot on the wooden planks and pass by him. "Yeah, sure." He joins me and we start walking to the house. Just before we get there, it starts raining very lightly. We reach the front porch right before it comes down a little harder. A sweet fragrance fills the air. I take a deep breath.

Matt sniffs too. "Know what that is?"

I've found my voice again. "Rain?"

"That's the cause, not what it is. I'm talking about the smell. It's called petrichor. It happens when it rains on dry ground, releasing bacteria and aerosols from the soil. I think of it as perfume."

I look at him. "You're strange."

He laughs. "Don't I know it!"

That little inner voice in my head says to shut up and say no more, but I'm often not smart enough to listen to good advice. "Guess that's why you agreed to take me in. That, and the money."

He quits laughing and keeps his eyes on me so long, I look down.

"I'd like to tell you the money had nothing to do with it, but I won't lie to you, it did. That doesn't mean I don't want you here."

This answer satisfies me. I'm so used to being lied to, I appreciate honesty. I wonder if he's going to ask if I want to stay here, but he doesn't. I'm glad for that. He just stretches and yawns. "You keep me on my toes. Speaking of money, I need to make some tomorrow so I'm going back to bed. The rain has already quit. I wish we'd gotten more. Are you going walking again or had enough?"

I keep my voice light. "I've had enough for tonight."

"Okay. Goodnight." Matt leaves me standing as he returns to his bedroom.

I stand for just a minute longer, enjoying the sound of the rain on the tin roof. I no longer feel the slightest bit antsy. I'm ready for bed now too. I head back to my room but not before making a detour to the kitchen, where I call softly to Sadie.

"Chewy?"

Chapter 16

SAM

It's Thursday, my standing appointment with Alex Coffey. While he's finishing up school work, I step into my boss's office to remind her I'll be heading out soon. I need to see if there's anything brewing with any of the other Phoenix kids that I need to be made aware of before leaving for the day.

Margo is my boss, but in our case, it's more a comrade-in-arms thing than a superior and subordinate. She's poring over spreadsheets on her computer. This means budget, something I try to distance myself from. I had enough of that when I was the superintendent of a corrections facility, thank you very much. That's why she gets the big bucks. Well, if there were big bucks, she'd get them.

Margo sticks a pencil behind an ear and motions me over to the visitor chair. As I'm lowering myself, she says, "You know when I hired you, it was with the idea you knew basic math. We aren't in this for fame and fortune, but Alex Coffey is costing us a bundle. Special school program tutoring, the high per diem for the foster parent, non-reimbursable medical costs." She thumbs through receipts. "A fireman uniform, entry fees, and ... "

I interrupt and throw back the line she gives out in her staff pep talks. "Whatever it takes, isn't that our motto? Wrap around services? The importance of pro-social activities?"

She pulls her glasses off, tosses them on the desk, and rubs her eyes. "Yeah, you can engrave those remarks on our bankruptcy papers."

Now I'm feeling guilty. I lean forward to try and get a look at the numbers. "Is it that bad?"

She puts her glasses back on and gives a little grin. "Actually, we're doing okay. But I worry if I don't bitch at you some, you'll keep this up till we are in trouble."

I relax. Good to know I'm not single handedly bankrupting our business. "Somebody in child services should have done something long ago. This kid was a walking emergency. I consider it an investment. We can pay money now or let the taxpayers pay millions over his lifetime for homeless services or incarceration because that's where this was heading."

Margo sits back, seemingly happy to have a distraction from her budget sheet. "You must be doing something right. I thought that kid would run off the first week. I do agree someone needed to step up. Placing him willy-nilly into foster homes, knowing they aren't going to last, is terrible. Not only is it awful for the kid, but that's how we blow out foster parents."

Now I've got her on a roll. "Not to mention, it makes foster care look so bad. Like we don't already have an image problem. Sure, the system has problems and there are some bad foster parents out there, just like there are bad teachers, judges, and policemen, but the majority of folks do this for the love of kids. In my book, they are heroes and they don't get the recognition they deserve."

She leans back in her chair and swivels side to side. "The need to get his eye fixed was a no brainer too. I enjoyed going to battle with the medical payment folks on that one. My blood boils to think they'd call it cosmetic surgery and say it's not an allowable expense because it wasn't medically necessary. Our kids have enough baggage to work through without something like that to deal with."

I lift an eyebrow and grin. "Glad to see you still enjoy going to war. There was something in the file where a previous worker made a run at it but dropped it when she ran into that particular roadblock. She obviously wasn't the bulldog you are."

"Are you calling your boss a bulldog?"

"Yep, I am. It's a compliment."

She grins. "I took it as one."

I stand up, thinking if I don't leave soon this will turn into a major bitch session. Something I enjoy at times, but Alex is probably ready to go. I nod at Margo. "If the kid does run off … hell, if he gets arrested again and gets sent off, I'll still know we made a lifelong positive change for him. His eye fixed, his tooth repaired, and the drugs the dermatologist prescribed have about got his acne mostly cleared up. These things alone will accomplish more than years of psychological therapy."

I walk out then turn around and lean against the door frame. "One more thing, while we're venting. There's not as much sympathy for kids like Alex as there is for kids who have suffered a major trauma. Kids who were terribly abused or watched a parent get shot, or any of the other horrors that come too often in this line of work. But a thousand small cuts can cause you to bleed to death as much as one major one. I read a recent study that showed kids in foster care have higher rates of PTSD than war veterans. And trauma isn't just about the bad stuff that happened. It's also about the good stuff that never happened."

Margo opens her mouth, I'm sure to chime in, but her phone rings, so I wave goodbye, and go to collect Alex. I'm pleased he's stayed put at Matt's as long as he has, but I know the battle is nowhere near won. In fact, it's just beginning.

Chapter 17

ALEX

Ninety-six days in the same foster home. A new personal best, well, at least for the past few years. Maybe my time in Placement Number 49 was longer. That was Ms. Francis. I remember her well because when she opened the door to meet me for the first time, she immediately hollered out, "Welcome!" Before I knew it, she had thrown her arms around me for a big hug. She was short and almost as wide as she was tall. Seemed like she always had a smile on her face.

The placements I remember most are the ones where I got moved when I didn't want to. I was doing fine at Ms. Francis's home but I'd gotten in trouble at school. It wasn't the first time, or the fifth. I'd been sent to in-school detention, suspended, then placed in an alternative school, but had trouble there, too. I'd gotten suspended again. This time my worker showed up to get me and instead of driving me to Ms. Francis, drove me to a psychiatric center for a "risk assessment." They only kept me about five days, so I don't know what risk they decided I was, but I was sent straight from there to Covington Academy, Placement Number 50, where their brochure advertised they served *troubled teens searching for healing and recovery.*

I was *not* searching for healing and recovery. I was really mad I couldn't stay with Ms. Francis. I didn't even get to say goodbye. If I was miserable, by God, everyone else was going to be too. I got thrown out of there in less than a month and it was on to Placement Number 51, which was actually a child welfare office where Placement Number 12, 28, 32, and 45 had been, if my memory is correct. They call it a *non-traditional placement*. Fancy name for a room with a cot in it. There wasn't even a shower. I got marched down the street to the YMCA for those. A security guard babysat me and any other kids that came along to join me. Out of boredom and tension, fights were common, so they always earned their money.

One day the guard on duty hauled me and two other kids into the social work supervisor's office and said, "I've had it. I'm done," and walked out.

Back to the present. I'm happy to see my bank account is growing. Matt is okay, although he has some annoying habits like hollering at baseball players on TV, like they'll hear him and it'll help them know the difference between a strike and a ball. Okay, sure, sometimes he can be funny, but it's always fun to watch his face tighten up when I call him Doc.

My biggest complaint is living in the sticks can get pretty boring, especially when you are sober and drug free. I go to Phoenix for school, go home, then do it all over again. I remind myself I'm getting paid for it.

Today is a break in the routine because we're making a stop on the way home to some hole-in-the-wall place on East Broadway, just a few blocks from Phoenix. Matt has to get something for his mother for her birthday. As far as I can tell, Matt doesn't talk to her or see her much, even though she apparently lives not that far from us. It doesn't take a rocket scientist to know Matt and his mother have "issues" as my many therapists through the years coin it. I don't know what the problem is because she seemed nice enough to me.

Matt parks right in front of the store. I take out my earbuds long enough to say, "I'll just wait here."

He turns off the truck and throws it into park. "Ah, come on in. I may need your opinion."

Oh yeah, like I know what to buy a mother. A bottle of OxyContin maybe, always the perfect gift for mine. Resigned, I drag myself in behind him. Matt says hi to the old guy at the counter then we start looking around. It's one of those stores that sells all that old shit some people like. Matt looks at the jewelry. *Boring, boring, boring.* I start walking around looking at stuff stacked everywhere. Old toys. Lots of kitchen stuff. There must be a million dishes in this joint. And then, something catches my eye.

I move closer and stare. It's a little ceramic bird. Nothing I'd normally pay any attention to except it looks exactly like the one my grandmother used to have sitting on the table by her front door. She's the only person who ever truly loved me. She and Mom didn't get along, but when Mom went on a binge, she'd sometimes drop me off there. My grandmother wanted to have me stay permanently but mom wouldn't do it. Just out of spite, I think. Those times with my grandmother were some of the happiest days of my life. Her little ceramic bird was right next to a framed picture of me as a baby.

One of my social workers let me know my grandmother had died, and that's why they couldn't place me with her once I entered the system. There weren't any other relatives either. This bird is just like the one she had. A thought pops into my head. *What if it was actually hers?*

It doesn't cost that much and I have the money but not on me. Matt had stopped to get gas after he picked me up, and I'd bought some chips and a drink, which now I'm kicking myself for doing. I could ask Matt to buy it for me. *Matt, will you please buy me a dumb bird thing?* No, too embarrassing. I'd look stupid unless I told him why and I don't want to share that info. I could come back tomorrow. But what if somebody else comes in and buys it before that? I'd be screwed. I can't take that chance. I *have* to have it. *Now.*

Matt has moved closer to me, picking up a few things and turning them over to see the price tag on the bottom. I move a little further away then return once he drifts to the next aisle. I keep an eye on him and make sure his back is turned to me when I make my move.

There's a simple solution to my problem and one I've used many, many times over the years. I quickly palm the bird and stick it in my jacket pocket. Then I casually walk away, lingering near some old cameras before heading up to the front when Matt lets me know he's ready to go. He's found something for his mother and the old guy is checking him out. After the guy bags up the purchase, he hands it to Matt and we start walking towards the door. Just before we get there, I hear "excuse me."

Dammit Matt, just keep walking. But he doesn't. He turns around and I turn halfway but keep looking at the door.

"Young man, have you forgotten something? The something that's in your pocket?"

I freeze for a second then try to look confident but confused. My initial plan is to go with total denial and call the guy a liar, but when I look towards him, I can see a video monitor just to his right and above is a sign that says, *Notice: Store Under Video Surveillance.* There goes Plan A.

It makes me furious. *Who puts video cameras in a store full of junk?* Do people really want to steal this shit? Well, people other than me, that is.

My mind whirls as I take stock of the situation. Matt is looking shocked. The old guy is calm. He doesn't look angry; he looks like he knows exactly what's going on in my head. Like he's a chess player and already is three moves ahead of me. I'm not sure what to do. Usually, I either get away with my shoplifting or if I don't, just take off running which puts me in the clear because they don't know who I am, or where I live. But that won't work now.

Shit. I pull the bird out of my pocket. "Um, oh yeah, sorry, I um, wanted to be sure it didn't get broken and I um, forgot it was in there. I'll pay now."

I reach into my jeans where I have a few quarters, a dime, and a penny left from my gas store purchases. "That's funny. I don't know where the rest of my money went." I start looking around like I must have dropped it on the floor or something.

Matt pins me with a look. He knows I'm lying out my teeth. He starts pulling his wallet back out. "I'm sorry sir, how much is it? I'll pay for it."

He shoots another look my way and says firmly, "We'll give it back to you, too."

"No!" I didn't even know I was going to say anything, but it just pops out.

There are footsteps on the wooden floor and a lady joins the man behind the counter. "Hey Dad, what's going on?"

The old guy doesn't take his eyes off of me. "This young man says he forgot to pay for something."

"Well, let's have a look, shall we?" She hits a button to rewind the video and then puts it in slow motion forward, as we all watch me shoplift. I also notice the sign above the cash register that says, "All shoplifters will be prosecuted."

Okay, running looks like a good option even if they do know who I am, but Matt has stepped between me and the door and I'm not going anywhere. I look out at the sunshine, the passing cars, people walking on the street and try to resign myself to what's next—that within the hour, I'll probably be seeing nothing but the four walls of a jail cell. Again.

The lady—who's pretty good looking—tilts her head to the side and smiles at Matt. "You don't remember me, do you?"

Matt switches his eyes from me to her. "I'm sorry, I don't. You are...?"

"Emily. Emily Morris. You sat behind me junior year in Mr. Rhorer's chemistry class. You scorched a hunk of my hair with a Bunsen burner."

Now it's Matt who looks like he wants to run.

Join the club.

Chapter 18

MATT

Well, doesn't this just suck? The whole day has been awful from the get go, and this is the icing on the cake. One of my crew this morning didn't show up. Mike gave me grief about our mother's upcoming birthday, so I had to try and come up with an idea for a gift she'll like, an impossible task. Alex has pulled another one of his stunts and now I'm going to have to atone for one of the sins of my past.

"Emily?" Now that I remember her name, I search my memory to recall something about her. Oh yeah, she hung out with Norah Lang and some of those brainier kids. Newspaper staff, Spanish Club. Yearbook staff. Not my peer group. I do remember that day in chemistry because I ended up in Saturday detention. I might have gotten suspended, but that would have meant I couldn't play in the Friday night game and that wasn't going to happen. I hadn't really meant to do any harm to her; I was just bored and messing around. I recall she accepted my apology and was a pretty good sport about the whole thing.

Now that I remember who she is, I give her a closer look. She looks good. Much better than when she was a teenager. I do recall those vivid hazel eyes. And she's filled out nicely since departing good old Western Hills High. She meets my appraising eyes, and I see the pleasure she's taking in ambushing me.

"It's okay. It grew back out." I can see it did. Auburn hair cut to her chin in one of those fashionable cuts that swings when she moves her head.

We've been lucky no one else has been in the store to witness our little drama, but the door opens and an older couple stroll in. Emily motions with her hand, "How about you all come with me for a minute?"

I nod and keep an eye on Alex to make sure he doesn't try and make a run for it. His face looks mutinous but from my days as a quarterback I'm good at sizing up guys, and I see fear there as well. What in the world was he thinking? Risking everything and going back to detention for a little birdie knick-knack?

We follow her to another room, set up as part storage room, part office. She motions to some chairs and we all sit. Well, she and I sit. Alex slumps, but I'm not fooled and stay between him and the door.

I smile at Emily. "How have you been? Sorry to meet again under these circumstances. Look, I'll pay for the um, bird thing. And Alex will put it back." I glare at him, daring him to say no again, but he turns away and looks at anything but me.

Emily smiles back. "Mom and Dad opened this place after he retired, but Mom died unexpectedly shortly after."

"Oh, I'm sorry to hear that."

"Thanks. I moved back to town a few months ago to help out. I'd been teaching seventh grade and decided to take a sabbatical. I'll probably go back to it eventually, but for now, this is a nice change of pace. We do generally prosecute shoplifters, but I think in this situation we can probably work something out. I have a son and I know I'd appreciate it if someone gave him a better option."

She turns her attention to the kid. "Would you please tell me your name?"

For a second, I don't think he'll answer, but he finally mumbles, "Alex."

"Well, Alex, I could use some help around here with some cleanup. If you'd agree to come work here for a bit, I'd be willing to forget about any charges. Matt, would you be on board with this?"

"That would be great ... and very generous of you."

She asks, "Alex?"

I shoot him a look telling him not to push it. *I'm going to kill him if he blows this.*

"Alright."

I breathe a sigh of relief. I was afraid he'd tell her to fuck off or something even worse. And I really didn't look forward to calling Sam and telling him his little project was back in lockup.

"Give her the thing, Alex."

He's been clutching his illegally gotten gain like he's some kid at a ballgame who caught a fly ball. But very slowly he sets it gently on the desk next to him and looks back down at the floor. He looks … sad? What is it about the stupid bird? This kid is an endless mystery but there's something off here. Something beyond his usual obnoxiousness.

After again expressing my appreciation and setting up the plan to deliver Alex to work off his debt, we start to leave. But Emily holds up a hand. She reaches over to pick up the bird then presses it into Alex's hand. "You keep it. I think it's calling your name." She smiles, winks, and whispers, "And this way I can make you work longer."

She gives me a look that tells me not to argue. She's petite and has to tilt her head at quite an angle to look up at me. I find myself staring into her hazel eyes and the way her whole face lights up when she smiles. She isn't my usual type at all and considering this situation, the last thing I should be feeling is attraction, but it's a sensation I've had a lot of experience with through the years so I call it as I see it.

This summer just keeps getting more and more interesting.

Chapter 19

ALEX

"Alex, bring me a little box ... make that a medium box. There's some stacked at the back."

I stick my phone in my pocket and go to find whatever counts as a medium box in order to make Emily's dad happy. Then I get stuck wrapping tissue paper around a bunch of green plates that look like gigantic leaves for the customer. *Then* I get stuck having to cart them out to her car.

"Thanks, honey," she says to me as she pushes the button to close her trunk.

The bad news: I had to work off my shoplifting debt. The good news: it wasn't all that bad and turned into working here a few hours a week. My bank account is getting fatter and fatter. The car I picture me driving keeps getting bigger and fancier in my head. The other plus is I don't have to sit around the Phoenix office waiting for Matt to pick me up. I can walk down here from there and have some time on my own without feeling like I'm constantly under surveillance. Plus, it's better than sitting out in the sticks at Matt's.

Emily is nice. In a weak moment one day when we were working together, I told her why I tried to steal the ceramic bird. She said, "Lots of people who come to the store might come to buy something practical, but end up with something that calls to them from their past. But maybe think of a different way to handle it. You could have asked me to hold it for you and I would have been glad to."

I nodded like yeah, that's what I'd do next time although probably not. I'd feel too dumb.

Her dad, Walter, is okay too if you don't mind being called "buckaroo" when he's in a good mood. And Emily's kid, Justin, is tolerable. Very weird, but tolerable. I sometimes think I've been kept on as much to keep the kid out of their hair as I am to unload boxes and sweep the floor.

At first, I just tried to ignore him and hope he'd take his nine-year-old self and go away. When no one was looking, I'd shoot him nasty looks and pretty much tell him to get the hell away from me. Truthfully, that's exactly what I whispered to him on at least three occasions. He didn't give a shit. And each day when he sees me, no matter how obnoxious I've been to him, he acts like I'm his long-lost best friend.

A big smile lights up his face when he sees me. "Hey! It's Alex! Hi Alex! Are you working today, Alex? Do you know that a cheetah can run up to eighty miles-an-hour, Alex?"

Then when I leave, it's "Bye Alex! It was good seeing you, Alex! What are you going to have for dinner, Alex?"

I'm gonna be honest. He broke me. His everlasting cheerfulness combined with the endless use of my name; I just couldn't keep being obnoxious towards him. Now I find myself saying, "Hey Justin, how's it going?"

Of course, that just gets him talking. And talking ... and talking. I swear he never shuts up, except when he plays games on his tablet. Then he just hums ... and hums ... and hums. And flaps his hands. A lot. He carts around a stuffed bunny wherever he goes. T. J. Funny Bunny is his name. Like Justin, T.J. has a lot to say.

I worked on a Saturday and was given money to go down the street to Subway and get him and me some lunch. His order: a six-inch turkey with provolone cheese, no tomatoes, and just a little mayonnaise. Sour cream and onion chips. When I get back, he unwraps it and fear strikes my heart when I see the cheese is cheddar. Even worse, I'd gotten ranch chips by mistake because the damn packages look almost alike, and I was trying to check out the hot girl sitting at one of the tables.

He unwraps the sandwich and goes instantly still and quiet. Holds up the sandwich like it's Exhibit A at a murder trial. "Alex, the cheese is orange."

"Yeah, Justin, I see that. Orange is good."

"It's supposed to be white, maybe a little yellow."

Uh oh. I'm in trouble. He scrunches up his face. "I don't like orange cheese. T. J. doesn't like it either."

I think I'm in luck because I got the same sandwich and mine does have provolone. "Look, I'll switch with you. You can have my cheese."

He shakes his head. "There's mustard on it. I don't like mustard. T. J. doesn't like mustard."

I peel off an inch that has some mustard on it. "See here, problem solved." He shakes his head more vigorously.

"Now it's not a rectangle. My cheese needs to be a rectangle."

Jesus! "Okay, I'll go back and have them fix it."

He pulls his food in closer to him. "No, I'll just take the cheese off. I won't have cheese today."

Thank God. He starts eating but after two bites, looks up at me. "Alex, did you know they put on the wrong cheese?"

"No, no, I didn't, or I would have had them make it right."

"Did you think of looking at it to make sure it was right before you left the store, Alex?"

"No, I didn't."

"T.J. thinks you should have. Do you think you should have, Alex?"

"Well, I sure as hell wish I had!"

"Did you know the chips were wrong too, Alex?"

It's time for a blatant lie. "They were out of sour cream and onion."

"Oh, that's too bad." He takes another bite of his sandwich. "Do you think they should have been careful to order enough sour cream and onion chips, Alex?"

It's all I can do not to scream. Untold questions later, lunch is finished. Showing how in control of myself I am these days, I didn't even reach over and strangle him … but I damn well wanted to.

When Justin went to throw away the wrappers and use the bathroom, Walter, Emily's dad, came over, grinning, "Did he have a *few questions* for you?" He does the air quotes finger thing. "I love the kid but never knew questions could be used like lethal weapons."

He sits down in the chair across from me. "I'm sure you've noticed Justin has some … um … quirks. He's on the spectrum. Autism spectrum. Do you know about this?"

I do, a little. There were kids in detention like that. The staff would explain how we needed to be patient with those kids. It wasn't always easy. There was one boy, Randall, who drove us absolutely crazy. That included one teacher who seemed to forget their little lecture about being patient. He lost his temper, nothing physical, but he started hollering at the kid. Staff aren't supposed to holler, but that doesn't mean they don't do it.

His face got all red and he raised his voice saying, "Randall, can't you just act normal for one hour today? Just one hour! How hard can that be? Do you even *know* what normal is?!"

The kid puckered up his face and yelled back. "Sure, I do! It's the button on the washing machine between low and heavy duty!"

The teacher just froze. The whole room went quiet. Suddenly, the teacher just laughed and laughed. Then he did something staff hardly ever do. He apologized to Randall for losing his temper.

I answer the question Walter is asking. "Yeah, a little."

"Well, good. Justin, and people like him just look at things a bit differently than you and me. Sometimes he can be a bit challenging. We appreciate you watching out for him while you're here."

A few hours later Matt arrives to pick me up, but I don't hurry to the front because I know he'll be talking with Emily. I'm pretty sure that's the other reason I got the offer to stay on and help out. During the slave labor I did as punishment for stealing, Matt stayed the first time to make sure I was a good boy. He and Emily talked … and talked … and talked. And smiled. And laughed. She made pumpkin muffins for us. He helped her fix some shelving. They stand closer and closer. Geez, get a room why don't ya??

Once school is out for the year, my tutoring time gets cut back, which lets me work a few more hours at the antique shop. I like the money and sometimes Matt hires me out to help with some of the jobs he doesn't use a crew for, sweetening my wallet even more. He tried to pull a fast one and have me work for nothing, saying it was part of the "deal." *Uh uh.* This is above and extra. He caved pretty easy so I think he knew that wasn't going to fly.

I'm working for him today and he's hollering from the kitchen to get my ass in gear. I wait a bit, like I always do just to annoy him, then throw on some clothes and go to eat his crappy burnt toast. He's sitting at the table with a cup of coffee and, lucky day, he bought some doughnuts yesterday which are sitting in a box on the counter. I beeline towards them. Chocolate glazed, my favorite.

Matt takes a sip of his coffee then sets his mug on the table. Waves the doughnut in his hand in my general direction. "You can't come to work dressed like that. Go put on your jeans."

It's still early morning but I can feel the sun through the window. "It's too hot out. I'm gonna wear shorts."

"This isn't the kind of work where you can wear shorts. Go change."

Leave it to Matt to ruin the good mood I was almost in. Just another stupid rule I have to put up with. I make a last try. "The regulations say you can't tell a foster teen what to wear. I'm not changing."

Matt shrugs and looks down at his phone. Probably texting Emily. "I can't tell you what to wear, but I can tell you no one works for me dressed like that. Suit yourself, if you don't want to earn some money."

"Fine! I'll change. Happy now?" I take my damn doughnut, grab a drink, and head to my room.

"Ecstatic," he mumbles.

"Put on socks too!" I hear him holler as I walk down the hall. *Christ, what a pain in the ass he is.* But I find a pair under the bed and yank them on, then stomp into my shoes without tying them.

The drive to the job site is nice. It's getting hot but with the windows down and the breeze blowing through the truck, it's comfortable. I like the wind. I stick my head out and close my eyes enjoying the feel of it rippling through my hair. We work through the morning with Matt digging holes to plant trees. When it's large enough we each take a side, lowering the root ball into the hole, then I push the dirt over it. It's getting hot so I'm glad I have the easier job.

When we break for lunch Matt parks the truck in a shady spot and we sit on the lowered tailgate. I reach into the cooler and get a Coke for Matt and a Mountain Dew for me. There are also chips, and some peanut butter cookies Emily made for us. This is the best part of the working day.

The afternoon switches to putting in shrubs rather than trees. The holes don't have to be as big and I'm bored with filling them in. I decide I want to dig. It's harder but I wouldn't mind having muscled arms like Matt. Girls like it. I seem to be thinking a lot about girls these days. Especially since during the summer they like to wear so few clothes. My imagination kicks into overdrive.

"Hey, give me a turn digging."

Matt smiles and hands over the shovel. "Have at it. Think you can handle it?"

I grab the shovel and toss it in the air a little, catching it on its way back down. "What, Doc, like it's hard?"

After two holes, having muscled arms seems less important. I'd be happy to go back to just pushing in the dirt, but pride keeps me going. Three holes later I'm breathing hard and the sweat is pouring down my face. Matt holds out his hand. "Here, you did good. I'll do the rest."

Pride is starting to not matter as much but I try to save a little face. "I'll finish this one."

"Fine," Matt says. "I'm grabbing my other gloves. I'll be right back."

Knowing I'm about to stop, I give the shovel a good push then lift my foot for another. *What the hell?* There's a funny sensation on my right leg, almost like a match has been set on it. Then another, and another, followed by a sharp pain on the back of my neck. I swat at it and something wiggles under my hand.

"Ouch! Shit! Ouch!" Now it's my hand that's stinging. I drop the shovel and back away shaking it out. Looking down, I'm horrified to see forty or fifty yellowjackets from the ankle of my right leg to my kneecap. Another dozen are on my shirt and I feel a sting on my head. The hole where I was digging is now a live thing with a swirling mass … like they're making their own little tornado. A buzzing and angry tornado. I bat at the ones buzzing in front of my face and start to run but Matt grabs me.

I push at his hands. "Let me go! I'm getting killed here."

Matt has one hand on my left arm and walks with me, quickly, but not past a walk.

"Don't swat at them. You'll just get them agitated and more will come after us. And don't run. They can fly faster than we can run and that just gets them excited."

I feel them stinging me through my pants. The pain isn't severe but I feel it. The ones in my hair are the ones that hurt. "They're stinging my head!"

The further we walk away the less of them are following us but the ones on my clothes show no thoughts of leaving. Finally, we reach the truck and Matt opens the passenger door. Take off your jeans and get in. Don't pull your shirt off, they'll sting you on your face."

I'm happy to strip. No one else is in sight and even if there was a crowd I wouldn't care. This is no time for modesty. I kick off my tennis shoes and drop the pants but I can't get them off that easy without using my hands. Matt uses his booted feet to hold them down so I can step out of them, then he shoves the ones off my shirt while he half pushes me into the cab. Now some of the winged demons from hell are flying around in the truck and I duck to avoid them. I can still feel the ones in my hair. *Ouch. Ouch.*

Matt has joined me from the driver's side. He has on his work gloves and bends my head down and starts yanking the yellowjackets out of my hair, crushing them and tossing them in an empty soft drink cup sitting in the cup holder. I see one light on his arm and start stinging him but he ignores it and keeps working on my hair.

The ones in my hair don't want to come out. Matt curses and yanks off his glove and reaches into my hair to yank out the last few.

Then he grabs his Farm Supply catalogue sitting on the seat and slams it on the one crawling up the dash then hits the starter. He drives about fifty yards away before opening his door and rolling down the windows to shoo the last of the fuckers out before quickly rolling his window back up. Some of the yellowjackets bang against the window, trying to get back at us. Geez, it's like something from a horror movie!

Matt is looking me over. "You okay? Where else did they get you?"

"My neck." I splay out my fingers and see red bumps coming up. "My hands."

Matt reaches behind the seat and grabs the first aid kit, then drives far enough away that the last of the wasps have given up the chase. He comes around to my side and opens the door. In his hands are a bar of soap and a water bottle.

"Hold your hands out." I do as he says and watch him pour the water over my hands then starts scrubbing with the soap.

"Bend over so I can get your neck." After the soap and water treatment, he reaches into the cooler and grabs an ice cube, wrapping it in a piece of gauze.

"Here, hold this on your hands." He grabs more ice and puts it on my neck.

"Better?"

I nod. He rummages in the first aid kit and pulls out a little red and white packet of Tylenol.

"Use your water bottle. Take these."

I don't argue. One of the few times I'm ordered to do something that I don't even think about it. We look back where we'd been and the yellowjackets are still swirling from the hole, the shovel right beneath them.

Matt grins and gives my arm a little shove. "Don't guess you'd like to go retrieve our tools, would ya?"

I grin back. I don't know why. But now that the danger is past, it *is* kinda funny. Also, like we had a big adventure. "No, but I'll film you doing it and put it on YouTube. Might go viral."

Then we're both laughing like idiots. Matt starts up the trucks and says, "Forget the shovel. We'll come back for it … and your pants … later when the little bastards finally go back to ground."

I'm still laughing which is saying something since I'm sitting here without any pants. "Hey, maybe somebody will see the shovel and try to steal it. I'd like to tape that!"

I act it out like looking around to see if anyone is watching me. Reaching out and grabbing the shovel, then screaming, "*Eiieeee!*"

Matt is looking at me and wiping his eyes. It feels good to be funny and for once, not in a smart-ass way, just … funny.

Even better, we blow off the rest of the day. I sit in the car outside of a store while Matt runs in and buys us bathing suits. He calls his mother to ask permission to go as her guests and a few minutes later we're in the pool at the country club. Another first for me. Matt says he hasn't been here in years. I notice some people looking at him … at us. I feel out of place and feel like they know it. I'm not sure why some are giving Matt a mean look. Matt either doesn't notice or ignores them but I don't. It makes me mad. If anyone is going to treat Matt badly, it's me, not these people. I stare at them until they suddenly decide they need to look at their phone or put on sun screen or something. I keep staring even then. *Stuck up turds.*

The cool water feels great and even better, on the way home we stop for burgers and fries. I've sworn off chicken nuggets, perhaps for the rest of my life. We sit in the truck and eat while parked under a large oak tree. I even know it's an oak tree. Before coming to Matt's and listening to him naming everything all the time, I'd have just called it a big tree.

I poke the straw into the cup lip and slurp until I hit empty, not to be purposefully annoying this time, just because it tastes so good. I pick up a French fry but before stuffing it in my mouth, look over at Matt. "Aren't you going to say it?"

"Say what?"

"That if you hadn't made me put on jeans and socks, I'd have gotten stung real bad."

Matt takes a last bite of his burger and wads up the wrapper. Looks at me all innocent like. "Oh, did I need to say it?"

"Ha, ha." I think a second. "What would have happened if I got stung that many times on my bare skin?"

"Well, it would have hurt like hell for one thing. And we probably would have made a run to the emergency room or at least to Mike. Or God forbid, my mother. She already thinks I'm negligent."

I look at Matt's hand. His finger tips are all red where he got stung pulling the wasps out of my hair with his bare hands. He didn't have to do that. He did that for me.

Matt smiles and takes a sip of his own drink. "Well, I guess now you'll listen to every single thing I say and do exactly what I tell you to do, right? Like clean your room. Eat your spinach. You'll say, 'Why, yes Matt, I now know how wise you are.'"

I roll my eyes. "Let's not get carried away."

As we drive home with the sun going down, I lean back in the seat, close my eyes, and listen to the music on the radio, feeling glad of something … maybe, just being alive. It's not a familiar feeling.

Later, after we're home, the stings start itching like crazy. I'm rubbing on them when Matt says, "Don't scratch; it just makes them worse."

I look at him pointedly because while he says this, he's scratching at his arm. He grins, "Do as I say, not as I do."

He holds up a finger in that wait-a-second gesture, walks out to the porch, then comes in with a spiky looking potted plant. Snaps off one of the spikes and squeezes it. Green slime comes out. He holds it out to me. "Here, rub this on your stings."

I look at him like he's lost his mind so he laughs and shakes the plant at me. "It's aloe. Nature's best remedy for all things itchy. Believe me, you'll like it."

I frown but I'm desperate. This seems really weird but I apply it and have to admit he's right. Feels great. Cool and some immediate relief. Matt goes into his room and brings out a box of Benadryl. I know the medicine cabinet in the bathroom is empty. All the medicines are in his room locked up. It's a foster care regulation. I can't get as much as an aspirin on my own. Stupid.

"Here, this'll help too, and it'll probably put you to sleep which will be good for both of us."

I try not to scratch. "Fat chance of sleeping."

He's nodding his head. "Yeah, between these stings, the heat, and the humidity going out the roof, even with the fans, it might be tough. But I have an idea. Come with me."

I'm not in the habit of jumping up and doing what I'm told in any hurry so I just stare at him.

Matt sighs, loudly and dramatically. "Remember how wise I am? Give me one night of doing what I say."

Rolling my eyes, I can be dramatic too, I follow him to my room and he yanks the bedcovers off my mattress and folds them up under his arm, then motions to the mattress. "Grab that end."

We haul it into the living room and drop it on the floor. He takes out a coin. "Heads you get the couch, tails you get the mattress."

He flips it. "Tails. You're on the floor." He turns on the window unit air conditioner, which he usually resists—like using it would make the room explode—and twists the knob. "I'm setting this to warp 10. *But Captain, the engines won't take it.*" Grinning at his own lame joke, he turns to me. "We're going to enjoy freezing our butts off tonight. My dad always called this 'hotel room cold.'"

He turns off all the lights and there's just the flickering of the TV screen and the hum of the air conditioner as it cranks out the glorious cool air. Sadie is excited about the mattress on the floor and gets the zoomies, jumping off and on. I decide to add to the festivities and bring us some soft drinks. I reach up and start scratching my neck but at the look from Matt, I put my cold Coke can on it. *Ahh, better.* I'm doing what Matt says. I hope I don't make it a habit.

That old movie, *Zombieland*, is on. We laugh as Woody Harrelson chases after the Twinkie truck. The movie ends and Matt switches over to a baseball game. The announcer drones on and on comparing this team to the one from some long-ago year. I feel my eyes growing heavy but I fight off going to sleep. It's a weird thing. I've been attacked, I've been in pain, and I could have died a few hours ago—not likely, but I *could* have—and the funny thing is this could be one of the best days of my life.

I don't want it to end.

That's my last thought of the night.

Chapter 20

ALEX

I wake before the sun is up. Still drowsy, I want to go back to sleep but the itching has returned even worse than before. So, I scratch a while, try to get comfortable again, scratch some more. Last night's contentment is history. And not just because my skin is driving me nuts. My thoughts are too.

I've been letting down my guard. One big sign is that I've quit counting down the days on *the deal*. A statement Matt made in passing about a week ago keeps bouncing around in my head. He needed the truck moved about a hundred yards to unload some trees. I'd offered to do it, knowing he'd say no. For a few seconds I thought he actually was going to let me. But then he smiled and said, "Very tempting because I could keep digging while you do, but better not. Sam might give me an earful if he found out. But soon you'll be old enough to get your license and I'll happily turn over the keys to you in these situations."

He tossed this out casually, the kind of thing you say without thinking about it. He might not have thought much about it, but I did. He acted like I'd be here long term. Like a permanent thing.

That, and what happened yesterday, have placed my internal warning signals on full alert. *Danger! Danger!* No, I've been down this road before. Fool me once, shame on you. Fool me twice, shame on me. Or in my case, fool me over and over, which makes me … what?

A complete idiot, that's what.

I had other upsetting moves, but it was the Flemings that broke my heart. Broke it apart and mashed that sucker flat. I had just turned eleven. For a while I thought I had it all. A nice teacher. A couple of friends at school and in the neighborhood. The dog loved me and slept with me every night. The Flemings' two kids were generally easy to get along with and I liked Sarah, the other foster kid who was close to aging out.

Mrs. Hughes, my caseworker back then, picked me up from school one day and took me to her office. Her co-worker, Mr. Scott, lingered within earshot near the door.

Mrs. Hughes kept twisting the ring on her finger. Then she'd smooth out her skirt. Would look at me then look down. Warning bells should have been going off in my head but young and stupid me, I had been lulled into thinking my life was going to be okay.

She talked about the weather and asked what the school had served at lunch. Then leaned forward. "Alex, I have some news I need to give you."

She glanced at Mr. Scott who eased his way a little more into the room. "Mr. Fleming has a new job and will have to relocate to California."

Now I get it. She knows what she tells me could make me upset. This is bad news and I look down at my hands in my lap and try to take it in. It means I'll have to leave my school and my friends. But I know enough about adults that their wants come first. From the way she's acting, this is a done deal. Me whining and crying isn't going to change anything. I try to focus on the positive side of it. California is nice, isn't it? Warm all the time.

Okay, I'll surprise her and show how tough I can be. What's that word my teacher said recently? *Adaptable*. Yes, that's what I'll be. I try to smile but can't quite be adaptable enough to pull that off.

I swallow. "Wow. I … um … always wanted to go to Disneyland. Guess maybe now I will."

Mrs. Hughes wets her lips and her eyes flick to the door. Mr. Scott is still standing there and each time I look his way, he hurriedly starts messing with his phone.

"I'm sure sometime you can. Or to Disneyworld."

I frown at her. "Why would we go to Disneyworld in Florida if we're living in California?"

She scoots her chair a little closer towards me. "Well, Alex, here's the thing. The Flemings can't take you with them."

Suddenly, she's talking really fast. "I'm so sorry sweetheart. I know you liked it there, but I promise we've found you a really good new placement!"

It's like the world stands still. Like the words she spoke just freeze and fall out of the air, smacking the floor. There's a roaring in my head … like a train coming down the tracks that's going to hit me head on. I'm frozen in place but tears I didn't even realize were forming start spilling out of my eyes. I saw Mrs. Hughes reach for a tissue but she didn't hand it to me. She started dabbing at her own eyes and I could see the tears running down her cheeks.

It was too much to process. I just want to go home and be by myself in my room. Hold the dog. I rubbed my tears away with my shirt sleeve.

Mrs. Hughes now hands me a tissue, but I don't take it. "Alex, it's okay to cry."

"No!" I push her hand away. "I need to go home and finish my homework. I have a math test in the morning. How … how long till they leave?"

She takes a deep breath. "I'm not exactly sure."

She wets her lips again then smiles. "You won't need to worry about your test. You see, I'm going to take you to your new placement today. We'll go here in just a little bit. The Marshall's live in a nice big house out in Beechmont, so you'll be in the Jefferson County school district, not this one. We'll get you enrolled there tomorrow."

My world was exploding but all I could think of were the small stupid things. "But what about my stuff?"

Mrs. Fleming packed it all for you. She gestures to the three black garbage bags in the corner. Tied up with the bright yellow tie.

That's when I knew, they weren't even going to come tell me goodbye. What about the dog? Who would he sleep with?

"I need to say goodbye to Snowball!"

"Oh, honey, I know this is really hard. I want you to know it's tough on the Flemings too. They felt it would be too painful for them … for you … so this seemed easier … better, I mean … a clean break. We should probably get going."

Her eyes flick to Mr. Scott again. Now I know why he's here. They expect there to be trouble. It's like that gives me permission to make it happen. I'm not going to disappoint.

Mr. Scott moves into the room. "Hey buddy, let me help you with your stuff, okay?"

He heads over to the garbage bags. I don't remember doing it, but I'm standing up. "No, just leave it. I don't want any of it! I don't want anything that reminds me of those fuckers!"

"Now, Alex, calm down." He reaches out to take my arm and I explode. The next minutes are a blur as I hurl everything off her desk then sweep everything off her bookshelves too, and watch it all tumble to the floor. Mr. Scott grabs me. He lifts me up with my back against his chest and I kick, making contact with his legs and knees.

"Stop this, Alex!"

I lean forward and bite down on his forearm. He tightens his grip so I throw my head back. I hear him grunt in pain and suddenly there's blood everywhere. I've busted his nose.

The next stop is the psych ward, my first time, but not my last. Mr. Scott filed assault charges against me. I never got to see the Marshall's nice big house. As a result of the assault charge, I went to court and was placed in a group home. Mrs. Hughes said they'd teach me "better ways of coping." I taught them I knew how to cope just fine, thank you, as I spent the next few weeks trying to attack every staff member there. That made me cope much better … feel much better.

Within a few weeks, they sent me to a residential center for disturbed children and put me on meds that made me quit hitting everyone. Instead, I just slept most of the time. When eventually

I was discharged, Mrs. Hughes got me a new foster home. I think she really tried her best to get a good placement for me, and I think they were nice folks, but I wasn't having it. I moved eleven more times before the year was out.

I made a promise to myself: Never again would I get suckered in.

◆ ◆ ◆

For the next three days Matt and I work. We bike. On the surface, everything is okay but I can't relax. Can't shake the feeling that if everything seems swell, it means disaster is probably right around the corner. Yesterday at dinner, Matt brings out a brochure and slides it across the table so I can see it.

"Here, have a look at this. It's the Frontier Cycling Classic. I do it every year. It's a couple of weeks away and with the workouts we've been doing, you should be more than up to it. How about we enter you in your age division?"

I slurp down some spaghetti and push it back towards him. "I can't do a race. There's no way I could win."

Matt shakes his head. "It's not about winning. Yeah, they give prizes to the first three with the best times, but that's for the serious riders. Most of the entrants would be people like you and me who just want to ride the course and finish. It's held on one of the biggest privately owned farms in the county so we get to ride where the public never gets to go. It's very scenic. Plus, the entry fee includes lunch and a cool T-shirt."

It does sound interesting, the chance to do something out of the norm, which sounds kinda good but also scary. "I don't know."

Matt grins. "Okay, if you'd rather just sit in a lawn chair in the heat and watch me bike, that's fine. Or we can skip it and work that day."

I turn up the side of my mouth. "Boy, you're really trying to sell this."

He nudges my elbow. "C'mon, it'll be fun."

Famous last words. I eat the last bite of garlic toast and push my plate away. "All right. What the hell, I'll do it." I say this, knowing I'll probably back out at the last minute. No one can stop me.

He stands up and sets his plate next to the sink. "Now you're talking."

That night I wake up after a few hours of sleep, soaked in sweat, after a nightmare. It was the Snowball dream. The one that started right after I left the Flemings. The dream varies but it always ends with Snowball in terrible trouble but just out of reach. But this time it was different. Snowball changed before my eyes to Sadie. Standing on a railroad track, looking quizzically at me while a train whistle-screams. I call and call but she won't come, doesn't move. I wake just before the train reaches her.

This can't go on.

But I know just what to do.

It's not like I haven't done it before.

Chapter 21

MATT

This is the time of year when work is the most challenging. It's a bad time for planting because the searing sun would have plants wilting as soon as they are put in the ground. In a few weeks when the days are shorter and the sun less direct, it will be the best time to plant trees. If you put them in during the spring, you have to water them constantly because they don't have enough roots to sustain themselves. In the fall, you can pretty much pop them in the ground and walk away. By the time spring comes, they'll have established themselves and unless there's drought, they don't usually require much attention.

Today, I've been driving around watering what I planted earlier in the year to make sure they make it to fall without frying. At some places I can use the resident's water source and hose, but for others, it requires hauling a huge tank of water in the truck and driving out to each specimen to give a thorough watering.

The Ross's project involved putting trees down their half-mile-long drive. They had been open to using natives, but initially they'd wanted all the same variety of tree. I'd talked them out of it, explaining that if some blight came along that affected that one type of tree, they'd lose them all. The devastation of the ash borer comes to mind. Much safer, even if you don't get that uniform look, to mix them up. With that information, they'd agreed and now there's a nice mixture marching down the sides of the drive. I'd put in several American yellowwoods. Why it isn't planted more I'll never know. A beautiful shape. Glorious, especially when it's flowering with fragrant, white, wisteria-like racemes. To it, I'd added tulip trees, sourwood, and various oaks. The oaks are slower growing but very long lived and important for birds. With nine hundred and fifty species of caterpillars, they are the foundation of the food chain for songbirds. People ask me about the damage to the trees from the insects. If there's a tree around, I point to it, and ask, "Do you believe you'll notice a hole in a leaf up there? It's not a problem."

Satisfied that all of the saplings got a good drink of water, I wrap it up for the day. It's Thursday so Alex had his standing appointment with Sam. I asked Sam if he could drop the kid at my place on his way home so I could finish up this job. Punching my cellphone screen, I call Alex to make sure he's home and let him know I'll pick up dinner on my way.

"Whatever," he says and hangs up. He sounds in a mood. Well, that's okay. He's been doing really well lately but I can't expect him to totally change his stripes. And honestly, if he wasn't acting grumpy at least half the time, I'd think there was a pod in the basement left by aliens. It wouldn't be Alex.

He's outside with Sadie when I pull into the drive. I give him a little wave but he just keeps walking and doesn't wave back. Yep, in a mood. His sessions with Sam can go either way. I notice sometimes he's in an especially good humor but other times, I think some of the talks on sensitive subjects brings up bad memories. Maybe we could go on a bike ride in a bit to get him in a better frame of mind.

I'm hot and sweaty. A beer would sure taste good but a Coke will have to do. If I bought a six-pack and put it in the back of the fridge, I'm sure it might "mysteriously" disappear. I let Alex stay home alone quite often now, but I'm no fool. Thinking of when I was his age, I don't know how my parents could be so dumb. Didn't they notice their liquor bottles going down. Did they think it was evaporation?

I head to my room to put up the truck keys. Not going to leave those laying in plain sight either. I'm diverted when my eyes catch something glinting on the floor. I move over for a closer look. *What the hell?!*

Twenty seconds later I'm dialing Sam. He answers on the second ring.

"Hey Matt. How's it going?"

"I'll tell you how it's going! It sucks! You need to come out here and see what that little pervert has done! Then you can take him somewhere else! I'm *done*."

◆ ◆ ◆

Sam was still in his car and close by so it doesn't take him long to arrive. I think I might have scared him this time. *Good*. He stands next to me looking at the evidence of the crime. No sign of Alex coming inside which is a good thing. The mood I'm in would be a detriment to his health.

My childhood trophies lay in pieces on the floor. Basketball, football, baseball, swimming, soccer, and even a few bowling ones, broken and scattered in every direction. They catch the light coming in from the window and gleam like they've just been polished when in reality I haven't touched them in ages.

Sam surveys the damage. "Well, I did tell you to put away anything sentimental, didn't I?"

I turn to him in disbelief. "Oh, so now this is *my* fault?" I pick up the one closest to my feet, "I got this one when I was eight years old!"

Sam's face softens. "Hey, I remember that one. Mike and I watched your team win the regionals. Okay, I'm sorry. I'll go round up Alex and see what he has to say for himself."

He pauses just a second and lowers his voice. "Unless you're serious about kicking him out."

I cross my arms across my chest and frown. "Just go get him."

A few minutes later Sam walks back in with Alex in tow. I can hardly bring myself to look at the kid. Sure, I'm unhappy my stuff got trashed, but it's the feeling of betrayal that has me sick at my stomach. The fact that every time I think we're getting somewhere, Alex goes off the rails. I actually thought he liked living here …

liked *me*. And damn it, despite everything, I was liking him. True confession: I'd begun caring about him as a person, not just my money maker, my obligation, my responsibility. Then he goes and stabs me in the back. W*hy? Why would you do this?*

Alex slouches in the door frame. He won't meet my eyes but he does take a quick glance up at Sam, and just as quickly looks away when Sam pins him with a look that reminds me he used to run an adult correctional facility and is as tough as they come. He motions to the floor,

"Alex, help pick these up. Set them here on the table."

Sam grabs a wooden base off the floor and picks up the little gold football player with the ball tucked under his left arm and his right arm stuck out like he's dodging tacklers. "You know what? I think some of them can be salvaged."

Pushing the two pieces together and setting it back down on the table, he says, "There. Maybe a little glue and it'll be almost as good as new."

As the words leave his mouth, the player tumbles over. The little gold football breaks off and wobbles end over end, crossing the table, then falling to the floor where it keeps rolling until Sadie, attracted by the movement, runs over and starts batting at it with her paws.

A gurgle comes from Sam. He's making a concerted effort to keep his head turned away from me, biting his lower lip as his eyes fill with tears. I want to hold on to my rage but he's making it hard. *Oh well, what the hell?* I reach over and grab one of the little basketball players. The ball is missing from his two outstretched hands and I place him on the soccer player so it gives the appearance the hands are choking him. Kind of like I want to do to Alex.

Why have I kept these things this long anyway? I was a good athlete. I know it and don't need these trinkets as a reminder.

Admiring my creation I say, "I never did like soccer worth a damn." I'm rewarded for my efforts by watching Sam crack up even more. I grab the smallest bowling trophy. "Shit, I got this one for winning my age bracket. There were only two other bowlers and one had just gotten over the flu."

I finally cast my eyes on Alex, and say, "A little creativity goes a long way, you know."

I dump the bowling trophy into the garbage can and rake the rest of the group in with him, proclaiming, "Now, my mother can never again tell me I should dust them."

Alex's face turns from Sam to me and back, blinking, and looking totally confused. I get some satisfaction from that. I point my finger at him. "I'm still pissed at you."

Sam wipes his eyes. "Yeah, we need to talk about this. Let's go sit down in the kitchen. I'm afraid if we stay here one of the little golden people will rise from the dead and crawl out of the garbage can."

Once more we do the sit-down-around-the-kitchen-table thing. Alex has had time to recoup from his surprise and has pasted his world-famous sneer on his face.

Sam leans forward and sets his elbows on the table, invading Alex's space a little. "Alex, would you like to tell us why you did that?"

Alex turns away and studies the floor. Sam says nothing. I open my mouth to talk but he gives a quick little shake of his head, so I close my yap and we sit and wait. And wait. Eventually Alex's eyes flick back up to us. He shrugs, "I was just messing around. No big deal. You all thought it was funny, didn't you?"

Sam leans back a little. "We made it funny, but I don't think the underlying reason for breaking someone's personal property is at all funny. I think you owe Matt an apology, don't you?"

Alex turns his head part way in my direction while still concentrating on the floor boards. "Sure. Sorry about your dumb trophies."

I turn to Sam. "His sincerity is overwhelming."

Sam gives a little sigh. "Alex, how about you tell us why you up and decided to go on a vandalism spree?"

The kid has folded his arms across his chest and makes it obvious he's said all he's going to say for now, but Sam keeps prodding.

"No? Nothing to say? Maybe you don't even know yourself why you did it? Well, that means I have to take some guesses." He squints the entire left side of his face as if deep in concentration while drumming his fingers on the table. "The most obvious reason is you're mad at Matt about something and this is your revenge." He swivels my way. "Did something happen?"

I finally get to chime in. "Not that I know of. I thought things have been fine. Good actually."

Sam returns to his thoughtful expression. "Okay, maybe that's not it." Suddenly he perks up and says brightly, "Maybe Alex is jealous he doesn't have any trophies."

Alex looks up in disgust. "Get real. Who gives a shit about that?"

Sam is in his full pit bull mode. He has grabbed hold and won't let go. "Hmmm. Okay, maybe it's because things *have* been good. I've worked with some kids where that makes them nervous. Like this is all going pretty well so maybe I should just wreck it while I have control. Could you be like some of those kids?"

There's a beat or two of silence then Alex shifts his chair under him. "No! I was just … just … in a bad mood! You're full of shit, you know that?"

Sam doesn't look at all offended. Even I can see Sam is on the right track. "Are you *sure* that wasn't it? It's a pretty good guess."

Alex is fully sitting up and glaring at Sam now. "I'm sure. I said so, didn't I?"

Sam nods but holds up his finger and thumb with hardly any space between them. "Yeah? But maybe I'm just a *little* bit right? A *teeny tiny* bit maybe? Maybe one percent?"

Alex lets his hands drop to his sides like dead weights and turns his head to the side. "Yeah, maybe one percent. There. Are you satisfied?"

This whole exchange has me thinking about fishing. Letting the fish run, then reeling him in a little at a time. But this fish seems to still have some fight left in him. Alex suddenly comes to his feet. His hands are clenched and he's standing in front of Sam, looking challenging. "I'm tired of this stupid talk. Just do what you're going to do and let's get on with it. I can go pack."

I don't like the aggressiveness he's showing. Sam continues to look nonchalant except I notice he has shifted his feet under him so he can stand up quickly if needed.

He says calmly and quietly to Alex. "Sit back down. No one said anything about packing. Maybe we don't know why you did what you did, but for right now it doesn't really matter. Regardless, you have to make it right. So, what would you suggest? How can you square it with Matt?"

To my surprise Alex's butt returns to the chair. He speaks under his breath so that I can hardly hear him. "They were just dumb trophies."

I feel the need to enter the dialogue again. "Yeah, dumb or not, how would you like it if I tore up something of yours that you'd had for a long time? That meant something to you?"

The sneer is back on full force. "Sure, go ahead. There's a shirt I've had for a few months. Have at it."

I can tell he wishes he hadn't said that. That he's said too much. I meet Sam's eyes. It's hard for me to keep a mad on when I think about how this kid has no connection to his past through people or even just the things the rest of us accumulate through the years.

There are a few beats of silence then Sam says, "Okay, then I'll suggest the least you can do is pay for the damages. That won't recoup the sentimental value but it's the next best thing. I'll look in a sports equipment catalogue and come up with a cost. Is that agreeable to you, Matt?"

"Yeah."

"Alex?"

"Whatever."

We're done. Sam departs. Dinner is short and silent, then Alex retreats to his room. It reminds me of his first weeks here when I barely saw him. Me, I work on some invoices and job estimates before turning on the TV and scrolling until I find an action movie in progress. I try to act casual when out of the blue Alex's door opens and he quietly slips out of his room. He comes into the living room and stands behind me with his hands in his pocket. I glance over my shoulder, acknowledge his presence, and turn back to the TV.

Some seconds pass by and he's still just standing back there. I'm back to thinking about fishing, when you see ripples around the bobber and hold your breath waiting to see if there's going to be a bite. Finally, he speaks. "I'm gonna get a Coke. Want one?"

I'm glad my face is turned away from him so he doesn't see my expression. A certain satisfaction. I keep my voice expressionless. "Yeah, that'd be good."

He comes back from the kitchen with our drinks and damn, if he doesn't sit down on the couch—at the far end—but still. He hands me the can and we both pop our tops at the same time. I reach back behind to the lamp and click it off so we're watching in the dark. Sadie jumps up and curls between us, resting her head on Alex's lap while he absentmindedly plays with her ears.

The movie has a long-protracted fight scene over a ravine. I tilt my can towards the TV. "Why do they keep fighting? Why don't they just toss the ladder down the hole so no more of the bad guys can come across and be done with it?"

Alex smirks. "It doesn't bother you this one guy is fighting off six and winning? You're overthinking this."

"Hmmm, you're probably right."

We watch till the end, with me dissecting the movie plot repeatedly while Alex castigates me for it. Our idea of a good time. The news comes on and I get up to let Sadie have her last outing of the night. She's asleep … and so is Alex.

Sadie jumps down when I cluck, but Alex doesn't budge when we leave or when we come back inside. I start to shake his shoulder but can't bring myself to wake him. That, and I know he doesn't like to be touched.

For a while, I just stare at him thinking about all the ways he's complicated my life and the chaos he's brought to my former peaceful existence. How he can get my emotions going from rage to delight, and everything in between, within a few short hours. When he offered me a drink, I felt I'd passed some kind of test. Maybe I have.

I have to admit Sam is really good at what he does. I'd told him so when I walked him to his car before he left this afternoon. I leaned my backside on the car hood and folded my arms. "So, do I require the most hand holding of all your foster parents?"

He grinned. "Nah, not by any stretch. I have some who call me every single day."

I furrowed my brow. "You're kidding."

"Nope. We have some tough kids. When we recruit, we promise to be there for our parents any hour of the day or night and we mean it."

"All these little tricks of yours. Is there a manual or are you just naturally good at it?"

He grins. "There are books and trainings, but I like to think I have a certain knack. I enjoy it which is half the battle. The important thing is to stick to techniques that don't get you into a battle of wills. I tell our new staff arguing with an adolescent is like mud wrestling with a pig. You both get dirty and the pig likes it."

"So, what's the name of the technique you just used? Badgering the subject to death?"

He laughed while he opened his car door. "Is that what it looked like? It does have a name. It's called the 'millimeter acknowledgment.' Get them to at least open the door to the possibility of what's really behind their behavior. Look, don't sell yourself short. You're doing great. Think of this little stunt as Alex's way of letting you know he's feeling closer to you."

"Great, if he feels any closer what does he do, burn the house down?"

He leaned over the top of the car door frame. "I'm going to give him some credit. He did something to send a message without doing any real harm."

As Sam took his seat, I slammed his door shut and conversed through the open window. "So, Mr. Know-It-All, is he ever going to change or will he be like this always?"

Sam snorted. "Of course he's going to change. We all do. You think anyone is a single individual from cradle to grave? For example, I used to know this guy who was a big star in his youth, thought he was hot stuff. Then he got knocked down a peg and it completely changed him." He smiled. "For the better, I think."

I refused to let him bait me. I can play this game too. "Talking about yourself?"

He laughed. "Maybe. But the point is Alex is young and has been through a lot. It's going to take time but hopefully, all we're doing for him is going to pay dividends on down the pike."

"I'm not asking for much. Can't he just settle in and act normal?"

Sam started his car, put it into gear, and peered at me through the top of his sunglasses. "Define normal." With that parting wise-guy remark, he drove away.

Good thing for the kid he has Sam as his caseworker. I also take some pride I haven't tossed Alex out on his ear long ago. Mike's right, I'm a stubborn cuss. Screw the money I get for the kid, I'm not letting him get the best of me. Then the big question pops in my mind. If I knew what I know now, would I take this on again? Crazy me, yeah, I would. Despite all his antics, I feel in my heart this kid is worth it. And he *is* better. Sam has told me this repeatedly and I can see it myself. At least he *is* still here.

Reaching over, I grab the throw off the back of the couch and toss it over him. If he wakes during the night, he can get himself to bed.

Chapter 22

MATT

Late August in the South means shorter days but it can be just as hot as July. And heat means storms. This morning started with lots of lightning, thunder boomers, and water coming down in sheets. Emily has planned a picnic for us and believes the forecast claiming it will clear by late morning. However, if it keeps this up much longer the road in front will flood and she'll have to come around the long way on the road behind us. Thankfully, her faith in the weatherman is justified when the storm ends as quickly as it began. The sun comes back out and the rain ratchets up the humidity to the point you feel you could take a knife and cut a slice of air. That's summer in the South.

The creek has come up but it's not over the road so we're good. Alex pretends he thinks a picnic is dorky, but I know it's all an act. He wants the good home cooking if nothing else. Emily's car pulls in the drive and before she can turn it off, Justin hops out, clutching T.J. Funny Bunny.

"Mom says we're picnicking in the *country!*"

Laughing, I run at him with my hands making horns on my head. "Yeah, watch out for the cows!"

He shrieks with delight. I love this kid. You can't beat his enthusiasm for just about anything. He's not your typical kid, but since when is *typical* necessarily good? Emily says he can run a stone man crazy, but she says it with love and affection.

She's gone to the back of her car, grabbing a big basket and checkered tablecloth. She's plenty strong but I believe in male chivalry. I hold out my hands. "Here, let me take that for you."

She extends the basket but keeps the tablecloth. At work she's typically in jeans and a polo shirt but today she's like an Easter egg, wrapped up in pinks, yellow, and greens. Shorts, tank top, and an opened blouse tied in a bow at her waist. She's like a shiny piece of candy ... one I realize I desperately want to unwrap. I've never dated any female this long without *unwrapping* her, but I'm either saddled with Alex or she's saddled with Justin, her dad, or the store. It's complicated.

I tug on the pink and white gingham cap she's wearing. "You look good."

She leans into me and exaggerates the southern accent. "Well, sir, that's what I was aiming for."

Anything brilliant and clever I was going to follow up with is lost as Alex bangs out of the front door. Did I mention these kids are a major stumbling block? He gives us a look like, *really?* Makes me feel like we're old people in the nursing home who shouldn't be having these thoughts.

Pleased he has made us break apart and scramble around grabbing for picnic items, he follows up with his usual grousing. "So, can we eat inside like civilized people or do we have to sit on the hard ground and fight bugs? I've already battled insects enough this summer."

Thankfully, Emily, of a large family of siblings, is made of sterner stuff and never seems the least bit rattled by Alex's mouth. She gives him a big smile and says, "We must suffer for our supper. And besides, I've already told Justin we're having an outdoor picnic in the country. Would you like to have him quiz you if we change plans?"

To Alex's credit he gives her a look that says *touché*. "Outdoors it is!"

I laugh and give him a little one-fingered salute. Damn, if the kid can't be engaging now and then when he's of a mind to be.

Justin dances around me in anticipation, waving T.J. in the air. "I want to see *real* cows."

I ruffle his hair and steal Alex's line. "Cows, it *is*. Tell you what. Bill Parkins next door has a whole herd. If we go around the creek and up the hill there a bit, we'll be high enough to see them all. And we might pick up a bit of a breeze as well."

"Great, a long hot walk," Alex grumbles but it's all for show. I'm on to him. He's into this.

It is a bit of a hike, longer because the creek is up and we have to skirt around it. We pass through fields full of goldenrod and asters lost in clouds of Queen Anne's lace and Joe Pye weed. Bumble bees and other pollinators have descended on the blooms like kids in a candy shop.

The morning rain was quickly absorbed by the dry soil and with the departure of the clouds, the sun comes down full force. The air has a dusky August scent, the smell of languid summer. Fall is right around the corner, but today you wouldn't know it.

As soon as we crest the hill, Parkins' black and white Belted Galloway cows come into view. Justin is ecstatic. I like the breed myself. Striking, with their middle section pure white, set off against the black on either end. I help Emily spread out the red and white tablecloth on a grassy spot under one of two large shade trees.

Justin claims his spot. "I want Alex to sit next to me!"

Alex obliges. Sadie sits next to the boys figuring they are more likely to sneak her some food. I lean over and fix my eyes on a point next to Alex. "Are those big black ants?"

He jerks around. "Where?!"

Then as he sees me grin, he purses his lips. "You're a riot ... *Doc*."

It's a lame comeback and he knows it. I've become immune to this particular insult. He went to that well once too often.

Emily is laughing and begins pulling her treasures out of the wicker basket. Classic picnic fare. Fried chicken and potato salad are the first to emerge. She opens plastic containers and we start to fill our plates. With a glance at Justin, she pulls out one last dish and presents it to me. "I made deviled eggs because you told me it's one of your favorites."

Justin freezes. Then his lower lip wobbles. "I *don't* like deviled eggs."

Emily nods. "Yes, I know, but we talked about this. Other people do like them. You don't have to eat them."

"I don't want to see them. Eat them where I can't see!" Sometimes Justin can get really wound up and lose it. I can tell Emily is worried he's going to go into a major tantrum.

Alex reaches over and puts his hands over T.J. Funny Bunny's ears and turns to Justin, "Don't let him hear you say that. He's into them. You *know* all bunnies dig eggs."

Justin's eyes go wide. "They do?"

"Well, duh! The Easter Bunny? Delivers them and everything, right?" Alex looks around like the Easter Bunny himself might magically appear. Then he whispers, "He might not like it if TJ wasn't on board about the eggs."

Justin looks stricken then rebounds. "Oh, TJ *loves* eggs." Then his brow furrows. "But Alex, I really don't like deviled eggs. Not. At. All."

Alex gives him a thumbs up. "It's okay. You aren't a bunny."

Justin shakes his head rapidly back and forth. "I'm not a bunny."

He props T. J. up where he'll be in plain sight of the eggs. For himself, he pulls down the brim of his baseball cap so the eggs are out of sight and then digs into the chicken on his plate. Crisis averted.

Emily silently mouths *thank you* to Alex. He just gives a little no-biggie shrug and starts eating. Darn, if I don't feel an urge to throw my arm around his neck and rustle his hair like I did Justin. He'd probably punch me if I tried.

Dessert is watermelon cut into little stars along with blueberries and whipped cream. She displays them with a little *voila*. "Yes, I'm on theme here. Patriotic since Labor Day isn't far off. Red, white, and blue."

Theme is all fine and good but she's wise enough to know the boys aren't impressed with fruit no matter how *Better Homes and Gardens* the presentation appears, so there are chocolate chip cookies as their option. Okay, mine too, although I eat a couple of watermelon stars to be polite.

After we finish eating, the boys and I toss around a Frisbee, with Sadie running back and forth trying to intercept, until we're all sweaty and ready to wrap it up. Emily finishes packing away the food. I grab the basket and we start back down.

She wipes her brow, "Goodness, it's hot. So did you say there was a shorter way back?"

I point down the hill. "Yeah, but we'd have to cross the creek which should be okay by now. There is one spot with some stepping stones we can use if you're game."

She is, and the boys sensing a challenge, are definitely on board. Halfway down the hill, we can hear the low mumbling chorus of the stream. When we reach the creek, the water has dropped significantly so we're in zero danger of being swept away, something that's a real consideration otherwise. I quote to people all the time that six inches of rushing water can knock a man off his feet. There's a zig-zag line of wet stones, some jutting above the water line and others just below. The boys are across in five seconds flat, then it's Emily's turn.

Just to poke at her I say, "Want me to carry you?"

I get the response I wanted. She curls her lip. "You know I have three brothers. There's nothing they could do, I couldn't do better."

She pauses. "Well, spitting maybe, but then ugh, gross."

Proving herself to be quite nimble, she's half-way across when out of nowhere Mr. Parkins barrels around the bend on his Gator. Startled, Emily slips, flails her arms, and with a loud splash, lands flat on her back in the creek. She immediately thrashes up to standing with the water almost to her knees, sputtering and pulling wet hair out of her eyes.

Justin jumps up and down and claps his hands. "Mommy went swimming!"

Water is dripping off the brim of her hat. I reach and pull a hunk of moss off her arm while trying desperately not to laugh. Alex and Justin have no such compunction. They think it's hysterical. Alex is practically doubled over. It hits me I don't think I've ever seen him really laugh like this before. It's good to see, even if it comes at poor Emily's expense.

Reminding me of the time I burned her hair back in science class, she is again a good sport and flings water from her arms at the boys, then at me. "Don't think I don't know you are laughing, too."

"Maybe a little," I say, trying to choke it back.

Mr. Parkins is not amused as he pulls up next to us. "I am so sorry. I should have been watching closer when I took that turn. Ma'am, my apologies. Can I give you a lift to the house?"

Justin quits laughing and is eyeing the vehicle with glee. "I wanna ride!"

Emily cocks her head at Mr. Parkins, which causes the water to flow off the left side of her hat. "Are you feeling guilty enough that you'd take him for a ride? He'd be thrilled. I'm nicely cooled off now and the house is close, so I'll just walk."

Bill is a nice guy and a good neighbor. "Sure, I'd be happy to take him for a spin."

Emily turns to Alex and says softly, "Would you mind going with him?"

Alex graciously says yes as he wipes tears out of his eyes. It's not a big concession. I can tell he wants to ride in the Gator almost as much as Justin but would never admit it.

I lift Justin on board. "Thanks Bill. Justin has a thing for cows if you'd like to show them to him, up close and personal."

Emily goes into mom-mode. "Not *too* close."

Alex hops in and Bill guns it. Justin squeals and even Alex grins. Off they go.

"I'll get you some dry clothes at the house. Alex is more your size and he'll be happy to loan you something."

I can't help but notice the wet clothes are clinging to her, flattering her curves. "Although there's some appeal having you in this state."

"Sure," she says with her hands on her hips. "You aren't the one having to wonder if there's a frog in your underwear."

We finish the short trek to the house and as soon as we step inside and shut the door, she kicks off her wet shoes while I go grab a towel. When I walk back to hand it to her, she's unbuttoning her blouse then lets it drop. Pulls her tank top off over her head and drops it to the floor too. She isn't wearing a bra. She grabs the towel and applies it to her wet hair, then wipes down her chest and arms.

I'm frozen in place, unable to take my eyes off her.

She looks me straight in the eye as she steps out of her shorts and shimmies out of her panties, leaving her standing there in her birthday suit. Draping the towel over her shoulders she asks, "Did you say you have some dry clothes for me?"
My voice sounds like I swallowed that frog she mentioned earlier. "Um, yeah…"

She tugs on my waistband, bringing me closer, then slips an arm around me. She gives a little grin. "I also presume you have a condom?"

I'm still having trouble finding my voice. "Um … yeah." *What am I sixteen?*

She starts walking down the hall to the bedroom. "Well, hurry up. I figure we've got twenty or thirty minutes tops till the kids get back."

I might have lost my voice, but I find my feet. "Right behind you."

Chapter 23

ALEX

"Hey, Coffee Cup!"

I'm on my regular route from Phoenix to Emily's store but as soon as I hear that voice, it has me doing a hard stop and turning around. Meaty Jones is there in the flesh. I haven't seen him since we were arrested. That seems so long ago.

He's with two other guys. One I recognize as Danny Collins; the other one I remember seeing before but don't know his name. His arms are heavily tattooed and he has rings in his nose. I stand in place and let all of them catch up to me.

Meaty has a cigarette dangling from his mouth. He reaches up and uses his two fingers to pull it free, taking a long drag before he does. "Hey, man, you got sprung?"

"Yeah, I've been out a while."

"I'm on probation." He laughs. "That means I'm not supposed to be with you … or anyone else with a criminal record. Which pretty much means I should dig a hole and stay there 'cause hell, everyone I know has a criminal record. So, fuck that."

He reaches in his pocket and pulls out a cigarette pack. "Want one?"

Why not? "Sure, thanks." I pull one out of the pack and bend over as he lights it for me.

Meaty gives me a long look. "Hey man, you look different." He leans in closer. "Your eye don't roll around funny no more."

I take another drag of the cigarette, glad to have something to do with my hands. "Yeah, got it fixed."

His gaze tracks me up and down and lingers on my shoes. "Those fakes?"

Proud to have brand name shoes, I try to play it casual. "Nah, they're the real deal."

A firetruck comes through the intersection with its siren blasting so we don't say anything else till it fades away. Meaty is talking to me but looking at the other two when he says, "You're doing all right then."

Here's the thing. When I hung out with these guys, I was at the bottom of the pecking order. Sort of like in baseball pick-up games when you're the youngest kid and they let you play right field but they don't let you bat. But the scales have tilted. In addition to my shoes, I have this expensive jacket. I have money in my pocket. Why not show off a bit?

I motion to the Subway down the street. "I was just going to grab a sandwich. You guys want anything?"

It's obvious from the looks they are exchanging, they haven't the dough to buy something for themselves. I ground my cigarette out on the brick wall behind me and get a ping of cheap satisfaction when I say, "I'll buy. Consider it a get-out-of-jail-free card."

They all grin and nod. "Sure, sounds good," Meaty says.

We get the food and go sit in the parking lot to eat. This is my second lunch but I'm happy to eat again. I'm always hungry these days anyway. Emily laughs and says boys have an empty leg to fill. Thinking of Emily makes me feel a little guilty. I'm supposed to be at the store by now. But hell, I haven't done anything really fun in like forever. Other than seeing some kids at Phoenix and the EMT classes, my time is spent with adults except for Justin, and he's too young to count. So what if I'm a little late one day?

The guys scarf down their food and Meaty reaches into his pocket. I think the cigarettes are coming back out, but no, it's a small bag of weed. "Thanks, man. How about we go down to the park for a bit?"

I know that park. There's a spot where all the kids go back behind a bunch of pine trees to get high. It's been a long time since I've been high. Too long. It calls to me. It's louder than that other little voice in my head saying, *you've got a good thing going right now, don't blow it.* But really, what's the big harm? I'll just get a little buzz going, then head to the store. I don't think Emily is the type to pick up on it. Something tells me Matt would know, but by the time he comes to get me, I'll be fine.

The weed is pretty strong stuff, just like Meaty promises. It feels good to be so relaxed, like returning to a familiar place, one with no expectations of me. It's been hard being this new Alex, one that stays in one place and does the things people tell him to do. I sometimes feel like a stranger to my old self. Slipping back into old Alex is like putting on a comfortable pair of old shoes. Like coming home.

Chapter 24

MATT

Emily calls to let me know Alex hasn't shown up. She's texted him and didn't get an answer. I'm used to the little game he plays, making me wait for him all the time, but hope it's not spreading to Emily. I try calling and texting and don't get any response either. I tell her to call me back later. She does, but it's to report he hasn't shown up at all and she'll be closing soon.

My irritation begins to turn to worry. He's never been this late before. I drive to the store just in time to say goodbye to Emily and Justin, reassuring Emily that Alex is probably close by. I drive around trying to spot him but no luck. I pull over in front of the Subway I know he frequents and go inside.

I'm told yeah, he was here, with a couple of other boys his age. So now, I'm less worried, but maybe I should be worried more? I sit there for a while to see if he'll show back up, then drive around town some more. No Alex. Eventually, I pull out my phone and call Sam. This is beyond my pay grade. Let him earn his money.

I explain the situation and hear him sigh through the phone. "Okay, I'll need to notify law enforcement."

This surprises me. "I thought he had to be gone like twenty-four hours first?"

"For kids in state custody, the rules are different. I'll take care of it."

I look up and down the street again, hoping to spot the kid, but nope, no sign of him. "What should I do?"

"You might as well go on home. He has his phone so he can call if he needs us. Hopefully, he will sometime tonight."

But he doesn't call. I eat a late dinner with Sadie then sit on the porch and watch the night come. I tell myself I should enjoy this quiet time, with things like they used to be before Alex graced my doorway. But there's a sick spot in the pit of my stomach I can't make go away when I think of what the next twelve or twenty-four hours might bring. They find his body behind the train tracks. He's in the hospital on life support from a drug overdose. He commits some serious crime and ends up back in juvenile detention, except this time he's facing adult court charges. Hell, even that is better than the first two options.

I go in and clean up the dishes, turn on the TV, and glance at my phone so many times I finally throw it down on the couch in disgust. All the mad has gone out of me. I just want him to be safe. When the eleven o'clock news is over, I head to bed. Sadie accompanies me, but on the way down the hall she circles around Alex's room before coming back and sitting down.

I pat the top of her head. "Yeah, I know. Sorry girl."

It takes a long time to go to sleep, twisting under the covers to find a comfortable position, while trying to quiet my mind. Eventually I drift off but wake when it's still dark. I reach for my phone and groan when the screen shows it's only three-forty-five in the morning. I turn back over, punch the pillow a couple of times, and try to fall back asleep but it never happens. By five o'clock I give it up, get out of bed, fix coffee, and wait for the sun to come up. At seven-thirty, I call Sam again.

He attempts to make me feel better. "Alex's an old hand at taking care of himself. We can just hope he doesn't do anything stupid while he's in the wind. This isn't my first rodeo with a missing kid. I have a trick or two up my sleeve. Holmes Street is where they all go to hang out. I'll drive around and ask some folks I know, see if I can turn him up."

It's irritating how nonchalant he sounds. "How can you stay so calm when the shit hits the fan?"

I can almost hear his smile through the phone. "Lots and lots of practice."

"Okay," I say. "Keep me posted."

What I should have said is: If you find him, *don't bring him back*. Any sane, reasonable person would probably have thrown in the towel by now. Maybe Sam will never find him. Hell, we may never lay eyes on him again. More horrible scenarios play out in my mind. I shake my head to purge the thoughts and head to work. Hard physical labor is what I need. I go through the mindless routine to get ready. Scoop up my pocket change, grab my wallet, lock the door, take two steps down the front stoop. Swivel back around and unlock the door.

"C'mon Sadie, I need some company and I can't stand those big sad eyes of yours."

She doesn't have to be asked twice. Hops in the truck when I open the door and claims shotgun. I can only hope on the way home today, she's riding in the middle, with Alex slumped and grumpy by the door. *Please.*

Chapter 25

ALEX

The sound of an engine wakes me up. Squinting through half open eyes, I see a guy with a yellow park employee shirt sitting on a big riding mower just the other side of the pines. He's got on earphones and is concentrating on his mowing so I know he'll move on in a minute without noticing me if I stay put. After he does, I sit up, looking around for the other guys. Everyone is gone. So is my jacket.

I scoot over and lean my back against a tree. It's a sycamore. The fact that I know this makes me think of Matt. And Sam. And Emily. And what a complete fuck up I am. Getting so high on the weed and a couple of pills for good measure, that I pass out. What do I do now? Do I call Matt? No, it would be better to call Sam. Could I come up with a good lie to explain where I've been? Thinking makes my head hurt all the more. I don't want to ponder the options. I don't want to consider the consequences for what I've done. So maybe it would be best to simply stay here all day. Longer than just today. Get high again tonight and just hang out for a few days.

There are little red welts on my arms. The mosquitoes must have enjoyed feasting on me during the night. Insects really have it out for me this summer. My stomach feels queasy. Or is it just hunger? The sandwich yesterday afternoon was the last food I had. Too busy getting high all night to think about eating. Well, if nothing else, I can go get some breakfast. I have money.

With that thought my hand automatically goes into my right-hand pants pocket where I keep my cash. It comes up empty. With rising despair, I realize my so-called friends have robbed me. I hit the rest of my pockets and groan as I realize the bastards took my phone too. I'm surprised I still have my shoes.

I lay down on my back and stare up at the sky. I listen to the kids on the playground down the hill, probably without a care in the world, and self-pity floods me. *Why couldn't I have had a normal life?* I slam my hand down on the ground next to me. *Nothing ever goes right for me!* My fist lands on a rock sending a sharp pain up my arm. I scream in frustration, not caring if anyone hears, hope they do. But the mower's too loud for the sound to carry.

The urge to move comes over me, like maybe if I walk fast enough I can escape everything—especially me. Cutting across the park, I enter one of the nice shady streets where folks with money live. I head back towards the rattier part of town where no one is likely to notice me or ask questions.

When I hit Holmes Street, my old stomping ground, I head behind The Cheapside Bar and Grill, making sure no one sees me, and then start pawing in the trash can. I luck out and find a half-eaten bag of potato chips. Now I'm thirsty, so a hose on the back of the building will take care of that problem.

"Hey, kid! Get the hell out of here!"

It's a guy, probably the owner or manager at this hour of the morning. I drop the hose, leave it running, and shoot him the bird as I vault the little fence leading to the alley. He's hollering but isn't chasing me. It feels good to do something mean and nasty. Anger is a good feeling, like a long-lost friend come to visit. It perks me up and I decide hell, I'm just going to see what trouble I can get into. *Screw it all!*

As soon as I'm out of the alley, my eye catches on a flier tacked to a telephone pole. I see the word MISSING in large block letters across the top with a picture underneath, and figure someone lost their dog or cat, but then something seems off which draws me nearer. I lean in to get a closer look.

No! You have got to be kidding me! Dammit to hell!

I march over and rip the flyer off the pole. The picture is me. I think it was when I was about five years old. I'm dressed in a dumb kiddie striped T-shirt and holding a little stuffed giraffe. Smiling big at the camera.

Thank God it doesn't have my name on it. Just says if you see this child, please call the Phoenix Foster Care Agency, and lists the number. I tear it into little shreds but even as I'm doing so, I glance down the street and see other fliers on other poles. I rip them off too, but around the corner, there's more. And more. They're everywhere!

Now I'm really pissed. This is Sam Murry's doing, I just know it. Does he think this is funny? This has to be some breach of confidentiality. There have got to be regulations against this. I have rights. I'll show him. I'll sue their asses! Filled with righteous fury, I head to Phoenix.

I walk through the side parking lot to reach the door. With satisfaction I see Sam's car is here. I have to hit the security buzzer and wait for the receptionist to buzz me in. It takes a minute and I fume, knowing she's telling Sam I'm here and he's giving the okay to let me in. Once the door makes its little telltale buzz, I yank it and stomp past her but she makes no attempt to talk or stop me, in fact, gives a little smile as she turns back to her computer screen. She obviously knows what's up. That pisses me off even more.

Murry is in his office sitting at his desk. I throw the stack of fliers in front of him. "What the hell game do you think you're playing? You can't do this! I'll report you to the … the … State!" This sounds a little stupid even to my ears since I know the State would be happy to be rid of me and aren't likely to jump to my defense.

Murry is leaning back in his chair with his feet up on his desk. Looks up and smiles at me. "Hi there, Alex. Glad to see you. We were worried about you."

"That doesn't give you the right to put pictures of me up everywhere! I want to call my lawyer!" I try to remember the name of that last one I had.

In one movement, Murry pulls his feet off his desk and pushes his chair back. Reaches into one of his desk drawers. "From what you're saying, I understand you'd like to file a grievance." He lays a form in front of me then plops a pen on top. "Just fill this out. Make sure and print legibly."

I grab the pen and move the form closer to me, bending over to read it.

Murry puts his feet back up on the desk. "Oh, and complete both sides please. You can sit down there to work on it if you'd like."

Does he think I'm bluffing? I'll show him. I start filling out my name, birthday, and today's date, but pause before: **Describe the incident in detail**. *Christ, I haven't done one of these in a while. I forgot they want to know everything but my shoe size.* I slow down and start chewing on the end of the pen while I read the instructions.

Mr. Murry picks up the baseball that's always sitting on the top of his desk and starts tossing it up and catching it as it comes down. "You know, I need to drop some papers off. If you'd like, you could come with me and we could grab something to eat while we're out. You could work on filling out the form later. There's no deadline on it."

Okay, I'm not stupid. I know he knows I'm hungry. And I know, he knows, that I know, filling out this form isn't going to really accomplish anything. And I know, he knows he's giving me a chance to save some face. My choices are pretty clear. I can go ballistic. Start tearing up his office. Reach across the desk and grab that ball and throw it at his face.

Or I can go use the bathroom down the hall, ride in Sam's nice air-conditioned car, and get something to eat. Maybe I could even go home … to Matt's home, I mean. But can I? Most of the time I've run, my previous foster parents wouldn't let me come back. In this case, I didn't really run away but *absent without leave* is pretty much the same thing, at least that's the way the adults see it.

I don't want to ask because it'll sound like I care. But I have to know. And *I do care*. I start cracking my knuckles. "Um, what about Matt? I mean…"

Murry always seem to know what I'm thinking. It's annoying. Yet useful sometimes too. He puts the baseball back on the desk.

"It's cool. I talked to him just a bit ago. I need to let him know you're here. He was very concerned about you." He brings his eyes level with mine and lowers his voice. "We all were, Alex. We'll need to talk about this more later, but for right now, the fact you're safe is what's paramount. You are okay, aren't you? I need to know if anything bad has happened while you've been gone."

Suddenly, I see a way to spin this more favorably. "Well, yeah, I got robbed. Some guys took my money, my jacket, and my phone. I couldn't call you … or Matt."

Murry doesn't look shocked. "Well, that is most unfortunate. I guess we need to file a police report. Do you know who it was?"

Shifting a little in my seat, I say, "No, never saw them before."

Murry smiles and I can tell he knows I'm full of shit. He once told me that after working in prisons, he can always tell when someone is lying. It's like a superpower. I believe him.

"Well, then I guess it wouldn't do us much good."

I look for a way to steer the conversation in a different direction. Murry has family pictures on his desk. There's one of a rider jumping a horse over a tall fence. I give it a little push with my finger. "Is this you?"

He leans over to see which picture I'm talking about. "Not hardly. If I tried that, I'd break my neck. No, that's my oldest son, Kelly. He's the horseman in the family."

I had just wanted to distract him, but now I'm a little interested. I've heard some stories from other kids here about Mr. Murry's children. "The one you adopted? How old was he?"

"Sixteen when the adoption was finalized. He has his own place now, but thankfully, lives close enough we get to see him a lot."

Without looking at Mr. Murry, I move the picture carefully back to where it was. "Sixteen is kinda old to be adopted, isn't it?"

I feel his eyes on me, but don't look up. He says, "Yeah, not as typical as most kids, but it happens, probably more than most people think. My wife and I feel very lucky to have him."

That statement takes me by surprise. I was thinking how lucky the kid was to have them. I look up and meet Mr. Murry's eyes. I don't want to talk anymore so I look for an exit.

"I'm going to the bathroom."

"Sure. I'll wait here till you get back."

◆ ◆ ◆

After lunch, life seems back to normal, and Mr. Murry and I are on the way home. The whole way I keep waiting for the lecture, the punishment, but Murry acts like it's just any other day. The only time he says anything about the past twenty-four hours is right before we arrive. He shifts his hands on the steering wheel and glances my way. "Matt was really worried about you. He combed the streets looking for you. Called and texted me a million times. You do what you want to, but the manly thing would be to apologize."

I don't say anything, just turn to look out the side window. I picture Matt roaming around looking for me. Mr. Murry making those fliers and going to the trouble of tacking them up. Perhaps I should feel guilty they went to so much trouble, but I kind of like it. Maybe that makes me feel just a little bit important. Like I matter.

We beat Matt home, so we take seats on the porch and wait. When I see his truck turn into the drive, my heart rate picks up. Am I nervous? Why would I be? He gets paid to take care of me, right? That's the deal. I see him emerge from the truck cab and realize I'm glad to see him.

Sadie jumps out of the truck and runs up to me. I pet her which keeps me from having to look at Matt. Nobody says a word as he pulls a chair over and joins us. As the silence drags on, I realize they are waiting for me to say something first. This makes me squirm. I'm used to being yelled at, lectured to, but not listened to. I think, *fine, we'll just sit here all day.* But Mr. Murry's last words in the car enter my head. About being a man. That, and I really *don't* want to sit here all day.

An apology. Okay, it doesn't have to be sincere. Just say it. Something like *sorry you all got so worked up about nothing.* I glance at Matt. He doesn't look mad or mean, or any of those things. Just maybe... wary. When I open my mouth, the words I planned don't come out. There seems to be a disconnect these days between my brain and my mouth.

I wet my lips. "Look, I screwed up. I'm sorry."

Mr. Murry looks at Matt then back at me. "Okay, I'm impressed. Good job. You even managed to throw some personal responsibility in there."

Matt laughs. "Well, it was sure better than the last apology. Hey, practice makes perfect. I've got an idea. Let's have him do about ten things wrong this week and apologize for each one till he gets really good at it!"

For some reason I laugh too. I'm not sure why. The joke wasn't that funny. Maybe it's a relief because for now anyway, things seem okay. I'm not going to be packing. I'm not going to be looking at sleeping somewhere else tonight. I think about how just a few hours ago, I thought my life was completely in the toilet, and now I'm sitting here with these two guys that I have to admit I like being around. It makes me feel ... *bold*.

"I just wanted to hang out with some ... you know ... friends."
Not that Meaty and those assholes are friends.

Mr. Murry leans back in the chair and nods. "That's a good point. I know friends are important. We probably need to see what we can do about fixing that. Maybe going back to public school this fall will be a start. Maybe some new friends might be a good thing, huh?"

I'm pleased with how things are going and remember another problem that can be solved. "I need a new phone."

I'm looking at Mr. Murry, but it's Matt that speaks up. "Sure, I can take you. Just make sure you bring enough money to pay for it. You can buy a new jacket too."

Guess my luck ran out. Mr. Murry grins. "Yeah, and don't expect to be paid for these last two days. And if you do this again, I'll dock you two days for every hour you're absent."

Honestly, that seems fair but I'm not about to admit it.

"Harsh," is all I say.

Chapter 26

ALEX

Thursdays are "Mr. Murry Days."

Our once-a-week meeting. I've gone through a lot of case workers in my time in the system. Some I liked. Some I really detested. But Sam Murry stands out as the best one ever. For one thing, he doesn't do the standard dorky question and answer show. The old sit-in-the chair-across-the-desk and ask, "*How's school? Have you been getting along with Mr. and Mrs. So and So?*" And the worst, "*Let's talk about how you feel.*"

Let's *not*.

Most of the time we don't even stay in the office. We go for a ride and get something to eat. We head to a park and throw a baseball. Or just take a walk. I know he tries to sneak in counseling. He harps on a few particular themes. Basically, it boils down to three things:

I'm a new and improved Alex.

I'm not a little kid anymore.

I need to be proud I've survived, man up, and think about the future.

This last one is complicated. Because it means letting go of a lot of *baggage*, as therapists like to say. That while I should be proud I've survived these years, it's okay to be angry because I was denied what most people take for granted. Mr. Murry said it's a type of grief. Mourning the loss of the childhood I should have had. Yeah, sounds good, but easier said than done.

Today it's pouring rain so we're here at the Phoenix office. When Mr. Murry sees me, he waves me down the hall, and we go in one of the meeting rooms where there are stacks of papers. He sweeps his hand in their direction. "We're mailing flyers about an upcoming field trip to Beechtree Bend amusement park. You and Matt should come; it'll be fun. These notices need to be mailed out. How about you help me with that?"

I fold my arms and frown. Sounds like work. "Do I get paid?"

Mr. Murry moves to one of the chairs and sits down, grabs one of the flyers. "Awfully mercenary, aren't you? I thought maybe you'd do it out of the goodness of your heart. Or because otherwise, you'll just have to sit there and watch me until I get done, which means you'll be here longer." He folds the paper twice then looks up at me. "I'll spring for a milkshake when I take you home. That's the best I can do."

What does he think I am? One of those guys holding a *Will Work for Food* sign? But the idea of just sitting here doing nothing for an hour doesn't sound like much fun. "Alright. What do I do?"

He shows me how to fold the flyer into thirds then stuff it in the envelope. After that, I peel off the adhesive address label and slap it on. Not exactly entertaining, but I really don't mind. Not that I'll tell him that. It's mindless work which in some weird way is sort of enjoyable. Keeps your mind busy without going to deep thoughts. I look at the walls while I'm folding and read all the corny posters. *Watch your habits, they become your destiny.* One that was also on the walls of the detention center: *A bad attitude is like a flat tire. You can't go anywhere till you change it.*

Often when you think you're at the end of something, you're at the beginning of something else. That one's by some guy named Fred Rogers, whoever that is. But it's my favorite, that is, if I have to like any of the damn things.

We talk while we work. It's easier to talk about stuff when you're doing something else, not just sitting there staring at each other while you do it. Sam wraps a rubber band around a stack of envelopes and adds it to the pile. "So, tell me about the bike event. I heard you looked good out there."

I shrug my shoulders. "It was just riding a bike. No big deal."

Of course I'm lying. It was just riding a bike but it was a big deal, at least to me. I woke up that day with cold feet and said I'd changed my mind. Matt didn't look surprised but said, "Well, let's just load up everything in case you change your mind. I haven't changed mine; I'm still riding."

Emily and Justin meet us at the event. Matt checks us in and we get our shirts and the numbers you pin on the back of them. There were apples and bananas and bottles of water you could grab if you were a rider. Matt pinned on my number and I liked being identified as one of the riders, being part of something, but I still wasn't going to ride. It was like I was just pretending to be one of them, an impostor. We watched the youngest division head off and it didn't look so bad. Just a bunch of kids all riding their bikes together.

Justin gets excited. "Alex is going to ride next!"

Matt picks up my bike from the back of the truck and wheels it over to me. Hands me my helmet. "You ready?"

I fully intend to say, "No, I'm not. I'm not doing it." But I don't. I take the helmet and put it on. I can't believe I'm doing this. I feel sick thinking about it, so why aren't I walking away?

What if I'm the last person to finish?

What if I *don't* finish?

What if I fall off and make a fool of myself?

Like I'm watching somebody else, I mount the bike and position myself about middle of the way back in the group behind the line. When the horn sounds, I start pedaling. Other bikers are too close to me for my comfort but in a few minutes there starts to be distance between us. Some surge ahead and some fall back. I'm still in the middle of the pack.

Pumping hard, I feel sweat start to trickle down my back. I hear Matt's voice in my head. *Pace yourself. You can always pick up speed close to the end when you know you have enough leg power left.* I'm still in the middle so after a few minutes I relax a little. Glancing back over my shoulder, I see there's plenty of riders behind me. I concentrate on a kid in front of me on a silver bike, determined to pass him. I do, then pick off a couple of others. There's an easy downhill section coming up, then a pretty steep hill to climb. I pass a couple more bikers.

Coming down the next hill, there's a long stretch of road in sight and I can see the leaders are way in front. I'm not going to reach them, but I don't care, because when I look behind me, I can see enough riders to know *they* aren't going to reach *me*. I relax and start to enjoy myself. Matt was right, the scenery is beautiful back here. We pass a big pond surrounded by flowering shrubs. A spray nozzle shoots water high in the air and some of the droplets fall on us. It feels good.

I pass a marker letting us know we are halfway through the course. Horses graze, standing side by side in a clump behind the black plank fencing. They look up as we go by. We make a turn and wind our way through a wooded section, and the instant drop in temperature feels good. The sun through the trees is casting shadows on the road in front of us. *This is great!*

The next big hill has me slowing a bit. My legs are beginning to tire some, but I'm okay. I know I have enough stamina to finish. Matt and I ride this much all the time. I don't know what I was worried about. When the finish line appears in the distance, at the end of a long straightaway, I pump as hard as I can and pass a few more riders that are on their last legs.

The finish is just ahead. *I've done it!* The last hundred yards I ride through people ringing cowbells and cheering. On the right hand side, I pick out Matt, Emily, and Justin. Matt's pumping his fist and Emily and Justin are both clapping and jumping in the air and screaming. I hear, "Yay, Alex!" as I glide by them and pass under the inflatable barrier.

Now that I'm done, I want to put on a cool front, like it's no big deal. Like I don't care. Like I just did it for the hell of it. But I can't pull it off. For starters, my mouth won't cooperate. I'm grinning so wide my face hurts. I couldn't stop it if I tried. I look back at my people and wave. *My people.* I believe at this moment I'm the happiest I've ever been in my life. It's a strange feeling, since in my wildest dreams I didn't believe I could *ever* be this happy.

Mr. Murry plops another stack of envelopes in front of me. "Penny for your thoughts."

Still in the glow remembering the event, I smile and decide to be honest. "I was thinking about the bike thing. It was pretty fun. I'm going to do another one sometime soon."

"Yeah? Good for you. Hey, let me know when it is. Would you mind if I came and watched?"

I pick up an envelope. "It's a free country. Do what you'd like." In other words, *that'd be great.*

Mr. Murry smiles. I look up at him from the top of my eyes and smile back. I know he gets it. I'm not fooling him. The stack of completed work gets taller and taller, then we're done. While Mr. Murry is putting the envelopes in a box to take to the post office, my eyes wander to the games and decks of cards stacked on one of the bookshelves. I remember when I met him at the juvenile detention center. That seems a long time ago.

I point to the book shelf. "So, when are you going to show me the card trick?"

He sets the box aside. "Well, since you've been so nice and helpful, how about today?"

He stretches out his long arm and reaches over to the shelf. He grabs a deck and starts shuffling. "The card trick can only be done with a trick deck which I'll show you in a minute. But first, this is a regular deck. Do you know how to play poker?"

"Yeah, I know. Are we going to gamble for money?"

"I'm pretty good, kid, so don't I wish. Maybe when you're eighteen and you come by my house on Friday nights when I get together with some of the guys, I'll be happy to take some of your money."

It could be the rainy day. It could be all the time I've spent in his company. It could be everything that's been going on in my life. I meet his eyes and hold them.

He stops shuffling and stares back at me. Gives a little smile. "Yeah, Alex, you're stuck with me for the long haul."

I stick my hands in my pockets and lean back in my chair. "What if Matt kicks me out?"

He resumes shuffling the cards. "I'd be disappointed, but you'd still be a Phoenix kid."

"What if I get arrested and sent off for a year?"

"I'd visit and be looking for a placement for you when you got out."

I look out the window and watch the rain bounce off the parking lot. Something inside me sort of settles into a calmness.

Mr. Murry starts dealing. "Poker is an interesting game, don't you think?"

He deals three sets of five cards, face up so we can see the hands. "Everybody starts with the same number of cards but each hand is totally different. For instance, this guy here, we'll call him Bob, got dealt two queens. This other guy, let's say Steve, got random cards with nothing higher than a ten. And this third guy, Bubba, has a pair of fives. You know the best thing about poker?"

I gesture to the cards. "If you win, you get money?"

He laughs. "You don't give it up, do you? That's one of the things I like best about you; you're persistent."

One corner of my mouth goes up because I like the praise. *Annoying* is usually the word I hear. Or *attention seeking*, a favorite of residential staff. My treatment plans always had a line that said: *Alex has a problem with attention seeking.* Persistent has a better ring.

Mr. Murry lays his hands over the cards. "The best thing is that any of these guys, no matter how bad the hand they were dealt, could end up winning the game. Bob has the best initial hand, so you might think he gets the edge."

He points to the left. "But Bubba here, he might toss three cards for three new ones, and end up with a full house. Steve might keep his lousy hand, but bluff everyone out so he ends up winning. This goes back to persistence. Hanging in there is half the game."

I give him a look to tell him, speaking of games, I know the one he's playing here. Sneaking in one of his little pep talks. He acknowledges my calling him out with a little wink and starts picking up the cards.

Sometimes there have been moments in my life, big ones. But sometimes there are moments, little ones. Little but significant.

Things that have stayed in my head for years and years. Most of them are things I'd like to forget but can't. But this is one of those moments that's going to be stuck in my brain in that much smaller file labeled "good memories." Sitting here with this man who came to me when I was at one of the lowest points of my lousy life. And it can't be denied that pretty much everything since that day has been better, just like he promised it would.

But it's more than that. His all-knowing attitude that I'm going to be okay … that I'm a survivor … that I should be proud I'm one. It might be corny, but I like the poker thing. It makes sense. I want to be a winner. I *can* be a winner.

Mr. Murry puts the regular deck up and reaches in a drawer for a different deck. He shows me the trick he did when we first met. Just like before, every card I touch and pull out of the deck is an ace of diamonds. I can't figure out how he's doing it, which is maddening.

"You promised the secret," I demand.

He gives his little shit-eating grin. He's enjoying himself. "Patience. Patience. All will be revealed in due time."

He turns all the cards face up and spreads them out in his hands. "Notice anything?"

Every other card is an ace of diamonds. "Yeah, but how do you know I'll get the ace of diamonds every time. It looks like half the time, I wouldn't."

"Ah, excellent question! All of the trick cards are just a shave smaller so when I flip the deck this way…" He flips from the bottom up. "…you see the regular cards because they are longer."

He flips this time from the top down and all I see are the ace of diamonds. "And when I flip this way, you see the trick cards. When you stick your finger in the deck it will always land on a short card. Simple science. It's called a Svengali deck."

He holds the cards out to me. "You can have this one. I have a bunch of them. Practice till you've got it down pat, then amaze your friends. Just remember a good magician never reveals his tricks."

I make a face at him. "But you revealed it to me."

He grins. "Who said I was a good magician?" Standing up, he reaches over and flicks off the light switch.

The rain is letting up. A few rays of sun are popping out. Steam is rising off the parking lot pavement. Time to go. I'm happy to have the cards. I reach over and pick them up. "Thanks, Mr. Murry."

Today is a day I'm feeling brave. "Or can I call you Sam?"

He's fishing his car keys out of his pocket. Puts on his sunglasses but lowers them so he's looking at me from over the top. "Well, now that depends. My friends call me Sam. Are you my friend?"

Out of habit a whole bunch of snarky remarks come to mind. But I don't want to say them. Honestly, I'm kind of tired of being a constant smart-ass. Nobody gives enough credit for how much energy you have to use to keep that up. That doesn't mean I can bring myself to say *yes, I'm your friend* so I reply, "I'm not your enemy."

He gives me a thoughtful look, which makes me turn my head away. "Glad to hear that. But that's not really the same thing, is it?"

I don't answer him. Just get up and walk by him heading to the door. He reaches over and opens it, holding it for me to walk through. I pause, look up at him, and say, "Thanks, Sam."

He smiles and gives me a wink. As I walk by, he reaches around and gives me a super quick little hug, instantly releasing me. The surprising thing is I don't mind. It's just one more sign that maybe I *am* a new and improved Alex. Like a car, an improvement on last year's model with better steering and gas mileage.

As we head to his car, I look up at him. "Don't think I'm going to forget you owe me a milkshake."

Chapter 27

MATT

I spent a good hunk of yesterday drawing up plans and preparing an estimate for a client that decides he's "going to think about it." I was hoping for a definite yes, but I'm in a good mood and don't let it bring me down. I've had several other well-paying jobs lately. Then there's Emily. I find myself wanting to be with her more and more and I think she feels the same way. Knowing we are getting serious, I had to do some confessing. One night I was venting to her about my trials and tribulations with Alex.

She gave some advice based on her experience of teaching seventh graders, and then said, "Did you ever wonder why I didn't ask you about your relation to Alex that day he shoplifted?"

"I guess I just didn't think about it."

"That's the thing about the store; it can serve as a gossip hub. Whitney Harrington told me you'd become a foster parent for a teenage boy. I have to tell you I was impressed. In all honesty, in high school, when all those girls were swooning after you, I had zero interest because I thought you were a jerk." She smiles and takes my hand. "I stand corrected. Anyone who takes in a troubled fifteen-year-old is anything but a jerk, so I owe you an apology. I suppose I should have known you can never judge anyone by how they were in high school."

I turn my hand so I'm holding hers, absently rubbing my thumb over the back of her fingers. "In all honesty, I was a jerk." I bite my lip and nod my head. I have to tell her. "Maybe I'm still a jerk. About Alex. It was never my idea. It was Sam Murry's and I only caved and took him because Sam offered me big bucks if I'd do it. So, don't put me on any pedestal because of that. My intentions were purely selfish."

There, I've said it. I wait for her reaction. Will she be totally disillusioned about me? Will this end what we've got going? To my surprise and relief, she just laughs. "Well, maybe your initial motives were less than one hundred percent pure, but I see how you are with him. Are you going to sit here and tell me you don't care about that boy?"

I'm relieved to be on safer ground and that I can give an honest answer to that question. "He's obnoxious as hell and makes it a full-time job running me crazy. Yeah, I'm nuts about him."

She smiles smugly. "See, I knew that." She tilts her head up for a kiss and I'm happy to oblige. Then she whispers, "If you'd said you didn't care a thing for him one way or the other, I'd have shown you the door."

I pull her in closer, wrapping my arms around her. "Glad I passed the test."

"I'll tell you what I tell my students. If you pass one test, don't rest on your laurels; keep studying."

She begins unbuttoning her blouse. "I was always good at sex education. Let me demonstrate."

And she did.

◆ ◆ ◆

It's late afternoon. I finish up work at noon and pick her up at her house in town. I like her place. A nice sized mid-century ranch with lots of windows and a big back yard. When I admired it, she'd said, "This was my parent's house but after Mom died and I came home, Dad wanted to move to something smaller. I didn't need all this room for just Justin and me, but Dad really wanted me to have it. He sold it to me for practically nothing. It was a win-win.

He loves to come and visit, and I get something much nicer than I could have otherwise afforded."

She took the afternoon off because her ex-husband, the lawyer, is making one of his infrequent visits to spend time with his son. This provides Emily and me with a child-free afternoon. It's obvious his coming makes her nervous because she's gone on a baking frenzy.

I ask, "Are you sure you want me around?" I slide out of her way so she can get eggs out of the refrigerator. "I can take off and come back in a bit after he's gone."

She shakes her head. "No, you might as well meet Brian." She grins. "After all, I know at least ten girls from high school you were well acquainted with back in the day."

Before I can think of a comeback, we hear a car pull into the driveway. I peek through the window blinds. He drives a Mercedes. Figures. I know he's an attorney working out of his daddy's big law firm so guess having an expensive car shouldn't be a surprise. He steps out of it, looking like something from a clothing ad. Expensive suit and shoes. Designer sun glasses. He looks fit enough, but like someone who plays tennis or golf, not digging hours a day. All he needs to do is cock his hip next to the car door and freeze for the photo shoot. I'm thinking I should have at least put on my better-looking work boots.

Justin runs to the door. "Daddy!"

He opens it while I put on my game face. Brian comes in and we all make nice-nice. Introductions, handshakes, and the southern staple … discussing the weather. He gives me the once over down to my foot attire. Nothing is said but I can tell I've been assessed and deemed "the loser the ex-wife has taken up with." At least he gives Justin a decent greeting before he turns his focus back on Emily.

"Doesn't he have anything better to wear than those old jeans?"

For a second, I think he's talking about me, but no, it's Justin's attire he's disparaging.

Emily gets this I'm-not-going-to-let-you-get-under-my-skin look, which means he did.

"It's what he wanted to wear."

"Well, then of course, that explains it. We wouldn't want to tell him 'no.'"

I'm glad Emily had me stay because there's no doubt in my mind that he'd have more to say on the matter. However, I inch just a *wee* bit closer and give him the look that Alex has perfected ... disdain with a slight taste of challenge.

Emily is glaring at him too, letting him know the only reason she's putting up with his crap is for Justin's sake. Mr. Debonair has the good sense to shut his mouth. He collects Justin, and they head out after Emily gives her son a good-bye hug and admonishes him to be good. As she does, she looks up at Brian with a stern expression. "You'll keep an eye on him, right?"

He puts his sunglasses back on and opens the door as Justin ducks under his arm and climbs into the car. "Of course. You always were a worrier."

Asshole. He may have dismissed me with one look, but I'm dismissing him after five minutes in his illustrious company. Emily sighs as she waves at the car backing out of the drive. "Okay, so now you know. I married a jerk. In my defense, in college he never showed me the real Brian. But in fairness, I never showed him the real Emily either. I kept pretending to be some version of me that appealed to him." She tucks a strand of loose hair behind her ear. "I was stupid."

She looks quite sad when she's usually so strong and self-assured. I pull her into my arms for a long kiss then look down at her. "I'm no one to talk, but I'd advise don't let him get to you. Screw him."

Looking up into my eyes, the mischief is back. "Never again."

With that, I help her pack up and we head over to my place to spend the afternoon. She's staying to fix dinner, so I've arranged for Sam to bring Alex home after school, leaving plenty of time for *other activities* in between.

When Sam and Alex show up, they both look at me with a knowing expression. I can almost hear the sing-song in their heads: *We know what you've been doing.*

After Sam takes off, Emily goes into full domestic mode, sweeping through the house scooping up hats, empty glasses, and scattered papers on her way to the kitchen. When she gets going, it's best to get out of her way. She has more energy than a power station. Soon I hear the sound of the oven door opening, the clattering of a baking sheet. A wonderful aroma fills the kitchen and spills into the rest of the place. Alex, proving he's no fool, lingers around. He's not disappointed. Chess squares, that southern cross between a brownie and chess pie, are soon out of the oven and cooling on top of the stove.

Emily knows he hasn't beelined it to the kitchen to see her. She hands him a small plate. "Help yourself, but not too many. I'm making a cake for after dinner."

I take a bite of one too. Still warm, it practically dissolves on my tongue. "You know you don't have to keep cooking for us all the time."

Alex, with a square in each hand, talks with his mouth full. "Don't listen to him. I could starve here."

I start to give a retort but stop when Emily's phone rings. It's on the counter and I can see her ex-husband's name on the screen.

She hurriedly reaches for it. "Brian?"

She's worried. Even Alex picks up on her tone and quits chewing.

She leans back, crossing one arm over her stomach. Her mouth is compressed in a straight line and her right foot starts tapping. The good news is she's no longer worried. The bad news is she's totally pissed. Brian's voice drones for some time but I can't make out what he's saying.

Emily unfolds her arms and stands straight. "Fine, bring him back to me. But I'm not home. I'm at Matt's. You'll need to bring him here."

She gives him the address, hangs up, then turns to Alex and me and says a little too brightly, "Brian says he can't take any more of Justin's shenanigans today. Something about a candy bar. Okay if Justin joins us for dinner?" She reaches over to the bowl, grabs the spoon, and takes her frustrations out on the innocent cake batter.

"Sure," I say, flicking a glance at Alex that warns him he better keep quiet. He doesn't need my counsel. He grabs two more chess squares and says, "I'll be in my room." He disappears fast and shuts the door behind him.

Emily's eyes are damp and after a few more seconds of punishing her cake, she takes a quick swipe at them. "I don't mind it for me, but I hate it for Justin. Someday he's going to put it together that his father doesn't see him much because he really doesn't want to."

I'm at a loss for something wise to say, but take a shot at the truth. "He's got you, and you more than make up for Brian's shortcomings."

She starts up again on the cake batter but tortures it less. "I hope you're right."

When we eventually see Brian's car come into view, she dries her hands on a dishtowel and heads to the front yard with me trailing behind her. I figure I should stay out of this as much as possible but I want to be there for support. Justin emerges from the passenger side about the same time Brian exits the driver's side. Brian is scowling. Justin is wailing.

He reaches his arms to Emily. "T.J! T.J! T.J Funny Bunny is gone. Daddy threw away T.J.!"

He's sobbing uncontrollably. Emily kneels and takes him in her arms, glaring up at Brian. "What the hell did you do?"

"I bought him a damn candy bar like he asked when I stopped for gas. But it wasn't the right kind and he wouldn't shut up about it, so I grabbed it out of his hand and tossed it out the car window. Then he started hollering and shaking that blasted rabbit at me, so I flung it out too."

Emily is so furious she's shaking. "You idiot! Don't you know what that means to him?"

Brian casts a scornful look at Justin. "He's too old to be carrying that stupid thing around anyway. It should have been tossed years ago. You don't have the guts so I took care of it."

By now Alex and Sadie have come outside to see what the commotion is about. Sadie goes straight to Justin, pushing her snout into his stomach then reaching up to give him a lick on his face. Brian kicks her with his foot. "Get away, you nasty mutt."

I lurch forward, but it's Alex who gets there first, his fists balled by his side. He gets into Brian's face. "Watch it, fuckwad!"

Brian shoves him away. "You watch your smart mouth!"

I'm hardly aware I'm moving, but in a split second, I have Brian's jacket lapels in my hands and push him back against his fancy car. I'm taller, I outweigh him, and I know I look like a homicidal maniac. Certainly, I feel like one.

I give him a couple of little bounces against the car. "If you *ever* put your hands on my kid again, I'll break your arms. You got that?"

His face is contorted with rage, but his eyes show fear. At least he's bright enough, law degree and all, not to be idiotic enough to take me on. To tell the truth, it's disappointing. I'd like nothing better than to go a few rounds, but not in front of Emily and Justin. I let him go before I do something I might regret. As I do, I grab his car keys out of his hand.

"Now, you and I are going for a little ride. You can show me where you tossed … the bunny."

If I weren't so mad, I'd have to laugh at how that sounds coming out of my mouth.

He tugs at his suit jacket and straightens it and his tie. "I don't have time for that."

I smile. "Oh, but since you brought Justin back early, I'm sure you have plenty of time."

With that, I slide into the front seat and motion to the passenger side. "I'll drive so you can look. Get in."

His eyes are starting to bulge out of his head. "Get the hell out of my car."

I know he's braver now that I'm sitting and he's standing, plus there's several inches of metal between us. I pull out my pocket knife and open the blade. "I said get in."

He doesn't think I'm that crazy. "Put that away." He sneers. "You aren't going to use it."

Oh, this is going to be fun. I smile and without taking my eyes off him, stick the sharp point of the blade into the headrest of the car. "Want me to keep going?"

His eyes get wide. Spittle flies out of his mouth. Mr. Debonair doesn't look so cool anymore. "That's damaging private property. I'll have you arrested."

"Yeah? Go ahead. I went to high school with the Sheriff." This is not a lie, but I don't elaborate that Johnny Ray would probably enjoy throwing my ass in jail.

I step on the brake, hit the starter, and the car roars to life. It *is* a sweet ride. I'm going to enjoy driving this. Keeping my eye on the bunny prize, I tone down the rhetoric. "Come on," I say in a voice only the two of us can hear. "The quicker you do this, the quicker you can get on your way."

There's a long couple of seconds, but I breathe a sigh of relief as he heads around the car. The passenger door opens. At the same time, the door behind me opens and Alex plops into the back seat.

I twist around. "Where do you think you're going?"

He crosses his arms signaling he ain't about to budge. "I can help look."

It's a pretty good argument and it occurs to me having a third party along with Brian might not be a bad idea. Alex must have the same thought because he slides over so he's sitting behind the passenger seat, which I can tell makes Brian nervous. I catch Alex's eyes in the rear-view mirror and give a little conspiratorial grin. He returns the look. It's a Hallmark movie moment, but there's no time to revel in the glory.

As I put the car in gear, I look out to where Emily is standing with Justin in front of her, her hands on his shoulders. I hope she doesn't think I'm being an ass. "We'll be back."

She pats Justin's upper arm. "Be careful."

I stomp on the gas petal and we peal out—thrilling Alex and horrifying Brian—but once on the road, I only exceed the speed limit by a little. "Where do you think you were when you tossed it?"

Brian, maybe deciding the best course is to semi-cooperate and get it over with, says, "Maybe ten miles back, but how am I supposed to pin point it? I can't tell one ratty house from another."

What a dick.

A few miles out, I slow and we all start looking to the side of the road. A few miles ahead Brian says, begrudgingly, "I know it was after this. I remember that barn…" and as if he's being too nice, he adds, "…with the dumpy-looking truck in the drive."

I glance over at the truck. It's not any worse than my old one was before the "truck-that-Alex-bought," as I've been calling it in my mind. I'm seeing nothing but Styrofoam fast-food cups and hay that's blown off farm tractor wagons, but from the back seat, Alex suddenly cries out, "Stop, stop! Pull over!"

I do as he says, looking in the rearview mirror first to make sure the coast is clear. Alex opens the door before I've come to a complete stop so I caution, "Be careful. Watch for cars."

I step out and watch Alex run about twenty yards back. He bends over and rises up triumphantly, holding up a blue and white scrap of cloth. "Found him!"

His face is split wide open with a grin as he runs back to the car with the object of our pursuit clenched in his hand. I smile because we found Justin's treasure, but also because seeing Alex acting like a kid his age should act, gives me a little zing. "Good eye! Way to go, Alex!"

Brian is out now and coming around to my side. "Great, now you can let me drive back to your house so I can get on my way."

I don't bother to look at him; just slip back in and shut the driver's side door. Alex gets in and finally Brian, with a frown, returns to the shotgun seat. Alex, who always knows when he can score the most "gotcha" points, leans forward with T.J. Funny Bunny. Having learned a thing or two from Justin, he mimics a high-pitched voice. "Hey dickwad. What else do you do for fun besides tormenting little kids and kicking dogs? Do you knock down little old ladies trying to cross the street? Or are you just always a jerk?"

Brian stares straight ahead but mutters in my direction. "Charming. You must be so proud."

Funny thing, yeah, I am. But I don't say anything, just keep driving. Emboldened by my silence and probably the notion his nightmare afternoon is coming to an end, he keeps spouting off, pretty much disparaging everyone and everything he sees, like the whole town is beneath him.

From the back seat, I can see Alex leaning forward to take another shot, but I give a little shake of the head and a wink. He leans back against the seat and smiles.

About a mile out, I pull the car over and turn to Mr. Debonair. "Get out."

He looks around quickly, like, *Where are we?* Then grasps what's happening. "Drive me to the house. I'll ruin these shoes!"

"You know, I would have but quite frankly, I can't stand to hear another thing come out of your mouth. I'll leave the car at the end of my drive. The keys will be under the front mat. I strongly suggest tomorrow that you call Justin and tell him you're sorry, that you're glad T.J. made it home."

For just a second, I think I've pushed him too far, but he clicks off his seat belt, opens the door, and gives a parting shot. "Boy, Emily really knows how to pick winners." With that he slams the door but not *too* hard; it's his precious car after all. It takes all my control not to screech the tires on takeoff.

Alex looks out the back and laughs as we drive off. "Oh, man, did you see his face?"

Suddenly, I feel parental and start thinking about what kind of role model I'm setting. "Alex, this maybe wasn't my finest hour. Sometimes I let my temper get the best of me. I'm working on it."

T. J. appears, rocking back and forth by the side of my head, and I hear that high-pitched voice again. "Oh sure, and all I want is world peace. Let's sing a song."

I can't help but laugh.

Damn, I love this kid.

Chapter 28

MATT

As promised, I leave the car for Brian, then Alex and I walk companionably up to the house. The screen door bangs as soon as we come into view, with Justin flying out like a little bullet, Emily not far behind. Alex, the triumphant hero who left no bunny behind, waves TJ high in the air so Justin can see the prodigal critter has returned to the fold. Alex and I both bend down when Justin reaches us. The little guy grabs T.J. and clutches him to his chest, and then puts his arms around Alex and hugs him tight. Alex flinches for just a second before letting his arms relax then wrapping Justin in a hug. I get a warm glow in my chest, but now it's my turn to be rewarded for our efforts. Justin flings himself into my arms and I stand up with him in my arms.

He leans back to look in my face. "Daddy was bad."

I nod my head. "Yes, he was. But he wanted me to tell you he's sorry. He was just having a bad day."

My eyes catch Emily who gives me a suspicious look, then shakes her head, telling me she knows I'm lying through my teeth. She claps her hands together, "Okay, everyone let's go eat. Just as soon as I put T.J. in the washer."

A few hours later we've wolfed down dinner, gone outside for a walk, and come back in to eat dessert. The summer twilight has given way to darkness. I'm sitting in my recliner with the kids sprawled on opposite ends of the couch, sound asleep, Justin still clutching a freshly laundered T.J. Funny Bunny. After all her time cooking, I'd offered to do the dishes but Emily said I'd done enough good deeds today and sent me out of the kitchen.

She walks out, wiping her hands on the dish towel, then carefully folds it and lays it on the edge of the counter as she enters the room. She smiles at me, holding up her finger to her mouth in the classic shush mode. She reaches over and drags the throw off the back of the couch, slowly and carefully, so as to not wake the kids. Once it's safely in her arms, she inclines her head to the door and heads outside. I follow, softly closing the door so Sadie can't follow. Not that she seems that interested. She raises her head for a second then wiggles into a more comfortable position on the couch.

We walk without saying a word to a little clearing, out of sight of both the house and the road. Once there, she spreads the blanket and sits down, reaching up to pull me down beside her, then wiggles into my lap. I enfold her in my arms and find her mouth, rewarded by a little moan. Clothes come flying off like we're about to go skinny dipping in the creek.

A little breeze arrives with the deepening darkness, keeping the mosquitoes at bay, not that I care right now how many there are or even where they bite me. From somewhere above, a screech owl gives its distinctive horse neighing call. It's a clear night so the sky is full of stars. Emily rolls on top of me. I have a full view of the star show, but my eyes have locked on her intense hazel eyes.

I'm not sure how it happened, when it happened, or what made it happen, but for the first time in my life I realize I'm truly in love. I would find that terrifying, but all I feel is a deep-down contentment that I'm exactly where I need to be.

Chapter 29

ALEX

I wake up when I hear Emily and Matt laughing and rattling around in the kitchen. I look at my phone and realize I've been asleep for quite a while. Justin is still next to me. I close my eyes, enjoying that drowsy half-awake feeling. It's hot, but the breeze from the oscillating fan feels wonderful as it sweeps over me, rippling my hair first in one direction, then in the other on its return trip.

A few minutes later, Emily and Matt appear. I squint, letting them know I'm mostly awake. Matt gives me a little wave then scoops Justin into his arms.

The kid mutters, "T.J."

Matt tugs on T.J.'s ears. "He's right here."

Emily smiles and touches Justin's arm. "Come on, sweetheart, it's time to go home."

Justin lays his head on Matt's shoulder. "Kay." Half asleep he pats Matt's back and mutters, "Matt's good."

Emily smiles at Matt. "Yes, he is." Then she turns to me and whispers, "Thank you, Alex, for being Justin's friend … and mine."

I think I may be blushing so I'm glad the room is dark. In a minute, I get up and stand looking out the screen door at them. I feel a pang because they look like the perfect little family. I wonder if there was ever one moment when I was a baby or little kid that my parents and I ever looked that way.

After Emily and Justin are gone, Matt and I watch TV till eleven o'clock then say our goodnights. In bed, I lie on my back with my right hand under my head, staring at the ceiling. The day's events start replaying in my head. I smile thinking of how Matt and I took care of that ... what's the word? Oh yeah, it was in a story I read for school. That *pompous guy.*

Feeling sleep coming on, I roll over and close my eyes, but something Matt said keeps scrolling through my head, over and over.

"Don't you ever put your hands on *my* kid."

Chapter 30

ALEX

It's back to school time. Real school. Public school. Mr. Murry was on board with it. I'm not sure I am, even though I was the one who asked for it.

On this, the last night before school starts, I'm feeling nervous. Thankfully, it's not a school I've been in before so I won't have the assistant principal looking at me in *that* way. The I-know-you're-trouble-so-you'd-better-watch-it look I know so well. Speaking of pointed looks, Sadie is standing by the door making it obvious she wants out.

"Okay, okay, I'm coming." She bounds out the door like this is something she's never gotten to do before in her life, and may never get the chance to do again. While she roams around smelling everything to try to find the really perfect spot that needs peeing on, I look up at the big dipper constellation. The stars are so much brighter here. I never even bothered to look up when I lived in the city.

The screen door squeaks as Matt joins me on the porch and glances up too. "No moon tonight but the stars make up for it." He leans against the porch rail. He puts his hands in his pockets, takes them back out, glances over at me, then quickly looks away. My radar shoots up. My muscles tighten. I bite my upper lip and wait.

He glances down and back up. "Alex, this is hard to say, but I need to be straight with you."

Oh no, this can't be happening! When will I ever learn? My hands have gone into fists. My chest constricts. There's a roaring in my head. I want to bang my head against the wall to stop it and to punish myself for being so stupid, once again.

Matt is looking back up at the dark sky. "You know you're going to be starting school, and it's the high school I went to. I was quarterback of the football team. I broke all sorts of school records. We won State my junior and senior year. I got a big college scholarship offer at Notre Dame."

Slowly his words get through to me. The roaring in my head ramps down and I go limp with relief. I'm not getting tossed out, but I'm going to get the don't-embarrass-me-at-the school lecture. The relief is so strong, it immediately turns to rage. *Go to hell!*

Matt finally looks at me. "Alex, I really screwed up. Like big time."

I blink. *What is he talking about?*

Pushing off the rail, Matt stands up and crosses his arms as he sighs. "I blew it all."

He gives a little half-assed chuckle. "I was a major fuck-up. I'm telling you this because even though it's been years since I was there, somebody might say something and I don't want you to get blindsided."

This is so not what I was expecting. *He's worried I'm the one who might be embarrassed?* Sadie bounds up onto the porch and I bend down to rub her ears, buying time to put my thoughts together. My mind goes to the worst possibilities. "Did you kill someone?"

"What? *No!* God, nothing like that." He leans back against the rail and softly laughs. "But thanks for that. Now, comparably, it doesn't sound so bad."

Sadie ambles over to him and he leans down to pet her. Dogs are good for talks that make everyone nervous.

"My mother went out of town for a weekend, but I didn't want to go, so I stayed home. That Saturday night a couple of guys and I got drunk. No, let me clarify that, we got plastered. Took a cooler to the country club around two in the morning. Scaled the fence, went swimming, and drank till we couldn't stand up straight. Then I got the bright idea it would be fun to take a couple of golf carts and play our version of Indy 500 on the golf course. We tore up several greens. That might have been bad enough, but next we saw one of the tractors and had the even brighter idea that driving it would be even more fun. I'd caddied for a summer and knew where they kept the keys and how to get in the shed to get them.

Matt pauses and looks out across the fields. I know he's having a hard time telling this story, but I wish he would hurry up so I know how it ends. I don't take my eyes off him.

He runs his hand through his hair. "By now, we've really torn the hell out of the golf course. We're laughing and whooping it up like the idiots we were. Then I drove over a gully I didn't see in the darkness and in my drunk-ass state, the tractor pitched over, pinning me beneath it. My so-called buddies ran off. I can't blame them too much. I think they thought I was dead and there was nothing they could do for me, so saving their own skins took precedence. They did, anonymously, call 911, so I can thank them for that."

He's looking at me and I think I need to say something, so I state the obvious. "But you weren't dead."

"No, but for a time I wished I was. I tore up my knee and was bruised all over, but miraculously, I wasn't seriously injured. As soon as I was checked out at the hospital, I was arrested and locked up. Sam, who was on the police force at the time, managed to get me released to him since my mother was out of town. He took me back to his house till she got home."

I'm glad we're having this talk in the darkness. I know Matt is glad too. Sam keeps telling me I'm the new and improved Alex, but for a second the old Alex has a thought. *Boy, I could use this as ammunition against him.* But maybe I *am* the upgraded Alex Coffey, because all I want is to say something to make him feel better.

"So, nobody else got hurt or anything. Just some dumb grass. What's the big deal?"

Matt's shaking his head. "What is Sam always saying? Actions have consequences. Notre Dame withdrew my scholarship and with all the pending charges against me, no other college would take me either. I wasn't allowed to go back to my high school for the rest of the year. The school put me in the alternative school for bad kids till I graduated a few months later. I thought I was going to be a legendary pro football player with a million-dollar contract, but ended up mowing lawns, while all my friends went off to college."

I think about the looks some people gave us the day we went swimming. Seems like some people do remember things a long time. Hey, I know what it's like to have people talk about you. About what a fuck-up you are. I figure everyone at child welfare knows my name. Sixty-five placements. It could be a record in the history of child welfare. Maybe *I'm* a legend. Maybe there are different ways to be a legend.

Shrugging my shoulders, I say to Matt, "Seems to me you got what you wanted. I mean, you *are* famous, aren't you? Everyone talked about you, didn't they? And here they are doing it all these years later. Shit, you might have sucked at football in college or broke your leg the first game and no one would remember your name."

Chapter 31

MATT

Alex's words ricochet around in my head. *Out of the mouths of babes*. Then slowly I start to smile; I lean my head back against the wall of the house, close my eyes, and *laugh*.

Once I get it together, I glance over at Alex and his face looks mutinous. I think he thinks I'm laughing *at* him ... like what he said was dumb ... but nothing could be further from the truth. In my haste to reassure him otherwise, I momentarily forget myself and risk losing life and limb by throwing an arm around him for the quickest of squeezes.

"Good God, kid. I might have wasted thousands of dollars on therapy, but you've nailed it for free."

Pleased with getting the compliment and credit, one corner of his mouth crooks up. "Therapy sucks. Take it from me." His face splits into a wide smile.

As I look at him, the thought pops into my head, *damn, his teeth look good*. For some reason this strikes me as funny, too, and I start laughing even harder.

But once the fit of laughter ends, it's replaced with a deep, abiding shame. Not for what I did when I was a dumb-ass kid, but for the all the wasted time I let it drag me down. Boo hoo hoo. Matt didn't get to play college football. He didn't get the big scholarship to Notre Dame. Here's this kid sitting next to me who has gone through all kinds of hell, and I've been poor-mouthing and making excuses instead of getting up off my butt and taking control of my life.

I had goals I didn't reach. So what? I have new goals. Nothing's stopping me from going to college now if that's what I want. The fact is, I don't *want* to go to college. I don't want a big fancy house. And I certainly don't want to work at some job where I put on a suit and tie each day and sit in an office. Or heaven forbid, work in a hospital. Mike can have all that, and welcome to it.

I want my piece of land. I want to work outside. I love being my own boss, even if it means I have no one to blame but me when things go south. I've taken risks with jobs and fallen flat on my face more than once, but the one thing I can be proud of is I've kept going. Putting all my money into buying this landscape business is a case in point. And shit, it might fail, too, but that doesn't terrify me. Well, not much.

Standing next to me, Alex smiles as Sadie gives a little grunt and flops at his feet. Taking on this kid was a risk too. If I'm honest with myself, there's been times if Sam had said I'll take the boy back now, I'd have happily helped pack his bags. But I'm glad that never happened. I first agreed to the deal for the boy as only a solution to a problem, but the emerging product—Alex himself—is worth it. It's no longer just about me.

I realize I have come to care about this kid. *Really* care. I know people have broken his heart. And it occurs to me he could break mine. Emily could as well. That, too, is a risk. A risk worth taking.

I'd dreaded this conversation, but the outcome is more than I ever could have hoped for. I look over at Alex, back lit against the light from the window. He's about to sit on the window sill, but I point, "Better not."

His gaze shifts left to where there's an orb weaver spider, at least four inches long, that's spinning a huge intricate web covering the entire window frame. Despite the scary appearance, the spider is harmless to humans, but I doubt Alex wants to be encased in the web.

"Holy shit!" He jumps back about three feet. "Why are all these bugs out to get me?!"

I laugh. "It's your magnetic personality." Opening the screen door, I ask, "How about a big bowl of ice cream?"

He cocks his head, reminding me of Sadie when I say the magic word *chew*. "What flavor?"

"The usual choices. Vanilla ... or vanilla."

He makes an exaggerated expression like he's deep thinking, then proclaims, "I'll have vanilla."

Throwing all caution to the wind, I clap him on the shoulder as he walks by. "Vanilla it is."

The next day, I am still in a risk-taking mode. Besides, I need an outlet for all these positive feelings. Something tangible. Alex keeps testing me; maybe it's time to turn the tables.

I have to take a few hours off in the morning to complete my task then Sadie and I pick Alex up from the store. Once we pull up in front of my house, I keep the truck running. "Hey, Alex, I've got to run over and pick up some wood chips for mulching the Wheeler's property tomorrow. I won't be long. There's something I need you to do while I'm gone. Look out on the back porch and you'll see. I left instructions."

Predictably, he starts grousing as he opens the car door and steps out. "Whaaatt? I just got home. I've been working. I'm not doing nuthin' else."

Enjoying myself, I smile. "I said I had something for you to do. I didn't say it was work, now did I?"

I put the truck in gear. "Do it or not. Suit yourself."

With those parting words, I'm gone, looking in the rearview mirror as I pull away to see him standing there with his trademark scowl on his face. I reach over to pet Sadie and lean in to talk to my partner in crime. "Yeah, he can scowl all he wants, but he won't be able to resist, will he? I bet you a package of rawhide you-know-whats, he'll go straight there."

Her tongue lolls out of her head and she nudges my hand for another pet. "What, you won't bet? Not even for a chew? You're no fun."

I made the mistake of saying the word *chew*, so she tilts her head and whines, meaning I have to dig one out of the glove box stash for her. She grabs it, then placing it between her paws, she starts vigorously gnawing. Peers up at me from the tops of her eyes.

I nod. "You're right What happens after he gets there is a question mark. No, I won't bet on that."

Chapter 32

ALEX

I use my key to get in the house. Every time I use it, I get a little thrill. Having my own key is somehow satisfying. I throw my backpack on a chair and head to the back porch to see what Matt is being so mysterious about.

The porch is always a mess. Shovels and other tools, old cracked hoses I think should go in the garbage, but Matt thinks they're still useful enough even with a hole or two in them. Dirty boots and shoes. Rags. Set against all the junk sits a gleaming brand-new bicycle. Black with red details on the frame and around the tire rims. The store tags hang off the handlebars.

I just stand and stare. Finally, I notice there's a folded note taped to a hammer that's sitting on the bike seat. My name is written on it. I lift the hammer and pull the note off and begin to read.

```
    I wanted you to have a bike of your own for the
upcoming event. I know how you react when I do some-
thing nice (this is nice, isn't it??). So go ahead,
here's the hammer to bash the shit out of the thing.
It's yours to do with what you like.
    Please, if you do bash it, take it outside so
there isn't a big mess on the porch. Please, if you
```

do bash it, don't video it. Please, if you do video it don't show it to me.

P.S. It's just a damn bike. Get over yourself.

I smile as I read it. Then despite my best efforts to stop them, tears pool in my eyes. I try and blink them away but as fast as I do, more come and spill down my cheeks. I use my elbow to wipe them away. That's the problem with starting to let yourself feel things again. You have to get used to how those feelings hit you. I quit trying to stop the tears and let them come. Now I'm sobbing and glad no one is here to see. When they finally stop, I use the bottom of my T-shirt to dry my face. I feel all hollowed out, but in a good way. I stare out at the fields behind the house and watch a couple of deer step out from a line of trees and begin to graze, twitching their ears, always on alert.

Maybe it's time to be brave. Maybe it's time to take what comes and hope for the best, to take a leap towards hope. Do I wish I had an easier life? Sure, I do. I remember when I was younger sitting in school, listening to the other kids complain about their silly problems. My mom wouldn't buy me some new video game. My sister borrowed my new shirt without asking. It was too hot during our recent trip to Disney World. I was always torn between envy and disgust. Usually, envy won.

What had Sam told me one day? During one of his many "survivor pride" pep talks? Most people only sip from the top of the drink of life. You've drunk from the bottom of the glass, and you're stronger for it. You know things most people will never know. Be proud of that.

I go find scissors and cut the tags off the bike, folding them into Matt's note, which I put in my growing accumulation of keepsakes. I carry the bike down the few steps, careful that it doesn't bang against the stairs. At the bottom I set it down, push up the kickstand, and go for a ride. With shock, I realize at this moment, I'm completely happy. I snatch it up to keep and treasure.

I feel the wind.

I feel the sun on my face.

I feel hope.

Chapter 33

ALEX

"I don't like the school."

Sam frowns at me. "Why," he asks. "Has something happened?"

"No," I answer. "I just don't like it."

Sam naturally has to play detective. "Is it the work? The homework? Do you have some for tomorrow you need to work on?"

Playing with two of the paper clips I picked up from his desk, I shrug. "I did part of it and that's all I'm going to do. I don't like the other parts."

He folds his arms, leans back, and says, "You can't go through life cherry-picking what you want to do and what you don't want to do."

I hold the paper clips still a second and look up at him. "Why not? Isn't that what everyone does?"

He opens his mouth, closes it, opens it, and closes it a second time. Narrows his eyes. Oh, this is rich. Ha! He doesn't have a ready answer! I decide to keep rattling him. While I click the paper clips together, I say, "I have a theory. The problem with schools is they are run by people who liked it when they went to school. I mean who *hates* school and becomes a teacher? I think they need to recruit some people who hated school. Then it would get fixed."

Sam reaches over and takes the paper clips out of my hand then stashes them in his middle desk drawer. I'm really on a roll with him today. It's usually pretty much impossible to get under his skin and I'm enjoying this.

All of a sudden though, he relaxes and gives me a big toothy grin. "Then I suggest you become a teacher. We can start working on that as a goal."

Proud of yourself, aren't you? I can't help but laugh.

He decides to get serious. "Look, I know it's tough after being out so long. There's bound to be a period of adjustment."

It's true I'm not liking school. I thought I wanted to go to public high school, but it's more challenging than just doing the on-line and tutoring thing I'd done with Phoenix. It's also not just the work; it's everything else. I didn't confess to Sam that thanks to redistricting, it turns out Meaty and his buddies attend the same school as me and are giving me grief. My third day there, Meaty spotted me in the hall and acted like we were the best of friends.

"Hey, Coffee Cup, how ya been? Hang around after the last hour and let's go somewhere."

I brush past him to my locker. "I'm busy."

He leans his hand against the locker door. "Hey, don't be that way, man."

I forcefully open the door, causing him to lean back. I toss my books in and say, "Yeah, I do. Maybe you can see my stuff gets returned to me."

"Aww, don't act like that. We knew you'd want to pay your fair share for the weed. You were out of it so we didn't want to wake you." He runs a comb through his hair. "And you seem to be doing good for yourself these days. Where you getting all your dough?"

He's so full of shit. The class warning bell rings. I shut the door and turn to him, ignoring his question about the sources of my funds. "I'd say I paid for my share and more. I'd like my phone back."

He gives an innocent little smile. "Phone? I don't know nuthin' about that."

Liar. "Well, if you find out something, let me know. Otherwise, leave me alone."

I start to walk away but he grabs my arm. I don't like to be touched so my body responds. I yank my arm back and shove him away.

Meaty's nice guy act is over. He snarls at me. "You'd better watch yourself. It would be a shame if being new to the school and all, someone was to report you for fighting." He looks pointedly at my locker. "Or say some drugs were found."

Before I can come up with a reply, one of the teachers comes out of a nearby classroom. Meaty gives a parting smirk and walks backwards a couple of steps before turning and fading into the crowd of other kids hurrying to beat the final bell.

Meaty's an asshole. It's not like I'm not acquainted with the species but he's rattled me. It's like I'm out of practice dealing with crap because things have been going so well for a change. I walk slow, preoccupied with my thoughts and trying to get my breathing back to normal. I end up getting to class after the final bell and get written up for being tardy. There's a dangerous moment when old habits jump to the front, and I almost tell the teacher to go to hell. Instead, I grab the slip of paper without saying anything.

I crumple the tardy slip in my hand and drop it in the nearby garbage can as I walk to my seat. The teacher doesn't like it. I stare at her issuing a silent challenge. I'm not in the mood to be messed with. She turns her back on me and starts writing on the white board. I take my seat but don't open my textbook and I don't do the assignment.

I don't need this shit.

Chapter 34

SAM

Becky, the Phoenix receptionist, pops her head in and says, "Code Blue." It's her way of telling me someone from child welfare is on the line for me.

I'm trying to finish some paperwork and am not happy to be interrupted, but decide I'd better take the call. If it's good news it will keep, but if it's bad news it never goes away. I might as well deal with it now as later.

"We've got a problem."

Okay, not good news. These are words I hear all too often in my line of work. Words that make applying to be a Walmart greeter appealing. It would be helpful if the caller would do some clarifying so I can anticipate in advance how bad the problem is. Like "we've got a little problem" or "we have a really major problem." Since she hasn't given any such clarification, I have to ask, "What's going on?"

The call is from Linda Snider. She's the child welfare social worker for about five of our kids, including Alex Coffey. We haven't really talked much since Alex came into Phoenix's care. I send the requisite monthly reports as well as the occasional incident report, but she's been happy to sit in the shotgun seat and let me do the driving on Alex's case. I'm sure that helps her have more time to deal with the rest of her caseload. Too many kids and too little time.

I've been on the police force. I've worked both juvenile and adult corrections. And now I work in the private sector with foster care. All of these jobs have been challenging and demanding, but in my mind, child welfare social workers have the toughest job there is. You can see it in their extremely high burnout rate. The majority of direct line workers start right after the ink dries on their college social work degree. By the time they get experience under their belt and get good at what they do, they often move on. Bail to another line of work entirely or move somewhere else in the agency where there's less stress and pressure. Some of them come work for us at Phoenix, where they deal with kids in foster care but don't have to do child abuse investigations.

Where they don't have to make what could be a life-or-death decision.

Where their caseload isn't so high as to be impossible.

Where they don't have to directly witness the atrocities inflicted on children.

I've had this discussion with my boss Margo, who once worked with a child welfare agency. I'd been complaining about how unrealistic the cop shows on TV are and I obviously hit a nerve. She pinned me with a stare. "You're worried about cops?! When a cop knocks on a door, he's got a gun, a Taser, a billy club, and most importantly, radio contact for instant assistance if needed. A social worker goes into a dangerous neighborhood and knocks on a door, not knowing if the person answering has a pit bull, is carrying a pistol, or is completely high and looking for a fight."

She picked up her mug but before she could take a drink, plunked it back on her desk. "And another thing. Have you ever seen a movie or TV show where a child welfare worker is portrayed in a good way? They're always shown as some mean official, with glasses and a tight hair bun, ripping a child from their loving, albeit dysfunctional, family *or* they're viewed as lazy, incompetent, or uncaring when a poor child gets the crap beaten out of them."

Margo definitely made her case in defense of child welfare workers that day and I try to remember it in my day-to-day dealings, though I still get frustrated with the whole child welfare system. I keep in mind, it's not usually the individual worker's fault, and I do like Linda and will try to help if I can.

I take a deep breath. "Okay. What's the problem? Who's the kid?"

I can hear her sigh over the phone. "It's Alex."

This makes me relax a bit. Alex is doing fine, so maybe this just means some bureaucratic form or payment voucher I didn't fill out right. "Okay, what can I do?"

"I don't know. The judge who committed Alex has set a court review. He says he wants to review the placement for, and I quote, 'appropriateness.'"

This is unusual … and concerning. I lean forward placing my elbows on my desk. "What brought this on? Is it about Matt King? He was fully vetted. Is there some allegation?"

"No, nothing like that. I think the bottom line is he doesn't think Alex should be in foster care. He believes he should be placed in a residential setting."

Okay, now I'm getting pissed. "This is stupid. Alex has his ups and downs but he's overall doing well. Why would we rock the boat when he's showing such progress?"

There's a slight pause. "Off the record?"

"Always. Tell me."

"The District Attorney, Andrew Flynn, is in real tight with the school superintendent. They play golf every Sunday. My guess is when Alex was enrolled and the principal got a glimpse of Alex's background, he complained to his golfing pal, who complained to the judge. I think Alex has done a few things at school that has also put him on the radar. If Alex is placed in residential care, he won't be in the public school. Problem solved."

My blood pressure keeps going up. "So, what does everyone expect, for Alex to remain in a residential setting until the day he turns eighteen? To never set foot in any public school again?"

"I think that's exactly what they'd like. But Sam, this may be difficult. He's brought up the runaway incident…"

I interrupt her. "It was one night and he came back on his own!"

"I know, but you and I have seen this before. People who expect these kids to be perfect when we know normal adolescents living at home with mom and dad have these same issues. The judge is calling this a 'placement review' and I have to submit a report in advance of the hearing."

Reaching for calm, I lean back in my office chair till it squeals. "You'll agree he should stay where he is, won't you? I mean, the judge can complain and make recommendations, but the Department isn't bound by them. All the judge can legally do is terminate the commitment and he won't do that."

I can hear Linda's sigh through the phone. "True, but my bosses on up the food chain are looking at the budget. They just contracted with an out-of-state provider that is offering residential care for less than we're paying you for Alex to be in foster care. There may be pressure to move him."

I can't hold back any longer. "Yeah, why don't you just rip his guts out and be done with it?"

Linda's voice goes up an octave. "You think I like this?"

Feeling ashamed of myself, I pedal backwards. "I'm sorry. I just get so tired sometimes of the system doing everything it can to take traumatized kids and keep retraumatizing them."

"Look, we're on the same side. I'll do what I can. I just wanted you to know what we're dealing with."

I end the call with more groveling to make up for losing my temper, but it flares up again as soon as I disconnect. "Dammit to hell!" I yell, as I pick up and throw my baseball against the door for good measure, then sit with my head in my hands. A minute later, Margo appears. "Hey, you okay?"

"No, I'm not." She takes the chair by my desk and I unload the story. As I finish, she closes her eyes and takes a deep breath. "Oh, God. This reminds me of Raymond Campbell, remember him? He wasn't one of yours, but you might have heard me trashing my office."

"Vaguely. He was the little kid with the robbery charge?"

"Yep, that's him. Eleven years old, seventy pounds sopping wet, and held up someone on the street with a handgun for their wallet and watch. He was the next thing to a wild feral animal. Had zero home life and had been pretty much surviving on his own for years. Never really been in school or sat at a table to eat a meal. They committed him to juvenile justice, one of the youngest kids ever, probably to at least get a roof over his head and have his basic needs met. DJJ didn't know what to do with such a young kid and in desperation, looked to us for foster care. I almost didn't accept him, but I felt something had to be done.

"We placed him in a family with a strong father and nurturing mother. I swear it was like the angels sang. I've never seen such a transformation in a kid. He adored them and his behavior completely changed. Six months successfully in foster care meant juvenile justice could contact child welfare and transition the case to them to meet his long-term placement and permanency needs. We let child welfare know we'd be glad for him to stay with us, and we'd just transfer the billing to them. They say, nope, we're cutting back on our use of private foster care and will be moving him to one of our child welfare agency foster homes. I went ballistic."

"I can't remember the specifics. What did you do?"

"Put everything in writing. Sent it to the judge in the case and to the top brass of child welfare with copies to the kid's public defender, and anyone else I could think of. One thing I've learned is always, always put things in writing. Spoken words they can deny, disclaim, or whatever, but they know when it's in writing there's a record that doesn't go away. They ended up letting us keep him. I did reduce our fee to meet them at least halfway. Happy end of story: he was adopted by the family."

Becky, who has apparently decided things have calmed down enough, peeks around the door of my office. "I brought some cookies; would you like some?"

Margo waves her in. "Sure, a cookie would make everything better." She takes one for herself and holds one out to me. "Seriously, a cookie will help."

Are they kidding me? A cookie will help? Suddenly, I bolt up in my chair as if electrified and grab the treat from her hand. "Yes! Exactly!"

Both Margo and Becky are looking at me like a psych hospital might do me some good.

I point my chocolate chip cookie at them. "Cookie. Cookie Van Patten! She's been the CASA volunteer for some of our other kids. If we can get Alex assigned to her, she'll eat the judge and child welfare for breakfast."

Margo claps her hands together. "Sam, that's inspired. I couldn't do that in Raymond's case because juvenile justice kids don't get a CASA worker, but since Alex is dually committed to both child welfare and juvenile justice, he qualifies. Cookie's a blue blood and well-known in the community. She supports the local theater, the humane society, and donates to political candidates she likes. And yeah, she's a force of nature. You think you can get the CASA folks to go for it?"

I smile. "I do. I have a secret weapon. My wife plays tennis with Cookie."

Becky gives a quizzical look. "Is her name really Cookie?"

I shake my head. "No, but whatever her real name is, it's a closely guarded secret."

CASA stands for Court Appointed Special Advocates. They are specially trained and supervised volunteers assigned to children involved with the child welfare system. They advocate for the child's best interest and are the one person in the court room with no skin in the game, other than seeing the child receives the best services and gets a positive outcome. It's a proven fact that kids with CASA have better outcomes. Unfortunately, there usually aren't enough CASA volunteers for every child, and Alex has never gotten one.

Hopefully, that's about to change.

Driving home an hour later, I'm happy to have a plan but I'm still feeling nervous. I'm not going to say anything to Alex about this. He isn't required to be at the hearing. No sense in getting his anxiety level up if I don't have to. I'll probably have to tell Matt, and I don't look forward to that. Not one bit.

Chapter 35

MATT

I drop by Phoenix at Sam's request and listen as he attempts to explain why Alex's case is going back to court, for what I see as no good reason. My brain tries to take it all in. A court hearing? Now? While Alex is doing the best he ever has? *Unbelievable.*

Then Sam goes into this CASA thing, which is less of a concern, but something easier to explode about. I scowl at him. "Cookie Van Patten. Are you shitting me? What is she again?"

Sam takes a breath and gets his patient look. "She's a CASA volunteer. She's being assigned to make sure Alex's best interests are being followed."

"*I* take care of Alex's best interests. I don't need any other people messing in my life. You're a pain in the ass enough."

"It's not for you; it's for Alex."

"Alex won't want anyone else messing in his life either. He'll probably cuss her out and that'll be the last we'll see of her. Plus, I'll feel the need to clean the place up real good. It'd be like entertaining my mother. Who, by the way, is an acquaintance of Ms. Van Patten. Bridge club or hospital auxiliary or something. That's enough to make me nervous right there. I don't need this hassle."

Sam has lost his patient look and raises his voice. "Look, you need to listen to me on this. Just shut up for once and do something you don't want to do."

Well, now this pisses me off. But before I holler back, I look at Sam a bit closer. He may have forgotten how long and how well I know him. Something is off. "You're hiding something."

He doesn't look me in the eye. "Don't worry about it."

"Oh, why doesn't that make me feel better? Worry about *what?*"

He leans forward and rubs his forehead. "The school and court folks aren't happy about Alex being in the public-school setting. They think he should be in a residential placement, one with an on-site school program."

"What the hell?!"

"I know. I know. That's why we need Ms. Van Patten. With her on our side, I think we can convince the judge Alex should stay where he is. It'll probably just be a formality. Judges in this state can't tell child welfare what placements to use, they can just make it uncomfortable for them. It might be good if you came to the hearing, too."

"Damn straight, I'll be there. And you know what, I'll bring my mother. If she hears Ms. Van Patten will be there, I probably couldn't keep her away if I tried. If there's one thing I can say about my mother, she knows almost everyone in town. Shoot, she may be Judge Stinnett's doctor."

Sam's expression lightens up a bit. "I like the way you're thinking. Let's ask Mike, too. Power in numbers. I'll run it by Alex's caseworker and attorney, to make sure they're on board. But let's not tell Alex. No sense in upsetting him. Cookie will be coming to see him a few times before the hearing, but she won't mention it to him, either."

Sam's biting his lip so I know there's more coming. "My worry is Alex will do something he shouldn't at school between now and then that could give ammunition to try and boot him out. We know he's been having a few issues. He's gotten a couple of detentions and his grades aren't very good because he keeps not doing the work."

Feeling defensive, I say, "I've nagged him about the homework but you know how he gets."

"Matt, I'm not blaming you. Personally, I think considering

everything he's been through, he's doing pretty well, but others don't see it that way. They see a kid causing them troubles. We'll just have to cross our fingers and hope he holds it together until we can get through this."

I hear the unspoken words from Sam: *If* we get through this.

Bad enough I've had to deal with Alex's issues, now we have to take on the court and child welfare system. But if they want a fight, we'll give them one.

No one is messing with *my* kid.

Chapter 36

SAM

The day of the hearing, it's hot and sultry. What else is new? Fall is here but no one told Mother Nature. By the time I've made the short walk from where I parked the car to the courthouse, my clothes are already sticking to me. The blast of cold air when I open the courthouse door is welcome. I take the marble stairs up to the second floor and head to Courtroom A. I find a spot in the waiting area outside the courtroom and take a seat. I got here first, so I could welcome my people as they arrive.

Matt is the first to show. He is also dressed in his Sunday best. I can't recall the last time I saw him in anything other than jeans. He looks quite good, which I tell him.

He tugs on his tie and grimaces. "I hate court."

"Yeah, I know. No one's idea of a fun time. Hopefully, the docket doesn't have us sitting here all day. The hearing itself probably won't take more than ten or fifteen minutes."

I motion to the seat next to me but he says, "Thanks, but I'll stand. Tugs at his tie again. "This is all stupid if you ask me."

"The expression on your face makes that very clear. I'd advise you look a little less deranged and homicidal."

He lifts his cheeks, baring his teeth. "Like this?"

I shake my head. "Ugh, go back to homicidal."

"Emily is coming too. She had to drop off Justin first and is now out there looking for a parking space. She'll probably have to circle the block ten times."

I wave at Mike and his mom as they get off the elevator and join us in the hallway waiting area. Dr. King, the female one, takes me up on the offer of a chair. Next, it's Emily, trotting up the steps. Her eyes don't go to Matt; instead, they go to his mom. It's obvious they've never formally met. Matt is standing there like a blob, so Emily extends her hand to Dr. King and initiates the contact.

When Linda Snider, Cookie Van Patten, and Amy Francis, Alex's public defender, arrive I make the introductions. Cookie first speaks to Matt's mom then engages Matt in conversation. I smile at the two of them. Despite Matt's initial reservations, she completely won him over, as she did with Alex. It didn't surprise me. She's a force to be reckoned with. I'm counting on that being the case in the courtroom today. I send up a silent little prayer: *Please Cookie, be on your game today.*

Ms. Francis speaks to me and nods towards where a tall gentleman is standing and talking on his phone. "That's the school superintendent, Paul Wharton. I wouldn't be surprised if the DA calls him as a witness."

Court starts, so Ms. Francis leaves us to join the parties inside the courtroom. We watch the parade of unhappy people enter the doors as their names are called. Juvenile court is confidential so only the immediate parties to each case are allowed in. I get more tense the longer we wait, and glancing at Matt, can tell he's feeling the pressure as well.

When the bailiff opens the door and proclaims, "Alex Coffey," we all rise to enter the courtroom. Superintendent Wharton looks taken aback when so many of us stand up for Alex's case. Judge Stinnett and the DA, Andrew Flynn, also seem surprised to see so many of us here. The judge's face lights up in recognition as he spots either Cookie, Dr. King, the other Dr. King, or hell, all of them. It's hard to tell since they are together. We all take seats in the front row. The judge is scribbling something on a piece of paper, which he hands to one of the clerks, then turns his attention to us.

"I see we have a number of folks here today on this case. The DA, Mr. Flynn, requested this placement review to determine if Alex Coffey is in an appropriate setting to meet his needs. For the record, please introduce yourselves."

We all dutifully say our names then wait for the judge to start the show. He doesn't keep us waiting. "I have several reports, including one from Alex's child welfare worker, Ms. Snider, and his CASA volunteer, Cookie Van Patten. Mr. Flynn, you asked that this case be docketed for review so please inform the court of your concerns."

The District Attorney stands and all our eyes swivel to him. "Your Honor, Alex Coffey has complex needs that have been well documented for many years. He has been in several psychiatric hospitals, numerous treatment-oriented group homes, and secure settings including private therapeutic facilities. The independent children's review assessments placed him at a Level Five, the highest possible level, and one that is almost always correlated with a residential setting.

"I'd like to also point out, Alex Coffey is not strictly a child welfare case. He has appeared on the delinquency docket on numerous occasions and recently served a one-hundred-twenty-day term in a juvenile facility. It was at the conclusion of this term he was placed directly into foster care. It would appear a step-down facility would have been much more appropriate. I believe all of us know that Alex has failed in foster care time and time again. It seems a disservice, not just to the community's public safety needs, but to this boy himself, to place him where he cannot access the intensive services he so obviously needs. Most importantly, this should include a program where he attends an on-campus educational program for the safety of the other students."

Sitting beside me, I feel Matt stir, and I place a hand on his arm, warning him to keep quiet. He scowls at me but keeps his mouth shut. Amy, Alex's public defender, speaks up. "Your Honor, I have read the reports filed by Ms. Snider and by Mrs. Van Patten, Alex's CASA volunteer. Yes, Alex has had numerous prior placements; however, it is not necessary for a child to be institutionalized to get necessary services. The whole point of therapeutic foster care is for the child to receive needed services *in* the community. The foster care agency has arranged for tutoring, counseling, and positive enrichment activities. I strongly believe moving him yet again would be very detrimental and that he should remain in his current foster home."

Judge Stinnett sits back in his chair and turns his attention to Linda Snider. "Ms. Snider, what is the Department of Children's Services stance on this matter?"

Linda wets her lips as she stands up. "We believe we placed Alex in an appropriate placement, but of course the Department is open to all options that assure the best services for this child."

I shoot her a piercing look, but she keeps her eyes straight ahead, ignoring all of us. I'm mad but she did warn me her supervisors were wanting to avoid any controversy. It's obvious this cop-out statement was vetted by her bosses, and she's just the messenger.

Beside me, Matt leans over to whisper. "That's all she's going to say? Why doesn't she tell them no one else would take him? That they still might not?"

I lower my head and whisper back. "It's true, but think about it. That doesn't help our case, does it?"

Shaking his head—I'm not sure if it's in disagreement with me or just disgust—Matt crosses his arms and leans back against the bench. He looks ready to explode. I understand the feeling but now is not the time.

The judge picks up one of the reports and turns to Cookie. "I'm always thankful when I have someone from CASA in my courtroom. I find CASA volunteers invaluable because they only concentrate on the child and are truly independent, which, no offense to the rest of you, is unique."

He leans forward and lowers his voice, almost as if he's sitting across the dining room table with a friend. "Ms. Van Patten, what do you have to say about this?"

With a smile, Cookie takes up the reins and speaks without hesitation or undue emotion. "Thank you, Your Honor. Since being assigned this case, I have spent time with Alex, his foster father, Matthew King, and Mr. Murry with the Phoenix Foster Care agency. You have the written report I filed, but I'm a firm believer that a picture is worth a thousand words. In this case, I have several photos that I believe illuminate the progress this child has made in his current setting."

She opens a pink folder. No one else would bring a pink folder to court but it matches her pink suit, which I'm sure she planned. She always has a distinct style. "Here is a picture taken of Alex on the day he was placed in Mr. King's foster home." She holds it out and the judge takes the photo from her hand and lays it on the bench in front of him.

"And this is a recent picture of Alex." She pauses and lets the judge study it. Stinnett actually smiles, looks at Cookie, then holds the pictures up to the D.A. before swiveling to let us all see them. Cookie had the foresight to have the pictures made 8x10 and affixed to foam board so we get a good look. No detail escapes her.

It was me who had taken the "before" picture on the day I'd picked Alex up from the detention center. The "after" picture was courtesy of Emily, who Matt told me is constantly snapping pictures of the kids. The picture in the Judge's hand was taken during a picnic. It's one of those off-hand pictures you snap that somehow hits all the right notes of lighting, expression, background. Even I had to look twice to make sure the smiling, attractive kiddo in that picture was Alex.

Satisfied with the reaction she got, Cookie dives back into the pink folder and begins placing other photos in front of the judge. Alex wearing his EMT uniform. Alex crossing the finish line at the bike event, laughing with pleasure and delight. Emily even caught one with Alex and Matt sitting companionably side by side. In the picture Alex is peering up at Matt. The reality was likely that something snarky was about to come out of his mouth but to the unknowing, it looks like he's hanging on his foster father's every word. Matt looks downright parental.

Cookie taps one of the pictures with her finger, pink nail polish, of course. "As you can see Alex has been actively participating in the community. These are opportunities he's had that he would be unlikely to receive in a congregate care setting. Alex has adapted well to being in a foster home with a single father. In my conversations with his foster parent, Mr. King, it's obvious he is very committed to Alex's success. It's to be expected, given Alex's background, there would be some testing and behavioral issues; but Mr. King has been unfazed by them, and has provided the needed structure and boundaries for Alex to continue to grow and overcome the many traumas this child has endured. I conclude that it would be extremely detrimental to move Alex from this placement."

The judge is nodding and opening his mouth to speak, but before he can say anything, Cookie continues. "Now, as to school, none of us should be surprised that adjusting after so many different schools, in so many different settings, would be a challenge. Alex and I had several conversations about the obstacles public school presents for him. I have also talked with numerous folks in the school system, and have a recommendation. Alex would seem to be a prime candidate for the Forward Thinking Learning Academy."

This is a surprise to me. Cookie kept it under wraps. It's run by the county school system but spots are very limited and extremely difficult to get. All of the other alternative schools are mostly for youth who have been expelled or have long term suspensions because of behavioral offenses. The Academy is geared for kids of trauma who might not have any behavioral issues at all, but need a supportive setting to succeed. Kids like Alex, with a long history of behavioral issues, are usually excluded so I didn't even try to get Alex in there. Maybe that was my bad.

I glance over at the school superintendent but can't read his expression. Is this news to him or did Cookie discuss it with him? Would he go along with it? I may soon get my answer because from the bench, Judge Stinnett asks, "Superintendent Wharton, is this a possibility?"

The superintendent and the DA exchange a look. I'm guessing Flynn was planning on calling the superintendent as a witness but disregarded that plan. I also believe in that look, the DA is sending the message: *This kid isn't going to be shipped off, so what's your Plan B?*

The superintendent stands up and says, "Yes, Your Honor."

Judge Stinnett looks satisfied. "Okay then. Does anyone else have anything to say before I bring this to a conclusion?"

As expected, the D.A. and the superintendent remain quiet. They know a losing game when they see one.

Judge Stinnet addresses Matt. "Mr. King, are you willing to have Alex Coffey remain in your home?"

Matt rises to his feet. "Yes, Your Honor."

"Very well. I see no reason to recommend any changes to the placement. I would like to see Alex in the alternative school setting and hope this can be quickly arranged. Thank you everyone for coming today. I'd like to add that I find it gratifying that so many people are invested in this young man's success. Mr. King, I wish we had more people like you to step up and foster some of these older teens. Ms. Van Patten, as always, thanks for your time and the thorough job you do. Dr. King, thank you for coming … and you too, the other Dr. King. We have lots of Kings in the room." The judge smiles at his little joke and everyone in the room chuckles.

We all file out as the bailiff calls the next victims into the room. No one says much until we step outside into the blazing noonday sun and convene at the top of the courthouse stairs. I feel a tangible relief and can tell Matt does, too. We were both more worried than we let on.

Emily volunteers to get her car and pick Matt up to go for an early lunch. I'm pretty sure her ulterior motive is giving Matt some alone time with his family. Since Matt isn't saying anything, I smile at Mike and Mrs. King, "Thanks so much for coming to show your support."

"Happy to do it," Mike says.

Mrs. King puts on her sunglasses. I move a little to the left so she isn't looking directly into blinding sun when she speaks to me. She opens her purse and gets her keys. "Yes, happy to. I'll tell Cookie how much we appreciate her."

She turns her attention to Matt. "How about you and Alex come to lunch on Sunday? I'll go by the bakery and get one of those key lime pies you like so well."

Matt pauses for a second. "This Sunday isn't good, but I'll call you sometime."

She's disappointed; any fool can see that. Any fool apparently, but Matt. I want to smack him upside his thick skull. "Oh, okay," she mumbles as she slips her sunglasses on. "Guess I'd better get going. Bye now."

Mike waits until she's at the bottom of the stairs and begins to cross the street before turning on Matt. "You are such an asshole."

Matt spits back, "Mind your own damn business."

Okay, this is awkward to be in the middle of another family's drama, but it's a family I've known almost as long as I've known my own. Mike isn't backing down. "When you hurt Mom, it *is* my business. You know what? Dad's been gone a long time now and you need to quit acting like he was some sort of saint. He wasn't. He had plenty of faults."

"Oh, like Mom didn't? Doesn't? She was the one who took up with another guy while they were still married."

Mike is shaking his head and raising his voice.

A couple of people are looking our way so I say, "Um, guys…" But I'm ignored so I keep standing here wishing I could be anywhere else.

"You have a very selective memory. Dad was screwing around with half the nurses at the hospital and everyone, *everyone*, knew it. You don't think that was humiliating for her? She found someone to try and be happy with, and it might not have lasted anyway, but you sure as hell didn't help by stirring up trouble at every opportunity."

Matt looks a little less sure of himself but isn't backing down. "You always take her side. And she always took yours. You and Dad…"

"I'll tell you about Dad and me," Mike interrupts. "He was my father and I loved him, but when I got old enough, I saw all the times he was a complete jerk." To my horror, he tilts his head in my direction, "Ask Sam. He knows it."

Oh Jesus, Mike, leave me out of it. But he's on a roll.

"You're too young to remember, but one Sunday when Mom was at work, Dad made me babysit you because he had golf lined up. Sam was there too, to keep me company. Right before Dad was to leave, you broke a glass and somehow sliced open your arm. I grabbed you up and ran to Dad."

I know where this is going but there's no escaping it, so I just paste on a non-expression and wait for the other shoe to fall.

Mike's face is completely red and his voice shakes. "Did he take you to the ER like he should have? No. That would have taken too much time and he didn't want to miss his goddamn golf game. So, you know what he did? He told Sam to go home and made me hold you down while he stitched you up—without anesthesia. There was blood everywhere. You were screaming; I was crying. He left me to clean everything up while he headed on to the country club.

I held it against him, and he knew it. Told me I was making a mountain out of a mole hill. I didn't tell Mom but she easily figured out what happened when she saw the stitches. She knew he hadn't taken you to the ER. They had a terrible fight that night. She never forgave him."

The blood has drained from Matt's face. "You're wrong, Mike," he says so softly I barely hear him. "I do remember that day, just bits and pieces, but I remember you carried me up to my bed and stayed with me all day. I was glad to have you there. I think as I got older, I just remembered it as getting hurt and Dad doctoring me."

Mike takes a deep breath and lowers his voice. "Yeah, I wish I had been young enough to forget most of it, but I never have. I didn't want to burden you with it, but neither of us is young anymore and it's way past time for you to know the truth."

I shift from one foot to another and suddenly they both seem to recall I'm standing here. Mike gives me a little push, "Sorry, Sam, to inflict this on you."

"Don't worry about it. You know I can compare war stories."

Mike has known me a very long time. I'm sure he hasn't forgotten the times he came to my house and saw my mother passed out on the floor from her heavy drinking. For a long time as a kid, I'd envied Mike what seemed like the perfect family, till I got a closer look behind the scenes.

Emily pulls her car up to the curb and gives a tiny honk of the horn. Matt waves at her. I'm sure he's thinking she couldn't have timed it better if she'd tried. "I'd better go." He holds out his hand to Mike. "I do appreciate you coming today."

Mike clasps his hand. "Of course I came. I'm still always here for you, you know."

Matt nods. "I know. I've always known."

As Matt descends the courthouse steps, I glance sideways at Mike and say, "I don't know about you, but between the court goings-on and this after-party, I could use some lunch. I'll buy."

"I wish I could, but I really need to be getting back to the office." He raises his eyebrows. "Besides, I see the school guy heading your way. Hopefully, he's not wanting another go."

As Mike departs, Superintendent Wharton makes his way to me and asks to have a word. I'm getting a lot of drama here today. I'm sure if these courthouse steps could talk, they could tell some tales.

"Sure," I say. I don't have any hard feelings and gain nothing by making enemies of the school folks. Often our foster care placements rise or fall based on how our kids are doing in school.

Our conversation is amiable. He's not a bad guy, and I know he has a tough job, balancing the interests of so many kids and staff, not to mention dealing with parents, social workers, and politicians. He asks if I'm familiar with the Forward Thinking Academy. I tell him yes, but I haven't been there. I don't mention that's because the tough kids Margo usually assigns to me have never been accepted. He asks if I'd like a personal tour. Today. Intrigued, I take him up on his offer to go straight there from the courthouse.

I like what I see. I let him know I'd be very pleased for Alex to have a slot. He says he can squeeze him in. We bob and weave around the elephant in the room, which is why didn't he put Alex here in the first place, instead of going the court hearing route. I used to do police work, but it doesn't take advance investigative skills to figure out it's because they'd prefer to use those precious available slots on "more deserving kids."

But who am I to throw stones? Don't we at Phoenix read the referrals and pick and choose who we take? It would be nice if there were enough resources for all the kids who need them, but this is the real world, after all. Right now, I'll work on helping those I can.

Starting with Alex Coffey.

Chapter 37

ALEX

I'm in a new school and to my surprise it's okay. When Sam talked about an alternative school, I got my back up. I've been in those before and at least half of the time they were awful. More like going to school in a detention center than anything like a public school. This one, like Sam promised, is small, and I don't miss all the noise and chaos of Western Hills High. The kids here are okay, too. None of the cheerleaders and star athletes making you feel inferior. In fact, no athletes at all because there are no teams. Sports are something that happens in P.E. class and here they tend to do things like yoga. I overheard a teacher telling a visitor that yoga is good for trauma.

They don't say it in our student guidebook, but all of us who go here know it's our troubled pasts that bond us. Every student has a story. There are quite a few foster kids. There's one boy who watched his parents murder his sister. He lives with an uncle now because they are in prison. His story humbles me.

One student makes going to this school really worthwhile, a girl in my history class. Her name is Hailey and in a funny twist, we have the same birthday. This was a starting point for our second conversation, which went much better than our first one. Here's how that first meeting went down ... and what happened after.

In the hallway on my second day, a girl said something to me as I walked by. I figured a girl who looked like her must be talking to someone else, so I put on my don't-give-a-shit face and kept going. A few minutes later, she cornered me before class started. She was holding her history book clutched to her chest. I tried ignoring her but could feel her staring at me. It went on so long it got weird, so I got ready to listen to some name she was going to call me and to give back as good as I got.

When I meet her eyes, she drops her arms to her sides, the right one still holding the textbook. She smiles and lifts an eyebrow. If anything, this makes her look even more attractive. Finally, she speaks.

"You're new so I'm not going to unload on you. But at this school we take care of each other, and no one is considered too high and mighty for the rest of us. So just because you're good-looking, don't go acting the snob like you just did. It's rude and unbecoming."

With that she spins around and heads into class. I stand there completely stunned. I have been called many things in my life but *good-looking* has never been one of them. I latch on to those words and the wild possibility I could maybe have a chance with her.

Now, I don't know what to do. I pay zero attention to the teacher's lesson on the Roman Empire and instead run sample replies to her through my head. I come up with a few but then doubt begins creeping in. What if she's just messing with me? Like someone sends the hot girl over as a prank. She'll report what I said and they'll all have a good laugh.

I'm grateful this happens at the end of the day, and I double-time it to the truck when Matt picks me up. He stops to get gas. I listen to music while he clicks the keeper on the gas pump handle and rests his elbow on top of the bed of the truck as the tank fills. The pump turns off and he removes the nozzle, returning it to its metal cradle. Then he leans in and says to me, "I'm going inside to pick up some stuff. Do you want to go get anything?"

"No, I'll wait here." I sit a few minutes thinking about Hailey. I pull down the sun visor, slide the flap over to reveal the mirror, and tilt it to see all of my face. Could what she said be true? I need a better view. I slip out of the car and pass Matt coming out.

"Changed my mind. I'm hitting the bathroom."

His mouth is full of peanut M&M's. He mumbles and holds the bag out offering me some. I take the whole bag out of his hand and keep walking. He must have swallowed because just as I get to the door I hear, "That better not be empty when you bring it back!"

Now I feel compelled to eat them all, pouring some into my hand. I like the blues and reds.

Thankfully, the bathroom is a one-person and no one is in it. I look at myself in the mirror, turning to the left then to the right side. I'm tan from all the hours working outside this summer with Matt. I've got some muscles too. But it's my face I look most closely at. Yeah, I look much better than I used to, but do I look *good*? I think I might, but I can't be sure.

I save two M&Ms for Matt. Both of them brown. He takes the bag and frowns. "Gee, thanks."

He tries to look mad but I know he's not. In fact, he thinks it's funny. I can see the wheels turning in his head, plotting his revenge. We don't keep an official score, but this is the shit we do. I wouldn't have left him even the two, but I've decided to use him. After he starts the car, I pull down the visor and look in the mirror again. "Do you think I'm good-looking?"

He swerves a little. "What?!"

"Relax Doc. Get over yourself. I'm not coming on to you. I need an opinion."

He frowns. "Where is this coming from? Is this a school assignment or something? Geez, what are they thinking?"

I know Matt has no problems in the female department. As long as we keep it light, I'm okay with this conversation. "Of course not. There's this girl…"

A corner of his mouth turns up. "Ahhhh, that explains it."

At the next stoplight, he turns to look at me with his elbow on the steering wheel, resting his chin on his thumb with a finger over his mouth. Looks me up and down. "Okay, is this a one to ten scale kind of thing or what?"

"Just answer the question. Don't overthink it."

The light changes and he glances to the left as he makes a turn, then looks back at me. "Smile."

"Shut up. Never mind."

"No, this is justified. You aren't going to look at a girl with your standard go-to-hell-look, are you? Won't you be smiling? And if not, I can tell you right now you won't be going out on any dates." He leans over with a cheesy look. "Pretend I'm a girl."

"Ugh, gross. Forget it."

"Can't. It's now forever burned in my mind." He makes kissy noises.

He's disgusting but I can't help but laugh at him. I give his arm a shove.

Pleased with himself, he nods. "There you go. Laughing is even better than smiling. Yeah, I'm used to always being the best-looking guy in the room, but you are now definitely competition."

He reaches up and wiggles his nose back and forth. "If only I hadn't broken this twice."

I roll my eyes at him, but I've gotten the answer I wanted. And I feel pretty good about it.

At the next light, without looking at me directly, he says, "Hey, seriously. You know it's easy to get a mental blueprint in your head about things, but you have to readjust that over time. I have the opposite trouble. I still think in my head I'm twenty but after a day of really hard work, when I get up the next morning, I find my body doesn't believe it anymore."

He looks over to check that I'm listening. "So, the caterpillar turned into a butterfly." Unbelievably corny, but if I'm being honest, I like the comparison.

Matt flexes his fingers on the wheel. "While we're talking about things being good, how about … you know … things in general?"

Looking for safe ground I come up with what I think is a good answer. I shrug and look out the window. "I've no complaints."

"Good, good. You know, you have your sixteenth birthday coming up in a few months. I was thinking after you got your license, we should see about getting you a car. Be nice if you could chauffeur yourself around. What do ya think?"

Both of us have been dancing around this conversation, because when I turn sixteen, it'll be after our six months *deal*. I guess this is Matt's way of again letting me know I can keep staying with him. I believe him, but I don't mind the reminders. It makes it seem more real.

I reach forward and start playing with the channels on the truck's radio. "Okay."

There, I said it. Matt's nodding and smiling. We drive on in silence for a bit while I picture myself picking up Hailey in my new car, dropping her off, then driving *home*. But I shouldn't get ahead of myself. The child welfare policies start rolling through my head.

"I don't know if they'll let me get my license. There's regulations. Caseworkers aren't allowed to sign for the permit. There's insurance and all that."

We're in the country now so Matt kicks off the AC, rolls down his window, and rests his elbow on the door. "No problem. I already checked with Sam. I can sign for you to get your learner's permit then you can go on my insurance policy. You have to go to something the child welfare folks put on called a 'Readiness to Drive' meeting, but that's no big deal."

Sometimes in late summer, it's like time stands still. The blazing sun on a windless day. The corn high in the fields as we drive by. The smell of freshly cut hay. Today is a good day. I want to hold on to it. I roll my window down and mirror Matt, resting my elbow on the door. He's been talking to Sam about me. Making future plans. Willing to put his name on a dotted line for me, even with all I've put him through.

I lean my head back against the head rest and close my eyes. A full minute goes by. When I open them, I turn to Matt, and purposely meet his eyes. "About the car … that'd be nice."

He takes his right hand off the wheel and gives my arm a little push. "Is that right?"

I push back with my left hand on his shoulder. "Yeah, and I'll be a better driver than you, too. Keep both hands on the wheel."

For a split second he takes both hands off the wheel, giving a little scream, then puts them back in the classic ten and two position. "Yes, sir."

Chapter 38

MATT

We've had an unusual early cold spell, a prelude to the changing season. It's tree planting season and an important time for my business. When winter comes there will be a big drop in referrals, so I need to make enough this fall to see me through till people's thoughts turn again to their yards and estates. A few weeks ago, I was thrilled when I landed the biggest job I've ever had at one of the largest property owners in the county. I've drawn up the preliminary plans and look forward to meeting with him this afternoon. It's a Saturday which may mean no work to some people, but for me—still building up my business—I'm happily at my clients' beck and call.

    The good news about getting jobs is word of mouth garners me more. This morning, I met with another prospective client and it looks like I'll land that project as well. That will help pad my bank account. All good, because the premium dollars I get for keeping Alex will be coming to an end soon. Sam and I talked and I'll go to a substantially less foster care rate. My bank account will take a hit but otherwise, I'm good with it. I won't feel so guilty when people tell me how swell I am for taking in a teenager. The nagging question is how Alex will take it when he, too, isn't tied by The Deal anymore. But I'll worry about that another day.

He's still making some pocket change working for Emily, but now that he's in school, his hours are much fewer. While I met with my new prospect, Alex spent the morning helping her load up items for an antique show at the fairgrounds. Emily already left for the show and locked up the shop early. She'd asked if I wanted her to bring Alex to me, but I'd told her no. I know she was secretly relieved because she wants to set up before customers start showing up. I'd called Alex and told him to run to Subway and get us a couple of sandwiches and I'd pick him up there. We can save time by eating in the truck on the way home. I need to drop Alex off, pick up my drawings, then hustle on to meet up with my prospective client. There's not much room for error which makes me nervous. It's bad form to be late when you're courting important business that will allow you to grow your company ... not to mention have money to eat, which I'm rather fond of.

What also has me antsy is the weather. It has rained the past several days, but the forecast today said it was all over with. I believed the local weatherman, especially since the day dawned with sun and blue sky. But out of nowhere, dark clouds appeared, and for the last thirty minutes, it has come down in buckets. It's stopped but I'm worried about the creek. I don't know how much it rained upstream. If I have to drive all around the back side of my property, I will really need to double-time it to be on time. It only rained a little in town so I didn't have to worry about Alex getting drenched and surely, he has enough sense to find shelter. I'd emphasized to him the need for promptness, but in order to make sure he doesn't dawdle, I text to remind him be ready to jump in the truck as soon as I drive up.

As I pull around the corner, I scan the front looking for him. Empty. *Damn it all, Alex.* I pull over and park, turning my head to check up and down the street for sight of him. Yank out my phone to call. No answer. I can see inside Subway's window that he isn't at the counter or a table, but I run in and check the bathroom. Empty. I get back in the truck and call him again. No answer.

I throw the cell down on the seat next to me, irritation turning to anger. He's played this game of keeping me waiting, but he's never done it when it involves my work. Maybe he's taken off again.

That thought makes me even angrier. I glance again at the clock on the dash. There's still enough time if he shows up in the next few minutes. Five more minutes go by. I try calling again.

Three more minutes. Three more, then I'm leaving without you. I've had it with this.

Three minutes later, still no sign of Alex.

And it's started to rain.

Chapter 39

ALEX

The last box is stuffed into the back of Emily's car. Justin is with Emily's dad so even the passenger seat is hauling cargo. I shut the car door. "There you go."

"Thanks so much. You want me to drop you off at Subway?"

"Nah," I say, "I've got plenty of time."

"Okay, wish me luck. Tell Matt I'll call him later."

I wave as she pulls away and head down the street. I'm hungry. It's started to drizzle just a little so I duck under awnings to stay dry. Pulling out my phone, I read Hailey's text from earlier today, smiling at her emojis. Distracted, I trip over a break in the sidewalk. When I turn the corner, I'm suddenly flush against a brick wall, with the pressure of a hand on my back. *What the hell?*

Twisting around, I see Meaty Jones inches from my face. I push back against his arm. "What the fuck are you doing?"

I take a closer look at him. It's been a while since I've seen him. He doesn't look good. He's lost weight and looks pretty strung out. Is he still mad about what happened that day at school?

Okay, if he wants a fight, we'll have a fight. I'm not taking any more crap off him.

Taken by surprise by his strength, he yanks me deeper into the alley, behind one of the green dumpsters, and grabs my phone out of my hand.

I am *not* having that again. "Give that back to me!"

"Screw you." His hand goes to his back, underneath his shirt, and when he brings it back around, he's holding a handgun. "Give me your money. All of it."

For a second, I freeze. He brings the gun closer to my face. "Now!"

Is he serious? Serious or not, fear begins creeping in. "Okay, okay, gimme a second." My hand goes into my pocket and I bring out all the bills I have and hold them up to him. He grabs them but frowns. "I need more than that." He looks at the watch on my wrist. Emily gave it to me a few weeks ago when I'd admired it at the store. "Give me that too!"

I'm reluctant to part with it, but afraid to not do what he says. I hand it over, but he's still not satisfied. "I think you're holding out on me."

I hold up my hands. "I'm not. That's all I've got on me." I shouldn't have added those last two words. He seizes on them. "Okay, let's go get the rest. Take me to it. Just start walking." He yanks his head in the direction of Holmes Street. I guess in the state he's in, he thinks I still live there.

My feet start moving and thoughts are bouncing around in my head so fast I'm having a hard time keeping them sorted. If I tell him I live way out in the country, what will he do? Is he so fucked up he'd shoot me? Matt is supposed to be picking me up soon. Should I head there? But what if I end up getting Matt shot? I couldn't live with that.

As we walk around a dumpster in an alley, I see the sliding door is open and it's about half-filled with black plastic garbage bundles. On pure instinct, I leap up and grab the top, dropping in with one seamless motion. I grab the handle on the inside with both hands, slide it shut, and hang on with all my might.

No surprise, Meaty is pissed.

"Come out of there, fucker. I'll shoot your ass off if you don't."

He begins tugging on the door. These past months I've been off drugs, eating regularly, and doing manual labor with Matt. I'm pretty sure I can win this tug of war. Not to mention, I'm scared shitless which powers me up.

Having no luck getting the door open, Meaty starts banging on the outside of the dumpster, probably with the butt of the gun is my best guess. The sound reverberates through the container something awful and my immediate reaction is to cover my ears, but I can't risk letting go of the handle. I cringe every time he bangs on the metal but keep holding on for dear life.

Then it goes quiet. I know I'm breathing heavily but I can't hear it because my ears are still recovering from his pounding. Did he leave? I don't think so. I think he's standing out there, frustrated, trying to figure something out. His next move is something I suppose I knew was coming.

I hear a shot. Only now do I start to wonder if the metal really can withstand the force of a bullet. I gaze down at myself to make sure I'm not bleeding, then examine the container to see if any little round hole of daylight has appeared. To my immense relief, I don't see any. I brace for more shots, but they don't come. Maybe he shot in the air just to scare me. Maybe the bullet ricocheted off and killed him. But now that I think about it, if he'd hit the dumpster with a bullet, it would have made far worse noise inside this big metal can than his earlier banging. It could be he's worried he's attracting attention.

He yells, "You're dead meat, Coffey! I found you this time and I'll find you again." Silence after that.

I don't know if Meaty is smart enough to try to lie to flush me out, but I'm taking no chances. I wait a few minutes then cautiously slide the door open just a tiny crack. When nothing happens, I open it a little more and peer out. Some guy leans out of a window above me. I yell up, "Hey, do you see a kid standing outside this dumpster?"

The guy gives me a funny look. "No, I just see a kid *in* the dumpster. Was that a shot I heard?"

I don't bother to answer, just slide the door and climb out. When I reach the end of the alley, I look to make sure the coast is clear, then start running. I don't quit until I get within sight of Subway. I go weak with relief at seeing Matt's truck parked in front. I slow down to a fast walk while trying to catch my breath. Matt will know what to do and I can't wait to get to him. I pick up the pace again and start jogging. My heart is still pounding and my hands are trembling, but I know as soon as I'm with him, I'll feel better.

I know I'll be safe.

Chapter 40

MATT

Too hyped up to sit in the truck, I get out and pace in front of the store, glancing at my watch over and over. Finally, *finally* Alex appears. My pent-up anger ignites at the sight of him. I've *had* it. I'm really sick of him purposefully keeping me standing around waiting on him.

As he gets within a few yards, I put my hands on my hips and lean toward him.

"Matt," he says, "You won't believe…"

Tired of his excuses, I unload. "I don't want to hear it, you hear me? You've kept me standing here twiddling my thumbs when I have somewhere important to be. You've made me late *again*! You think the world revolves around you? Well, it doesn't."

I wait for the scowl but instead he looks upset. Good, maybe I'm finally getting through to him. But rather than calming me, it revs me up more. "*Not another word!* Get in the truck. *Now!*"

I yank open the passenger door and he climbs in. I hurry to my side and slide into my seat, starting the truck up almost simultaneously. Only after I've gotten up to the speed limit and on a straightaway, do I look at him. He's slumped against the door with his head down, looking rather pitiful. My anger has diminished now that we're in motion, and my instinct is to soothe, but I stop myself. Maybe it's good he looks cowed, like a kid who got chewed out should. My football coach gave it to me far worse, and that was in front of the whole team.

We keep up the silent treatment. The houses and used car lots have faded to fences and barns. The rain has let up a bit. If the creek's not up, I'll have a chance of being on time. I give the truck a little more gas, going more over the speed limit than I'd like on wet roads. I keep looking at the clock for the time, then checking Alex who remains wedged to the car door. Even in my rattled state, something seems off. Once we get within a half mile of home, I decide to make an overture.

"Alex, I'm sorry I yelled at you, okay?" I reach over and touch his arm and he shakes me off. Mad, I guess. I'd prefer that to how he's looked since we left town. I reach the end of the drive and realize I'm screwed when I see the water is rising above the level of the road and quickly gaining steam. One look and I completely deflate but accept there's nothing I can do. If I'm late, I'm late. Being a little less late isn't worth taking chances especially with Alex in the vehicle. I take out my phone and text Mr. Schwartz, letting him know I won't be on time. His reply comes right back.

> Actually, glad to hear it because I'm on a virtual meeting that's running long. Could we wait and meet Monday at 9:30?

I reply:

Sure, see you then.

That done, I turn my attention back to the boy. "Alex, look, let's talk about this, okay?"

He looks up at me fiercely and says, "Fuck off!" To my horror I see he's crying. Now I feel like a complete piece of shit. "Oh, Alex, I'm…"

I don't get anything else out because he's pushed opened the truck door and has started running up the drive. By the time I step out of the truck, he's already past the point I can grab him.

"Alex, no! Come back! The waters too high! Please, Alex!"

I can see the water's not completely over the drive. There are strips still showing solid ground and he's almost made it across. I relax. He's going to make it. Quite a few people have told me I'm too paranoid about the water and maybe they're right.

No sooner than I have that thought, a wall of water comes roaring down the creek, knocking Alex off his feet. He manages to reach up and grab a small branch of a tree flanking the drive. I rush towards him, but a new gush of water pulses through, causing him to lose his grip, pushing him into the roiling brown water. I watch him go under the surface and come up a few seconds later, coughing and shaking his head—his face, his eyes shocked wide.

I watch in horror as he is swept downstream.

I'm running down the side of the raging water trying to control my panic and desperately trying to figure out the best thing to do. Dive in to try and swim to him? Or go further down the streambank and try to snag him? The decision is made for me. He snags himself. There's a three-board plank fence and he's managed to grab onto it. How long can he hold? My stomach is sick because I know if he lets go, I'll never have another chance to reach him.

"Hold on, Alex, hold on! I'm coming!"

I sprint down the bank, then throw myself into the water and begin pulling myself along the fence to reach my kid.

Please, dear God, let him hold on.

Let me get there in time.

Chapter 41

ALEX

Water fills my nose. I suck a breath before going under again. Gasping, I rise above the water one more time. I clutch the fence board as best I can and manage to pull myself along to one of the fence posts, which I'm able to cling to with both arms.

The relief I feel vanishes when I realize the water is still rising and soon, I'll be holding on underwater. Using all the strength I can gather, I try to pull myself towards the bank but it's very slow going. I manage to make it to the next fence post and need to rest. I'm cold and I'm tired. My arms aren't working so good. I'll rest, just for a minute, then I'll try again. Laying my head next to the post, I close my eyes. Rest, just a little more rest.

The water keeps swirling around me, pulling at me. It's like something evil, like it wants me. My left hand slips off and I quickly re-grip. Opening my eyes again, I can see gray sky and Mr. Parkins' house on top of the hill. Some part of me is thinking rationally: *I'm probably going to die*. This funny thought pops into my head: *I'm having a really bad day*.

Above the roar of the water, I hear Matt's voice screaming my name, but it sounds far away.

I think about trying to move again but can't bring myself to take action. Really, it would be easier to just let go. To let the water have me. To end all my struggles. To give in.

Again, I hear Matt. It still seems far away, but I concentrate on his words: *Hold on, hold on, I'm coming*! I grip the post a little tighter. Suddenly, I realize I'm hearing the voice better; it's closer. I turn my head against the flow of the water and see Matt pulling his way towards me. The sight of him, the determination in his face, gives me strength. I don't take my eyes off him. I can't talk but I hear myself let out a sob, and the voice in my head says, *I don't want to die. Not now. Please save me, Matt. Please save me.*

His voice gets louder and louder.

His hands reach towards me.

His arms close around me.

Chapter 42

MATT

"Let go, Alex, let go of the fence. I've got you … I've got you."

With a sob, he releases his hold on the post. I draw him in as he wraps his arms around me. Using all my strength, I lower my head and pull along the fence towards the closest bank. It's like my football days, with three guys hanging on trying to take me down, but I refuse to give in to their wills. In a few seconds, or an eternity, my feet hit solid ground, but the water still doesn't want to let go. It pushes me up against the fence, but as long as I have the fence, I'm okay. A horrible vision pops in my head of the fence giving way, but I shove it aside, praying it holds. It's held this long through countless storms, but then it's never had someone my size and weight ramming into it either.

Once my hips get above the water line, there's no stopping me. Without the water holding him up, Alex is heavy in my arms, but once I'm completely clear, I struggle several yards further uphill to make sure we're safe before I collapse on my butt and pull the boy into my lap. Overcome with emotion, I sob and rock him, muttering, *Thank you, God. Thank you.*

He starts to retch and I turn him sideways as he coughs up water. His face is white, his hair plastered to his face. My fingers holding him are bleached and wrinkled, and I feel an all-over ache, which could be shock or maybe even the beginning of hypothermia.

It concerns me that Alex was in the water longer than I was. I need to get him somewhere warm. He needs to see a doctor to make sure he's okay.

Sitting there, I can see my truck on the other side of the torrent, useless as the tits on a boar hog. There's no way I can walk up the hill, certainly not while carrying Alex. My mind isn't thinking real clear, so when I hear a voice, I wonder if I might be hallucinating.

No, it's a real voice attached to a real person. Dan Parkins.

"Jesus, Matt, are you all okay?"

I raise my head to him. "Help me with the boy."

Dan helps lift Alex and twitches his head to the left. "I'm in my Gator." Between us we carry Alex to his vehicle. He holds him up while I climb in the back, then I let him hand the boy to me.

"Where do you want to go?" Dan asks.

"My house. I think getting him dry and warm is the first step."

Alex's teeth are chattering so hard he can barely speak. The effects of the cold water but also the adrenaline that I know flooded his system is being dispelled through shivering.

His eyes meet mine. "I'm sorry ... so sorry ..."

"No, no, it's okay buddy, everything's going to be okay. I'm here." I smile down at him. "You can't get rid of me, can't you see that?"

He starts to cry again which breaks my heart, and I pull him tighter, absorbing his shuddering body. As soon as we all get inside, I say to Dan, "Get the shower going, good and warm. He runs ahead and I follow with Alex. The three of us stand there without speaking for several agonizing seconds while waiting for the water to heat up. I use my foot to kick off Alex's one sodden sneaker, guessing the other one must be halfway to the Mississippi River by now.

As soon as it's warm, I step into the flow of the water and begin stripping the outer clothes off the boy. I'm glad to feel the warm water too, as my fingers aren't working all that well. They feel like little rubber balls. Alex's jeans are stuck so hard to his body, I'm about tell Dan to get a knife, when they finally give way with a sucking noise. Dan reaches in to help, pulling Alex's T-shirt over his head.

The steam rises around us and the warmth works its magic. Alex becomes more alert and his head comes up to look at me. I smile down at him. "Bet this is something you never saw coming, all of us in the shower together, huh?"

I'm rewarded with a snort from Dan and a giggle from Alex. He's coming around. Fifteen minutes later, dressed in dry clothes, I have Dan drive Alex and me the long way around to get back to my truck. Then we're off to the ER. Dan offered to drive us to the hospital, but I assured him I was okay.

Alex is the one that swallowed enough of the creek to have me worried. I've read about secondary drowning, also known as delayed drowning, when water gets into the lungs. This can prevent the lungs from exchanging oxygen and carbon dioxide and can happen up to forty-eight hours after a person has suffered an almost drowning event. I call Mike to let him know what's up, and I'm not going to object to getting preferential treatment when I arrive at Central Methodist Hospital, where both he and Mom work. I also ask him to call Sam since I have a responsibility to notify him because of Alex's status as a state agency child.

Alex gets checked out. I get a list of symptoms I should monitor for the next twenty-four hours or more: coughing, breathing issues, lethargy, changes in mood or behavior. I laugh at the last one. Guess if he starts acting all pleasant, I need to call the doctors.

Once home, I insist he lie down and he doesn't argue, choosing the couch over going to his bed. Only after he's comfortably situated, with Sadie pouting because I make her stay on the floor beneath him, do I sit beside him and get the story of what happened while I was waiting for him this afternoon.

I try to stay calm as I hear his tale, but my hands turn into fists. What incredibly bad timing, after everything else he's put me through, that I picked *this time* to completely lose my temper at him. Once he's finished the story, I tell him, "Okay, don't worry. I'll handle it." I shake my head, "Boy, you've had a bad day."

This gets a bigger laugh than I expected, and he explains he had the same thought while he was floundering in the creek. Then he says, "Go to the city and there's drugs and guns but I come to the country and about get stung to death and drowned. Can we move to some place in between?"

"We just may need to do that."

This gets a smile. He thinks I'm kidding, but the truth is, that's the plan. I want Emily on a full-time basis and she feels the same. We were waiting for the right time to tell the boys, and I guess this is as right a time as any.

I pull the comforter up to his chest. "Do you like Emily's house?"

For a second, he looks puzzled, then puts it together. "Oh."

He gets a thoughtful expression and looks away. I see a flicker of fear in his eyes. I anticipated it and I'm ready. "Hey kid, this is a package deal. You and me. Emily and Justin ... and let's not forget T.J. Funny Bunny. Our own version of The Brady Bunch without the corny song, thank you very much."

Reassured, he looks back up. "I thought you loved this place."

I nod and shoo Sadie back to the floor as she tries to slowly sneak onto the couch. "Yeah, I do, but Emily's place is much bigger. You and Justin can each have your own room. It won't be such a long drive to school and other activities, plus it's closer to Emily's shop. But I'll keep this place for the business. I'll have the land for the plant inventory and the house can be my office. We can come out for weekends, like a cabin vacation. So, what do you say, should you and I become civilized human beings and move to the burbs?"

He reaches below to pet Sadie, before giving a little smirk. "Well, I have some practice with moving. I guess I could do it one more time."

I flick some dog hair off my sleeve and use my most nonchalant voice. "There are some strings attached." I enjoy his wary look. "Changing houses is one thing, but us?" I point to him then back at me. "This is permanent. You got that?"

A small smile. "Okay, Doc. I mean ... Matt."

I lean back and cross my arms over my chest. "You know Murry's been messing with us, don't you?"

"How's that?"

"He's got a savior complex. He never meant for us to just put up with each other. He was out all along to have us end up together for the long haul. Just because it worked out that way, doesn't mean we should let him get away with it. Don't you think we should do something about that?"

He nods in agreement. "Absolutely. But what?"

I give my best evil villain smile. "I think it's time he got a little comeuppance. And I know just how we can do it."

The kid grins. "I'm on board as long as it doesn't involve water … or bugs … or guns."

"Alex, my lad, we need none of those things. This calls for brain power."

I start to explain my little plan, but he's not listening. His eyes blink a couple of times then close. As his breathing becomes steady, I tuck the comforter around him, and sit a few minutes watching him sleep. I'll fix us some dinner later and will keep a close eye on him all night.

I step outside and gaze down the drive at the creek. The water level has dropped back to something closer to a pleasant little brook, not a death trap. I hear the sound of geese overhead and scan the sky until I can see the penciled V, high against the blue, heading southward. Another marker of the changing season, another tally as the year marches on. Halloween, Thanksgiving, Christmas, and the New Year will be here in the blink of an eye.

I suppose it's only fair I wax poetic about life after watching someone almost die. Someone you care deeply about. Life happens, the good, the bad, the ugly, and sometimes by chance, the wonderful. You may not get your dream job, or the super model girlfriend, or travel the globe, but with luck and determination you can have a job you do well and go home at the end of the day to the people you love. Who really needs anything more?

Emily will be here in the morning, bringing cinnamon rolls, and we will talk about our plans for merging households. A long-term commitment is new territory for me, but I'm going to give it my best shot. I'm realistic enough to realize there will be bumpy spots ahead, especially with the kids. Alex has come so far but he remains a work in progress. Justin will have challenges as he gets older. I've made mistakes and no doubt I'll make more. But maybe I'll be forgiven because I'm only human. This parenting business isn't for the faint of heart.

With that thought, my phone rings. I look at the screen, smile, and answer.

"Hi Mom. Guess Mike told you about today. Yeah, we're both fine but thanks for calling. Hey, we'd really like to come to dinner. Can I bring Emily and her son, too? I'd like you to get to know them. When would you like us?"

Chapter 43

SAM

It's been a good day. After three years, Phoenix finally secured a contract with the Department of Juvenile Justice to provide foster care for some of their kids. Some states like Oregon and Kentucky have done this for years, but in many others, it's been a hard sell. So often the kids in child welfare and juvenile justice are one and the same, but the kids who end up falling into the juvenile justice side don't get many of the benefits child welfare youth do. Relatives and friends who agree to take in a child or teen involved with child welfare are considered kinship care and can usually get financial payments like foster parents. There's no such arrangement for the justice kids. If they have no home or can't go home following a stay in a juvenile facility, the caseworker might ask a grandmother or aunt to take the youth in, but no compensation comes with it, so it might not happen. It's one reason these kids end up on the streets homeless, or worse, incarcerated again.

I'm also happy the foster parent recruiter I recently hired has turned out to be worth her weight in gold. She's a foster parent recruiting machine. Signed on three new families this week alone. We need every home we can get. We turn away five times as many kids as get referred to us.

I'd spun that story to Alex about how he'd be good public relations material for Phoenix as a ruse, but it turned out to be true.

Every day, child welfare workers send me a new batch of challenging referrals, but sadly there's no way we can serve them all. I hate reading the files of the ones we turn down, knowing the kid is likely heading to residential care because we don't have a suitable home. That thought is depressing, but I try to focus on the kids we have been able to help and the ripple effect of helping one child. Not only do you help that child, but you touch the lives of the generations to come through that child's children and grandchildren.

It's Friday, late afternoon. I have one last appointment before starting my weekend, but it's an easy one. Just Matt and Alex stopping by. I have to say, I'm more than a little pleased with myself on how that has all worked out. Alex has come so far from that kid I met in the detention center. Caring adults and positive experiences can help overcome trauma. That and a healthy dose of Vitamin H. Hope. How can you thrive if you believe life holds no promise? I give myself some credit while giving Matt his just due for doing the heavy lifting. But the real hero of the story is Alex himself. For not giving up on himself. For facing all the obstacles and rising above them.

Mike's also noticed the changes in Matt since Alex's arrival and admitted my crazy idea wasn't so crazy after all. He's also gratified Matt's relationship with their mom is much improved.

I bragged, um I mean, *talked* to Bonnie last night. She poked me in the chest with her finger. "Okay, you pulled it off, I admit it. You're also insufferably smug which is very unbecoming in the male species."

I'm feeling pretty cocky. "Hey, bring me a beer, would ya?"

The next thing I know I'm taking out the garbage. She sure knows how to humble a guy.

I hear our receptionist buzz in Matt and Alex, so I holler down the hall, "Hey guys, come on back."

They walk in and take seats, saying nothing. Matt doesn't engage in any of the usual start up banter. Crosses his arms. Alex looks at the floor. I give a little laugh, "You guys look kinda serious today."

No one laughs or smiles back. Matt looks at me soberly. "Look, this thing with Alex and me isn't working out. He and I have both talked about it. We want to end the contract. Today. Right now."

Oh, come on, they can't be serious. After all they've been through and how close I've seen them become? Demetrie Jones, aka Meaty, was in court this week and is heading to a juvenile correctional facility. I feel for the boy. He has a lousy home life, along with a pretty severe substance abuse problem, and I hope a therapeutic setting can do him some good. But I'm glad to have him away from Alex for the foreseeable future.

Alex is doing well in his new school and is loving the EMT program. He's even been going out on some ambulance calls. Matt and he are doing some bike events. Things couldn't be going better. So maybe they had a little bump in the road this morning, something I can smooth over with them like I have before.

I use my calming voice. "Hey, let's talk about this. What's the problem?"

Matt shakes his head. "No more talking. We're done with that. Alex and I discussed things and we've both made up our minds. Right, Alex? "

Alex's hand goes to his back pocket and pulls out the written agreement. He looks me right in the eye, and slowly tears it in half, saying, "I've had enough of this shit."

Feeling a rising panic, I steeple my hands on my desk and say, "Now, sometimes, when people have disagreements…"

Matt waves his hands. "Don't start up with that psychological crap. You aren't talking us out of this."

I lean back. Both of them are glaring at me.

Shit!

My mind is scrambling furiously at how to fix this, but then I realize something's off. My eyes narrow. Despite their body language and stern stares, they look too … too … *twinkly eyed.* Collapsing back against my chair, I say, "You guys are messing with me."

Matt grins. "You think you're the only one who can be clever?"

"Whew." I let out a breath I didn't know I was holding. "You two really had me going."

The two of them exchange a look, pleased with themselves at my expense. Matt says, "But we are serious about the contract. We don't want to negotiate a new one like you recently suggested, and I don't want to be a foster parent anymore."

Alex leans forward and picks up Sam's baseball. "And believe me, I'm really tired of being in foster care."

Matt and Alex smile at each other then turn expectantly back to me. I reach over and take my baseball back from Alex but grin at him. I toss the ball in the air and catch it before laying it back on the desk.

"Then, let's talk adoption."

Chapter 44

ALEX

My name is Alex King. I am sixteen years old. I had sixty-five placements once I entered the foster care system many years ago. I exited the system five months ago when I was officially adopted. I shocked everyone at the adoption hearing when I asked to hold one of those dorky signs. Surprised myself too. I just decided, what the hell, I wanted one. It is after all something I never expected and don't mind celebrating. The picture with the judge has me standing next to my newly married parents, Matt and Emily, my little brother Justin, my grandmother, my wonderful CASA worker, Cookie, former caseworker (and now good friend) Sam, holding a piece of poster board.

"*Adopted after 4,224 days in care.*"

I even wrote and read a statement in open court. Kinda got embarrassing when I got a little choked up, but when I finished and looked up, turns out I was the most together person in the room. Everyone, even the judge, was crying. This was the same judge, who locked me up twice before. Go figure.

I'm glad the judge doesn't do traffic court. The ink on my driver's license was barely dry when I picked up a speeding ticket and got it yanked for six months. Matt confiscated my keys and chewed me up one side and down another, you know, like a father does. In a sign of my growing maturity, I took it really well. Okay, that's a lie.

Maybe the truth is I hollered back some choice words as I went to my room, slamming the door behind me hard enough to rattle windows. After thinking about it, I soon realized I had to take responsibility for my actions so I came back and apologized. Okay, that's a lie too.

I pretty much sulked around for three days, giving everyone the cold shoulder. I really hated losing my license and the freedom it brought me. Getting my wings clipped so early after getting it really sucked. Matt and Emily gave me a wide berth, but boundaries are not Justin's thing. At dinner, on the third night, he started up.

"Alex, are you still mad?"

"Alex, Matt says he's waiting for an apology. Are you going to apologize?"

"Alex, I really think you *should* apologize, don't you?"

"Alex, are you going to apologize *now*?"

"*YES!*" I couldn't stand any more of it. Setting down my fork, I looked at Matt and Emily and said, "I'm sorry for how I've been acting. I was mad about getting the ticket, and I shouldn't have taken it out on you because I did a dumb thing." Turning to Justin I asked, "Satisfied?"

He nods and goes back to attacking his lasagna. Matt stares down at his plate smiling, then looks up at me with a smug expression.

"*What?!*"

He tears apart his garlic bread, sticks a large bite in his mouth, then starts to chew. Out of the side of his mouth, he says, "I just love that you've met your match and that he's half your size and half your age."

I roll my eyes, but true confession, he's right. Justin has my number. I was also glad to have a way to quit acting like a jerk and get things back to normal. At least, what passes for normal at our house. I don't want the bar set too high for me. I know I'm going to still screw up sometimes, but hopefully not in a big way. I have too much at stake now to go back to the dark place I was in. I have plans. I have goals. I have people who care for me and people I care about right back.

Life has been out there patiently waiting for me. Took a while, but I found it.

Author's Note

My first novel, *The Car Thief*, took a deep dive into the juvenile justice system. During my time working in that field, I was privileged to work with some dedicated professionals. However, it can't be emphasized enough: the best way to help kids is to keep them out of the system whenever possible.

Of special concern are "dual system youth"—those kids who start in the child welfare system then move into the juvenile justice system. Youth who have four or more foster-care placements enter juvenile justice at very high rates, some stats say as much as 85 percent. I recall one youth with sixty-four placements in foster care (the number I chose for my character, Alex) before coming to my state's Department of Juvenile Justice. If we know these stats, why do we continue to casually move kids from foster home to foster home, and worse, to congregate care like group homes and other residential placements? I'm not saying there aren't times when residential care is necessary, but it should be used very judiciously.

We know children thrive best in family settings. I have been blessed to witness the unbelievable success of some kids who were deemed "lost causes." Two youth come to mind—a boy and a girl—who went straight from our most secure-care juvenile facility (where both spent much of their time in isolation) directly to a foster home successfully. Too often there are youth like these who are low-level offenders but because of their extreme behavioral issues wind up in maximum security settings where they only get worse. Like most juvenile justice agencies at the time, state-run foster care was off the table. Fortunately, this was just when private agencies had come onto the scene with therapeutic foster care (TFC) which could be accessed by juvenile justice. TFC was viewed very suspiciously by many residential and community justice staff who kept saying, "What are we, child welfare?"

At the time, I was the Director of Classification for my state's juvenile justice agency. In this one boy's case, I figured there was no way he would be accepted by a private foster-care agency. However, having nothing to lose—and constantly begged by the superintendent to get this kid *out*—I contacted our recently acquired foster-care resource and spoke to the director, Beau Necco. I didn't spare any of the details about the problems with this kid. To my surprise, he told me to send a referral packet. He said, "We know about these kids with an alphabet soup of diagnoses and a trail of failed placements. We call them 'paper monsters' but the bottom line is they are just kids."

Forty-eight hours later they sent a proposal. They'd take the youth for several times more than the usual per diem payment because they needed additional funds to provide the resources needed to manage this challenging youth. These services included a back-up respite foster home (who would be reimbursed whether they were used or not) and aides who would provide positive youth activities. These aides were usually some big twenty-something guys who would take the boy out during the days and play basketball, go hiking, or whatever else would wear the kid out before they'd deliver him back to his foster home.

Did it work? Yes, it did. Of course, the boy wasn't an angel, but he never ended up back in juvenile court again and stayed in the home till age eighteen. The girl's trajectory was very similar and in fact, she later became a foster parent for this same agency who took her into care. Her specialty? Taking in teenage girls.

A caseworker I knew who was used to dealing with troublesome teens and knew the most important thing was to initially keep the newly placed kid from running. So, he'd whisper to them if they'd stay a certain amount of time, he'd give them money. All kids going into care get an initial clothing allowance, so this money came to them regardless, but they bought into it, because they thought they were getting away with something. This was the inspiration for "The Deal" with Alex.

All these experiences and observations during my career went into *Sleight of Hand*. As with *The Car Thief*, although a work of fiction, many of the scenes within the book are based on true occurrences with some adjustments to maintain confidentiality.

The biggest difficulty in writing this book was the need to point out the difficulties in the system while also acknowledging the extraordinary work of foster parents, child welfare and juvenile justice staff, CASA workers, and others who strive to do their very best with the often-limited resources they are given. The reality is, just like in any occupation, there are good and bad people in the system. Foster care has caused negative ramifications for many children, but it has also saved many a child's life—not just literally by rescuing them from abuse and neglect—but by exposing children to how a good family operates. Even a few days' stay can be something that inspires a child for the rest of his life.

Speaking of CASA, when I wrote *The Car Thief*, my local CASA director read it and said, "This boy needed a CASA volunteer!" She was right and I wanted to be sure to include one for Alex. I've witnessed the dedication of many CASA volunteers and how they can make a huge difference in a child's case.

If you enjoyed some of the "techniques" used by Sam while working with Alex, I want to point you in the direction of Charlie Appelstein's books and resources available at www.nobadkid.org. I've been using some of his teachings for years and they work! The card trick, however, is my own. During college I took an elective out of the university's recreation department. Each week we did something new. One week we learned magic tricks. These were meant for fun and not for use with at-risk kids, but out of all my college classes this one had the most lifelong impact. In my first job as a juvenile probation officer, I had a first-time meeting with a tough kid who would barely speak or even look at me. In desperation, I pulled that Svengali deck out of my purse (yeah, you never know when you'll need a card trick…) and within minutes that kid was chatting away with me. It truly never failed me in the decades that followed. Kids can't resist.

Finally, let me touch on the other aspect of *Sleight of Hand*. My love for horses was used in *The Car Thief,* but for this book I turned to other important things in my life including gardening with native plants. Doug Tallamy has written several great books on the subject, and I urge everyone to see how essential it is that we encourage insects into our yards by planting native flowers, shrubs, and trees that sustain the food chain. It's literally a matter of life and death. No insects, no life.

Thank you for reading my book. I hope it inspires you.

Acknowledgments

All books are a team effort. A huge thanks to my wonderful friends and Beta readers: Betsy, Christie, Karen, KKJ, Leslie, Linda, Lisa, Margo, Melynda, and Steve. Each one of them made a major contribution (and kept finding those pesky mistakes!) and I couldn't have done this without them. I'm equally grateful for Mary Knight, award winning author and my writing mentor, for always steering me in the direction I should go. Credit for the wonderful cover goes to publisher Jonathan Scott. And I'd be remiss if I didn't thank my readers for the encouragement to keep writing these types of stories. I hope you like this one.

Vicki Reed

With a master's degree in criminal justice and decades spent working in child welfare and juvenile justice, Vicki Reed takes readers behind the closed doors of systems the public seldom sees. Her debut novel, *The Car Thief: A Boy's Perilous Journey through the Juvenile Justice System*, was the winner of two national awards. A sought-after speaker, Vicki continues to write while also consulting in the juvenile justice field.

Vicki lives with her husband and son in Lexington, KY, the self-proclaimed Horse Capital of the World, where she enjoys riding her horse, hiking and biking, and gardening extensively with pollinators and wildlife in mind.

Resources

To learn more about juvenile justice in the U.S., contact the following national organizations:

National CASA (www.nationalcasa.org)

National Partnership for Juvenile Services (npjs.org)

Annie Casey Foundation (www.aecf.org)

Coalition for Juvenile Justice (info@juvjustice.org)

Juvenile in Justice (juvenile-in-justice.com)

www.ingramcontent.com/pod-product-compliance
Lightning Source LLC
Chambersburg PA
CBHW031412290426
44110CB00011B/357